WITH FIRE & SWORD

THOMAS DUNNE BOOKS
ST. MARTIN'S PRESS
New York

WITH FIRE

& SWORD

*

*The Battle of Bunker Hill
and the Beginning
of the American Revolution*

JAMES L. NELSON

THOMAS DUNNE BOOKS.

An imprint of St. Martin's Press.

WITH FIRE AND SWORD. Copyright © 2011 by James L. Nelson.
All rights reserved. Printed in the United States of America. For
information, address St. Martin's Press, 175 Fifth Avenue, New York,
N.Y. 10010.

www.thomasdunnebooks.com

www.stmartins.com

Library of Congress Cataloging-in-Publication Data

Nelson, James L.
    With fire and sword : the battle of Bunker Hill and the beginning of
the American Revolution / James L. Nelson.—1st ed.
        p. cm.
    Includes bibliographical references and index.
    ISBN 978-0-312-57644-8
    1. Bunker Hill, Battle of, Boston, Mass., 1775.   2. Boston (Mass.)—
History—Revolution, 1775–1783.   3. United States—History—
Revolution, 1775–1783—Causes.   I. Title.
    E241.B9N45 2011
    973.3'312—dc22

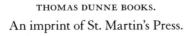

2010040653

First Edition: March 2011

10   9   8   7   6   5   4   3   2   1

To Stephanie Nelson,
my sister, my first friend, for all your love,
kindness, and generosity over all these years;
you are the best of us.

Contents

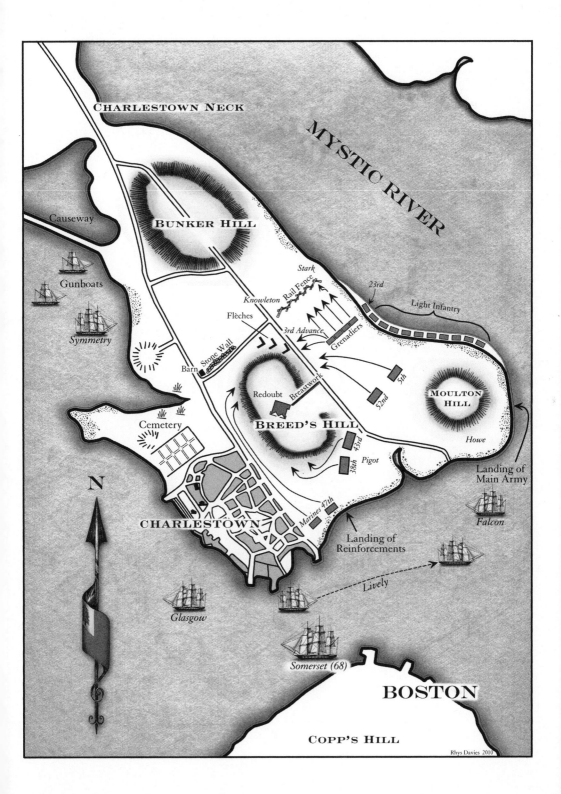

CHARLESTOWN NECK

MYSTIC RIVER

BUNKER HILL

Causeway

Gunboats

Symmetry

Stark

Rail Fence

Knowleton

23rd

Light Infantry

Flèches

3rd Advance

Grenadiers

Barn

Stone Wall

Breastwork

5th

52nd

MOULTON HILL

Redoubt

BREED'S HILL

Cemetery

43rd

Pigot

38th

Howe

Landing of Main Army

Falcon

N

Marines 47th

Landing of Reinforcements

CHARLESTOWN

Lively

Glasgow

Somerset (68)

BOSTON

COPP'S HILL

Rhys Davies 2010

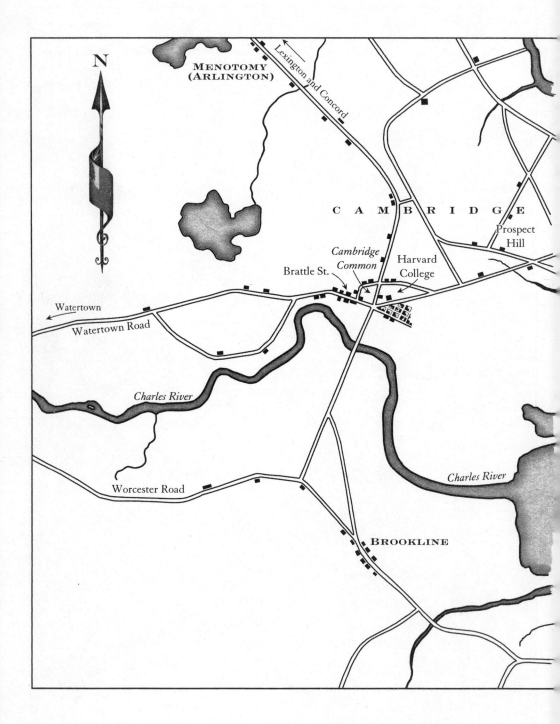

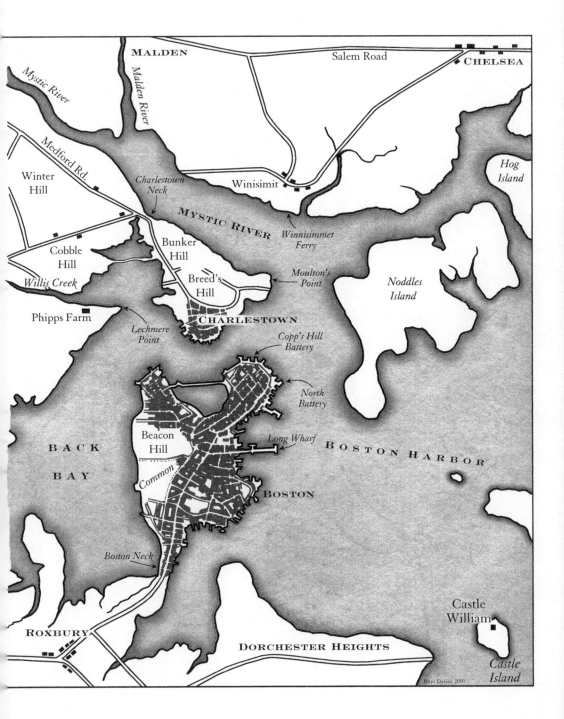

MALDEN

Salem Road

CHELSEA

Mystic River

Malden River

Hog Island

Winter Hill

Medford Rd.

Charlestown Neck

Winisimit

MYSTIC RIVER

Winnisimmet Ferry

Cobble Hill

Bunker Hill

Breed's Hill

Moulton's Point

Noddles Island

Willis Creek

Phipps Farm

Lechmere Point

CHARLESTOWN

Copp's Hill Battery

North Battery

Beacon Hill

Long Wharf

BOSTON HARBOR

BACK BAY

Common

BOSTON

Boston Neck

Castle William

ROXBURY

DORCHESTER HEIGHTS

Castle Island

Rhys Davies 2010

WITH FIRE
& SWORD

Prologue

THE BATTLE
OF BROOKLYN

On August 27, 1776, in the cool of the predawn hours, five American officers stood on the Old Jamaica Road that ran from the small town of Brooklyn to the west, through a cluster of buildings that made up the village of Bedford, and past Howard's Tavern just a mile or so behind them. The night seemed preternaturally calm, though far off in the dark they could hear the occasional dull, flat bang of a musket fired by a nervous picket at some moving shadow.

The five men made up the left flank of a line of American troops positioned along a ridge of hilly ground called the Heights of Guana, or, today, Gowanus Heights. The heights were comprised of a series of hills around one hundred feet in elevation, densely wooded and covered with thick brush. Their steep slopes and thick cover made them all but impenetrable to an army attacking in a line of battle. They formed in effect an outer work, a second ring of defenses beyond the extensive works that had been constructed to the north on Brooklyn Heights.

There were only four ways for an army to pass through the Heights of Guana. One was up the Gowanus Road, which ran along Gowanus Bay at the western end of Long Island before swinging inland around the marshy area known as Gowanus Creek. The next was Flatbush Pass, a mile and a half from Gowanus Bay and a mile north of the town of Flatbush. Less than a mile to the east of Flatbush Pass was Bedford Pass, south of the town of Bedford. Finally, at the far end of the Heights of Guana, was Jamaica Pass.

The four passes were bottlenecks of varying degrees, points in the line where the enemy could be held at bay. When organizing the defenses on Long Island, George Washington, commander in chief of the American forces, and his officers had looked to this high ground as a way of holding off the British advance from even reaching the chief defenses at Brooklyn, or at the very least making them pay a high price to get there. Washington had instructed Major General Israel Putnam, in command of the American troops on Long Island, that "your best men should at all hazards prevent the enemy's passing the wood; & approaching your works."

Washington, of course, did not know where that enemy would strike. When the British first arrived in June from Halifax, after having been driven out of Boston, they put their troops ashore on Staten Island, across New York Harbor from Long Island. There they remained while the Americans continued to furiously dig in and wait for the attack to come. Finally, on August 22, the enemy began to shift troops to Long Island; a great flotilla of ship's boats, flatboats, bateaux, anything that could float and carry troops was employed, carrying 15,000 men across the water to Gravesend Bay. A few days later another 4,000 were sent over, bringing the total British force to around 19,000. They were some of the best of the British troops, the light infantry and the grenadiers, as well as some newly arrived Hessian units. Still Washington was not sure where they would attack.

The fact that the British had a navy and the Americans had none, or at least none that could pose any threat to the British, meant that the enemy had almost unlimited flexibility in where he could strike. Transports could carry men up the Hudson River to land above Manhattan, or up the East River to the eastern side of the island. They could disappear over the horizon, as they often would during the course of the war, leaving

Washington to guess where they might land. Or they could launch their assault on Brooklyn, as appeared to be their intention.

On the day before the Battle of Brooklyn, Washington wrote to his cousin Lund Washington, caretaker of Mount Vernon, about the current situation:

> The Enemy . . . , landed a pretty considerable part of their Force on Long Island; at a place called Graves end bay about Ten Miles from our Works on the Island; and Marched through the Flat & level Land . . . till they (or part of them) got within abt three Miles of our Lines, where they are now Incamped.

He explained to Lund that he did not know "what there real design is . . . whether it is intended as a feint—or is to form part of their Attack." Washington was willing to speculate on one point, writing, "A few days more I should think will bring matters to an Issue one way or other."

The majority of Putnam's approximately 8,000 troops on Long Island were behind the earthworks in Brooklyn, but about 2,400 men were arrayed along the Heights of Guana, most of them guarding the passes. On the American right, posted on the Gowanus Road, were 500 men under the command of William Alexander, Lord Stirling (Alexander claimed a Scottish peerage, though the British House of Lords refused to recognize it). General John Sullivan in the center was watching the Flatbush and Bedford passes with around 1,000 men. To the east of Sullivan, Colonel Samuel Miles of Pennsylvania was positioned with around 800 troops. At the Jamaica Pass, the easternmost gap in the Heights of Guana, there was no one, save for the five officers nervously watching the road.

Part of the problem for the Americans was a confused command situation. General Nathanael Greene had been responsible for establishing the defenses on Long Island and understood the situation better than anyone else, but by August 20 he had become so deathly ill that Washington was forced to withdraw him and gave orders that "General Sullivan is to take command on Long Island till Gen. Greene's state of health will permit him to resume it."

Four days later Washington replaced Sullivan with Israel Putnam, who, as one of five major generals, was entitled to the command. Joseph Reed, Washington's aide-de-camp, wrote to his wife from Manhattan that "General Putnam was made happy by obtaining leave to go over— the brave old man was quite miserable at being kept here." Putnam may have been happy, but he knew very little about the defenses on Long Island that Greene had so laboriously established.

The American command faced problems much bigger than not knowing the lay of the land. Some time earlier, Washington had written to Congress with regard to some of John Sullivan's weaknesses as an officer. He had excused them by saying, "His wants are common to us all; the want of experience to move upon a large Scale; for the limited, and contracted knowledge which any of us have in Military Matters stands in very little Stead." In that, Washington was right.

Many of the men pacing the ground on the Heights of Guana, or back in the earthworks in Brooklyn, or manning the various posts spread across Manhattan, would end the war as seasoned veterans, soldiers as good as any in the world. Some, such as Sullivan, Henry Knox, Nathanael Greene, and of course George Washington, would earn their place in the pantheon of heroes who helped found the nation. On that August night, however, on the eve of the second major battle of the Revolution, they were mostly untried beginners with little experience in the type of warfare in which they were engaged. Nothing served to illustrate that lack of experience better than the shocking oversight of leaving the left wing of the American line undefended and flapping in the breeze.

This was not a mistake the enemy would make, nor was it a mistake the enemy had overlooked.

THE BRITISH COMMAND

Just half a mile away from where the five American officers stood on the Jamaica Road, their eyes turned toward the east, searching the dark for movement, the vanguard of the British army was halted and waiting for word to advance. This one column alone, around 4,000 strong, outnumbered all the Americans defending the Heights of Guana. At its head was Sir Henry Clinton, the second in command of the British forces.

Clinton was around thirty-eight years old (there is some question as to when he was born) by the time of the Battle of Brooklyn, and like most senior officers he had been born into the aristocracy. His father, Admiral George Clinton, was the younger brother of the Earl of Lincoln, and the family was also connected by marriage to the Duke of Newcastle-under-Lyne. Such a bloodline was certainly enough to assure Henry a decent military career.

In 1741, when Henry was still a child, his father accepted the governorship of New York, where Henry lived until returning to England in 1751 to join the British army. Ironically, Clinton's first military experience consisted of service in the New York militia, which now made up part of the force opposing the British on Long Island.

Admiral Clinton died in 1761, leaving behind a considerably smaller estate than most suspected, thus leaving his son less well off than he might have hoped. Maintaining oneself in the style that was expected of an officer and a gentleman of the British army, particularly one from a noble family, was no inexpensive proposition, and Sir Henry spent most of his life plagued by money troubles. There was money enough, however, to purchase commissions for Henry, and before his father's death, he was serving as a captain in the Coldstream Guards. Just a few years later he held the rank of lieutenant colonel.

During the Seven Years' War, Clinton served in Germany as aide-de-camp to the Prince of Brunswick, where he managed to distinguish himself for his brave and gallant service, ending the war as a full colonel. In the interim between the Seven Years' War and the American Revolution, Clinton married a woman named Harriet Carter. They had five children, but soon after giving birth to the fifth Harriet died, and Clinton was nearly driven mad with grief.

Sir Henry Clinton was a good soldier, never wanting in physical courage or thoughtful strategy, but he was not the ideal subordinate. By his own admission he was reticent, "a shy bitch" as he once called himself.

At the same time he was given to strong and often contrary opinions, and he expressed these opinions in less than tactful ways. He and his superior at New York, William Howe, were already chafing in their roles, and even before the fighting started were barely on speaking terms.

Clinton was a freethinker when it came to devising strategy, and his ideas often differed from those of everyone else. In his memoir he wrote that "though a subordinate officer" he felt it his duty "to sometimes exercise my own eyes and understanding in examining the face of the country and the positions and strength of the enemy and take the liberty of humbly submitting to the Commander in Chief, when he permitted me, such measures . . . as my observations suggested."

The various commanders in chief did not always appreciate the humility with which Clinton made his suggestions, and his lack of social grace led to his ideas being frequently dismissed. "My zeal may perhaps on these occasions," Clinton admitted, "have carried me so far as to be at times thought troublesome, nor will I presume to say that my plans were always best or even practicable."

Awkward though he might have been in expressing them, Clinton's plans were often solid, sometimes brilliant. The flanking movement that he led along the King's Highway to the Jamaica Road was a case in point. Clinton had taken it upon himself to reconnoiter the American strength along the Heights of Guana and found "but a few passes through them by which they could be penetrated." Among them was "a pass to their left about a night's march from us which I thought practicable."

Clinton drew up plans for a cavalry attack on the Jamaica Pass, which, he assured Cornwallis, "once possessed, gives us the island." Clinton's plans called for the American left flank to be turned by a column that was "in very great force, for reasons too obvious to require detailing." The attack would begin with a demonstration on the enemy's right, the end of the line farthest from Jamaica Pass, and include assaults and artillery barrages all along the line. These feints would be "vigorously but not too obstinately persisted in," in order to distract the Americans from the real purpose. With the Americans looking to the west, the flanking column would advance around the eastern end of the line, and once it got "possession of the pass above Howard's House, the rebels must quit directly or be ruined."

Clinton understood that he was obnoxious and disliked and that any plan coming from him would be immediately suspect. So, at Clinton's request, the plan was carried to headquarters by Sir William Erskine, a commander of dragoons; there, Clinton wrote, "it did not seem to be much relished." Indeed, the plan seems to have been met with something akin to derision. Major General James Grant, for one, a tough Scotsman and veteran of the French and Indian War, saw little need for such fancy maneuvers. Grant had commanded American militia during the previous war and had been taken prisoner in part because of the failure of his men to fight, which left him with no high opinion of American fighting capabilities.

Grant was famous for having stood up in the House of Commons at the outbreak of the Revolution and announced that with 5,000 British troops he could march from one end of the continent to the other. At the time he said it, it was likely true, but now there was a genuine army of the United States, with more than 20,000 men under arms. Still, Grant's opinion had not changed. He favored a direct assault by overwhelming force on the passes through the Heights of Guana.

The responsibility for that decision, however, was not his. That honor rested with William Howe, commander of the land forces in North America (save for Quebec, which was still under the leadership of Governor Guy Carleton). Howe's older brother, Admiral Richard, the Fourth Viscount Howe, had six months earlier been made overall commander in chief in America.

William Howe came from a family that was about as prominent and well connected as one could be. His mother was thought to be the illegitimate daughter of George I, and though that was never officially acknowledged, the Howes were treated like a branch of the family. Howe's mother received an annual pension from court of £750, which was later increased to £1,250, and she was a member of the household of George III. Admiral Lord Richard was well connected in court in his own right, having been shipmates with the king's brother, Edward, who had served in the Royal Navy. George III's daughter Charlotte was godmother to Richard Howe's first child. The king often turned to him for advice with naval matters, which were not a peripheral matter but rather a central concern to the king of an island nation.

William Howe, youngest of the Howe brothers, enjoyed the benefits of his family's wealth and royal connections, one of which was the certainty of advancement in the military service. Army commissions in the eighteenth century were purchased, not awarded, as a means of keeping control of the army in the hands of the aristocracy (advancement in the navy was greatly aided by influence such as that of the Howes, but rank could not be purchased).

Commissions were not cheap. A lieutenancy of an infantry company might go for five hundred pounds sterling, a commission as a lieutenant colonel five times that amount. The Howe family wealth allowed them to buy William a lieutenancy at eighteen, a captaincy at twenty-one, and a post as lieutenant colonel at twenty-eight.

The now seemingly odd system of purchasing rank rather than earning it would appear to invite incompetence in the leadership. That certainly happened, but for the most part the British army was as competent and professional as any in Europe. William Howe was an example of the British system at its best. Wealth and connections assured him of rank commensurate with his status, but his position of command in the army was also well deserved. During the French and Indian War he served with bravery and distinction both in Europe and in America. Under General James Wolfe he led the first troops, the "forlorn hope," up the narrow path outside Quebec to the Plains of Abraham where the battle for the city was fought and won. In numerous actions following, William Howe added to his reputation for daring and intelligent leadership.

Howe was a big man, six feet tall, with the same heavy features and dark complexion as his brother, who was known in the navy as "Black Dick." Like most sons of the aristocracy they attended Eton, though neither showed much aptitude for scholarship, and they were known for being inarticulate. Their native intelligence lay in other directions, and both men had well-deserved reputations as effective and fair leaders. Both would introduce changes and innovations that greatly improved their respective services.

There was a third Howe brother as well, the eldest of the three. George Augustus, the Third Viscount Howe, had also served as an officer in the British army in America during the French and Indian War. His skill and leadership were so esteemed by the colonists that when he was killed in a skirmish at Ticonderoga in 1758, the General Court of Massachusetts voted £250 be raised to erect a monument to him in Westminster Abbey. The younger Howe brothers never forgot that kindness, and it shaped their view toward the colonists, which was largely friendly and sympathetic.

As a result of their affection for Americans and their liberal political leanings, the Howes were not much interested in taking part in a war against the colonies, and it was only when George III personally requested that they go to America that they relented. On their insistence, they were given the authority to make peace as well as war, but the concessions they were authorized to offer as peace commissioners were limited, so limited that they made no progress at all in negotiating an end to the fighting.

So, in late August of 1776, a few weeks after he turned forty-seven years old, with thirty years of service in the British military, William Howe prepared to lead the largest army ever deployed from England in what would prove to be the biggest battle, numerically, of the American Revolution. The 19,000 British and German troops ferried over to Long Island represented a little more than half of the men under Howe's command, while Washington had 8,000 defending the Heights of Guana and the defenses around Brooklyn, and 19,000 total. Nearly every general officer who would play a significant role in the Revolution on either side was in New York that day.

Despite the superiority of numbers, Howe was not of the same mind as James Grant. He did not hold his enemy in contempt, and he did not relish trying to simply fight his way through the Heights' narrow and easily defended passes. In the few days since receiving Clinton's suggestions for a march around the American left, Howe had begun to see the wisdom of it, particularly after being assured by Loyalist cavalry officer Oliver De Lancey that it was feasible. Though in his report to American Secretary George Germain he failed to mention Clinton's part in the planning, Howe followed his second in command's ideas almost to the letter. On the evening of August 26 the first column advanced toward Jamaica Pass. The Battle of Brooklyn was under way.

JAMAICA PASS

Clinton led the vanguard, which consisted of a brigade of light infantry and the light dragoons. They marched off from Flatlands, about four miles southwest of Jamaica Pass, at 8:00 P.M., moving fast and as quietly as they could. Three Loyalist farmers served as guides at the head of the column.

Behind Clinton came Lord Charles Cornwallis with the reserves, consisting of "the First Brigade and the Seventy-First Regiment, with fourteen field pieces." The narrow lanes on which the armies moved did not permit "two columns of march," so the main body of the army, under the command of Hugh, Lord Percy, followed some distance behind Clinton and Cornwallis, ready to sweep into the American rear once the advance troops had secured Jamaica Pass. General Howe would also accompany the flanking column.

"Between eleven and twelve o'clock," Clinton wrote, "being in a lane, we heard much firing in the rear of the column." The gunfire likely came from American militia standing sentry at Flatbush who accidentally fired on other American troops in the dark, but it was enough to make Clinton fear that surprise was lost. He hurried his column along, leaving the road and crossing open fields on a direct line to Howard's Tavern and the pass beyond.

The troops continued over the cleared fields until, as Clinton wrote, "my guides informed me we were within a quarter mile of Howard's House, which was a few hundred yards from the gorge I wished to lay hold of." Clinton sent a patrol forward to scout the approach to the pass and see if it was occupied by American troops. The men moved quietly though the dark night, keeping their bearings by the few lights glowing in the windows of the tavern.

The five American militia officers never heard them coming. Watching the Old Jamaica Road that ran to Howard's Tavern from the northeast, they did not see the light troops approaching from the southwest over open ground. Then suddenly they were surrounded, and even in the dark they could not miss the gleam of bayonets. They surrendered to Clinton's patrol without a shot fired, without an alarm raised, with hardly a sound.

The British patrol returned to the head of the column with the prisoners and the news that Jamaica Pass was unoccupied, that the five men now in their custody were all the defense the Americans had posted there. Clinton sent a detachment into the pass itself and stationed units along the Bedford Road that ran through the pass to make sure the flank remained unguarded, then "waited for daylight to take possession in force."

Even before Clinton had secured Jamaica Pass, six miles to the east, the Battle of Brooklyn had already begun.

Major General James Grant commanded around 5,000 men on the British left, just the number he claimed to need to march from one end of the continent to the other. Though Grant was eager to have at the rebels, his orders were to simply make a vigorous diversion to draw attention from Clinton's flanking maneuver, at least until it was clear that Clinton's column had come in behind the enemy. Then Grant could turn his diversion into an all-out attack.

Opposed to Grant was Alexander, Lord Stirling, with 500 men, a mixed group of Pennsylvanians, Delawarites, Marylanders, and others. Allegedly Lord Stirling was in the gallery of the House of Commons when Grant made his boast about marching across America. Now it was Stirling's chance, as well as his duty, to prove that Grant could not even get as far as Brooklyn.

As Grant's men were advancing toward the American right, a guard of 120 Pennsylvanians from the regiment of Colonel Samuel Atlee were sent ahead of the lines to watch for the enemy's approach. A public house called the Red Lion Tavern stood near the crossroads, and it was there that the Pennsylvanians took up their post. Around 11:00 P.M. on the night of August 26, the sentries "descried two men coming up a water-melon patch, upon which our men fired upon them."

Whether the men were advance pickets from Grant's column or British soldiers in search of a uniquely American snack is not clear, but either way they retreated, and Grant now knew where the American lines began. Around 1:00 A.M. on August 27 Grant sent about 300 men forward to attack the guard at the Red Lion. A sharp fight ensued, with the Americans holding their ground and exchanging fire with the British troops until it was clear that the enemy were working their way around the American flank in an effort to surround them. The Pennsylvanians then "retreated to alarm the remainder of the battalion."

Brigadier General Samuel Holden Parsons was the commanding officer for the men charged with holding the western approach. At first light some of the guards who had been driven off rushed to Parsons's quarters and informed him "the enemy were advancing in great numbers by that road." Parsons turned out at the alarm and found the British "were through the wood & descending the hill on the North side." Parsons rounded up twenty of the guards who had been driven from the Red Lion Tavern, all that he could find, and "took post on a height in their [the enemy's] front at about half a mile's distance—which halted their column & gave time for Lord Stirling with his forces to come up."

General Israel Putnam was posted behind the earthworks at Brooklyn Heights when he received word of the attack. He immediately sent orders to Lord Stirling to oppose the British advance. "About 3 oClock in the morning of the 27th," Stirling wrote, "I was Called up and Informed by General Putnam that the Enemy were advancing by the Road from flat Bush to the Red Lyon, and ordered me to March with the two Regiments nearest at hand to Meet them."

The two regiments closest were a battalion of Marylanders under the command of Colonel William Smallwood and Delaware troops commanded by Colonel John Haslet. Stirling led his men south toward the

Red Lion just as the sun was coming up on a perfect summer morning, "cool clear & pleasant," as one observer noted.

Stirling and his troops were about half a mile from the tavern when they ran into Atlee's Pennsylvanians, who had first been sent there to guard the road. "Col: Atlee . . . Informed me, that the Enemy was in Sight," Stirling reported. "Indeed I then Saw their front between us and the Red Lyon." Stirling sent Atlee's men ahead to take position on the left of the road while he formed up his other regiments along a ridge in the woods.

Atlee's men were in open country, and they found themselves exposed "to the great fire of the enemy's musketry and field pieces, charged with round and grape shot." Though Atlee's men had never been under fire before, they stood their ground until Stirling's men had formed up, then fell back to take position in the woods to the left of the other brigades. Despite the intensity of the fighting, Atlee lost only one man, "shot with a grape shot through his throat."

Stirling had about 1,600 men deployed against Grant's 5,000 or so. Grant sent a column of men to move around the American left to try to flank Stirling's line. Seeing this, Stirling repositioned Atlee and Parsons to meet this threat. The officers, with around 300 men, took position on a hill to the left of Stirling's line, where they were assaulted by the 44th and 23rd regiments. The Americans "repulsed them in every attack with considerable loss," Parsons wrote to John Adams. "The number of dead we had collected together & the heap the enemy had made we supposed amounted to about 60." In fact, the British lost 27 men killed and 103 wounded to Parsons and Atlee's 1 killed and 2 wounded. Among the British killed was a Lieutenant Colonel Grant, which gave rise to the rumor that James Grant himself had been cut down.

For two hours Grant's men, with their superior numbers, and Stirling's men, with their superior position, exchanged fierce fire with musket, rifle, and cannon. Grant was discovering that his movement across America was not so unrestricted as he supposed. Of course, he was not trying to break through Stirling's line. He was trying to do exactly what he was doing—pin down the American right flank while Clinton swept around the left.

General John Sullivan, in command of all the American troops arrayed along the Heights of Guana, was headquartered near the center of the line between the Flatbush and Bedford passes. Opposed to him were a little over 4,000 Hessian troops under the command of General Leopold Philip von Heister, who, unlike Grant, was not making much of a diversion. By sunrise on the 27th the Germans had not advanced enough even to drive in the America pickets, but rather contented themselves with cannon fire at the American lines.

Aware that a sharp fight was taking place on the American right, Sullivan rode down to the Flatbush Pass to get a sense for what the Germans were up to. Seeing that little was happening there, and that the brunt of the enemy's attack seemed to be against Stirling's men, he shifted a brigade to the right flank to bolster Stirling, leaving about 800 men to hold off the Hessians if and when they finally advanced.

At sunup, just about the time that Samuel Holden Parsons was making his first stand against Grant's troops with 20 of Atlee's riflemen, Clinton was sending the entire vanguard ahead into the Jamaica Pass to secure it against any American attempt to hold it, but none came. Now in full possession of the back door to the American lines, Clinton waited for Howe and the main column to join him so that they could press their attack down the Jamaica Road to Bedford.

It was about two hours later that Howe finally arrived and the entire column, 10,000 strong, began to roll forward. Howe was still wary of the entire operation. Indeed, according to Clinton, Howe "did not expect any good to come from the move" and seemed reluctant to advance his men through the pass. Even as they did, Howe "seemed to have some suspicion the enemy would attack us on our march." Clinton dismissed Howe's concerns, certain that "as they neglected to oppose us at the gorge, the affair was over." This might be what passed for humility with Henry Clinton, but in fact he was right.

The American left nearest to Jamaica Pass was held by a Pennsylvania regiment under the command of Colonel Samuel Miles, a veteran of the French and Indian War. Miles would later claim that he saw the disaster coming and warned Sullivan of it. Writing some time after the Revolution, Miles recalled that Sullivan had visited his camp on August 26, at which time Miles informed him that the bulk of the British army lay to the left of his position, and that he was "convinced when the army moved that Gen'l Howe would fall into the Jamaica road, and I hoped there were troops there to watch them." Miles's regiment was at least two miles west of the pass.

Unfair as it now seems, after the disaster on Long Island, Miles came in for a good portion of the blame for allowing Clinton to flank the American line. Miles certainly felt the criticism was unjust, and he maintained that despite his warnings of the army's vulnerability on the left, Sullivan did nothing to correct the problem. "If Gen'l Sullivan had taken the requisite precaution," Miles wrote, "and given his orders agreeable to the attention of the Commander-in-chief, there would have been few if any prisoners taken."

Much of the blame has to do with the fact that the Americans had no cavalry on Long Island. Washington had been offered a small cavalry unit, but it was so difficult to find fodder for the horses that he declined their service. Thus the Americans were deprived of the traditional eyes and ears of the army. Mounted troops sweeping the perimeter of the defenses certainly would have noticed a column of 10,000 redcoats flanking the American lines. It was yet another example of the American command's "want of experience to move upon a large Scale."

Miles was closer to the Bedford Pass than the Jamaica Pass when the Hessians in his front finally began to move, around 7:00 A.M., which brought on fire from the American lines. "I immediately marched towards where the firing was," Miles wrote, but he had covered no more than a few hundred yards when he was stopped by Colonel Samuel Wyllys, who ordered him to defend the road that led from Flatbush to Jamaica Road.

Both officers were colonels, but Wyllys held a Continental commission and Miles a state commission, which made Wyllys the superior. Still, Miles argued that the enemy was most likely to come through the Jamaica Pass, and if he could not advance toward the gunfire he should be allowed to turn and march for the pass. To this Wyllys agreed, and Miles turned his men around and marched off through the woods toward Jamaica Pass to the east.

Miles's men marched for about two miles before coming out of the woods onto the Jamaica Road, and they were stunned by the sight that greeted them. "To my great mortification," Miles wrote, "I saw the main body of the enemy in full march between me and our lines." Miles's column, hidden in the woods, had marched right past Clinton and now came out at the tail end of the British line, with the baggage guard ahead of him and the rest of the troops already to his west, between him and the works around Brooklyn. Clinton was already through the pass and behind the American lines.

OPPORTUNITY MADE AND LOST

After Clinton's men had advanced unopposed through the Jamaica Pass, they "halted for the soldiers to take a little refreshment," then continued on. They reached the town of Bedford, directly in the rear of the troops guarding the Flatbush and Bedford passes, around 8:30 A.M. Howe wrote, "The attack was commenced by the Light Infantry and Light Dragoons upon large bodies of the Rebels."

Once Clinton and Howe struck in the rear, the Hessians in the Americans' front, who had been biding their time, rolled forward with the grenadiers and jaegers (German light infantry) in the lead and von Heister following behind at the head of the brigades. They quickly formed into their lines of battle, the sharpshooters in the front as they advanced, but they met with little resistance. The Americans had turned to meet that greatest of threats to an eighteenth-century army—an enemy in the rear—and now their front was unguarded. Sullivan's troops were trapped between two advancing armies, and they began to retreat.

Off to the west, Stirling and Parsons were still making a bold stand, holding Grant's troops in check. Stirling wrote, "In this possition we stood Cannonadeing each other 'till Near Eleven oClock, when I found that General Howe with the Main Body [of] the Army was between our men and Our lines." Now, as Sullivan's defense of the two central passes collapsed, the Hessians began to advance against Stirling's lines as well.

After the battle, stories of terrible brutality began to circulate, many of them credible. One British officer wrote, "We took care to tell the *Hessians* that the Rebels had resolved to give no quarter to them in particular, which made them fight desperately, and put all to death that fell into their hands." According to that officer the disinformation worked on the Germans, and the British needed no such inducement. "The *Hessians* and our brave *Highlanders,*" he wrote, "gave no quarters, and it was a fine sight to see with what alacrity they dispatched the Rebels with their bayonets after we had surrounded them so they could not resist."

Seeing that the lines were collapsing and the army flanked, Stirling ordered most of his men "to make the best of their way thro' the [Gowanus] Creek," while he and five companies of Smallwood's Marylanders flung themselves at Cornwallis's 2nd Grenadiers and the 71st Highlanders, who had come up the road behind them. It was Stirling's hope that the Marylanders could both cover the men's retreat and fight their way to safety.

The performance of Stirling and the Marylanders was the most extraordinary of the day, and the only real bright spot for American arms. Again and again they charged the superior British forces, only to be driven back with heavy losses. Finally, with most of the men under his command safely across the creek and heading for the Brooklyn Heights, Stirling ordered the Marylanders to disperse and try to get back to the lines. Some did, but many were killed or taken prisoner. Stirling, finding himself trapped, made his way to the Hessians and surrendered himself to von Heister.

In the confusion, word of the retreat was never sent to Parsons and Atlee, fighting on Stirling's left flank, and they suddenly found themselves alone and nearly surrounded. They ordered their men to fall back as they tried to reach the American lines at Brooklyn, but soon they were completely cut off by Cornwallis's men. Atlee and some of his troops surrendered, but Parsons and seven others managed to hide in the swamp overnight and get back to their lines the next day.

John Sullivan was not so lucky. He, too, was surrounded leading a rearguard action and taken prisoner. Off to the east, Miles and the 230 men under his command tried to fight their way through the flanking column and back to Brooklyn. It was only after hours of bloody fighting that he was finally forced to surrender.

Around 1,500 American troops were killed, wounded, or missing. The rest were put to flight, racing back down the dusty roads and through the plowed fields for the imagined safety of the earthworks on Brooklyn Heights. On their heels were the grenadiers who had formed the vanguard, the Hessians, and the light infantry. It was a messy, confused rout, as the retreating men poured into the earthworks, throwing the defenders there into confusion.

At that point an extraordinary opportunity opened up for William Howe. Rather than simply driving the Americans from their outer lines, he now had the chance to storm their works and carry all of Long Island, capturing half the Continental Army and George Washington himself. "Our men were most eager to attack them in their lines," one British army officer wrote, "and I am convinced would have carried them." Clinton was all for pushing on as well. "I had at that moment but little inclination to check the ardor of our troops when I saw the enemy flying in such panic before them," he wrote.

Howe did not feel the same. Quite unexpectedly, he ordered a halt to the advance. It was a decision many found shocking.

Most of the British officers who had fought that day were as surprised as they were furious. "I was also not without hopes," Clinton wrote, "that his Excellency, who was on a neighboring hill and, of course, saw their confusion, might be tempted to order us to march directly forward down the road to the [Brooklyn] ferry, by which, if we succeeded, everything on the island must have been ours."

Clinton made it clear that he did not mean to "insinuate that Sir William Howe was in the least wrong," before going on to explain the many reasons why Howe's decision was stupid on its face, concluding that "there is no saying to what extent the effect resulting from the entire loss of that army might have been carried in that early stage of the rebellion, or where it might have stopped."

Most did not bother with the kind of disingenuous civility that Clinton displayed. Charles Stedman, the British officer turned historian, wrote that the Americans raced to their lines "in evident confusion. It is to be lamented that this advantage was not pursued; for in the confusion into which the enemy were thrown by the rapid march of the English army, a most decisive victory would have undoubtedly accrued to the British arms."

Perhaps more reflective of the anger that the other officers felt were the words of Sir George Collier, captain of the forty-four-gun ship *Rainbow,* anchored off Long Island:

> The Americans, *frightened, defeated,* and *dismayed,* were pursued to the edge of a ditch of a temporary work they had thrown up, into which the victorious troops *would* have entered with them, *had they not been restrained* by the most positive *orders* of the General. The retreat was sounded, and the conquering army *halted.* Their ardour was, by this means, *cruelly checked;* and one of the most glorious opportunities for ending the rebellion *lost.*

Historians have generally agreed with the officers under Howe's command that Howe ignored the chance to strike a decisive blow, one that might have changed the course of the war. Instead he began a formal siege, laboriously digging trenches, or "regular approaches," toward the American works. Two days later, in the course of a single night, Washington moved his entire army to safety across the East River. It was one of the truly extraordinary maneuvers of the Revolution, and Howe did not even know it was taking place until it was over.

The question remains, why did William Howe pass up an opportunity that everyone else recognized as an unparalleled chance to bring the enemy to their knees? In his report to Germain he wrote, "Had they [the British troops] been permitted to go on, it is my opinion they would have carried the redoubt; but as it was apparent that the lines must have been ours at a very cheap rate by regular approaches, I would not risk the loss that might have been sustained in the assault."

Howe had no doubt that his men could have taken the American entrenchments by direct assault, but he also believed they would pay too high a price if they tried. The commander in chief had learned a hard lesson about launching a frontal attack against American troops hunkered down behind earthworks, and that lesson saved the Continental Army from ruin after the disastrous rout on Long Island.

It was a lesson that William Howe had learned at Bunker Hill.

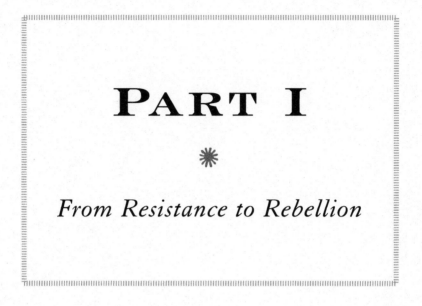

PART I

*

From Resistance to Rebellion

Chapter One

THE LEXINGTON ALARM

Bunker Hill. It must have looked like the promised land, glowing golden in the setting sun, to the 1,800 or so British soldiers who staggered across Charlestown Neck and along the base of that high ground on the evening of April 19, 1775. They were men of the 4th Regiment of Foot, known as the King's Own, the 5th, or Northumberland Fusiliers, the 10th, 18th, and 23rd, the famed Royal Welsh Fusiliers, and others. There were Royal Marines and artillery. They were exhausted, starved, wounded, and choking with thirst, dogged and harassed to madness by American militia all the way from Concord, sixteen miles away.

At their head rode Brigadier General Hugh, Lord Percy, the thirty-two-year-old son of the Duke of Northumberland, colonel of the Northumberland Fusiliers, heir to one of the greatest fortunes in England, and a skilled and experienced soldier. The fabric of his fine waistcoat was torn where a bullet had carried a button away, but beyond that he was unhurt. The same was not true for many of the men under his command.

Percy had arrived in Boston on July 5, 1774, as part of the buildup of troops sent to enforce Parliament's disciplinary measures against the city.

A number of things surprised him, including the price of necessities in that embargoed city. For the "handsomest" horse in the country, by Percy's reckoning, he told his father, "I was forced to give 450£." He also "got some tolerable chaise-horses from N.Y., for there were none good eno' in this country." Additionally he was able to rent the home of the former governor, but used it only for dining, "for we are all obliged to remain at other times & sleep in camp." Percy entertained his fellow officers as well as "occasionally the Gentlemen of the country." It was a busy schedule. "I have always a table of 12 covers every day. This, tho' very expensive, is however very necessary."

Percy was a Whig and a man of liberal tendencies, generally sympathetic with the struggles of the American colonies, but he arrived with some preconceived notions about the people of Massachusetts that meeting them did not change. Just a few weeks after arriving in America, Percy wrote to his father, "The people in this part of the country are in general made up of rashness & timidity. Quick & violent in their determinations, they are fearful in the execution of them . . . To hear them talk, you would imagine that they would attack us & demolish us every night; & yet, whenever we appear, they are frightened out of their wits."

The ten months Percy spent in Boston only reinforced this view, and during that time he was able to see firsthand the deterioration of the political situation. By the end of October, still five months before the fighting at Lexington and Concord, he was writing to his friend and distant cousin the Rev. Thomas Percy, "Our affairs here are in the most Critical Situation imaginable; Nothing less than the total loss or Conquest of the Colonies must be the End of it. Either indeed is disagreeable, but one or the other now is absolutely necessary."

On the night of April 18, General Thomas Gage, commander in chief of the army and governor of Massachusetts, ordered his troops to march on a secret mission. They were to seize military stores, particularly gunpowder, small arms, and artillery, secreted in the town of Concord. Though it was not committed to writing, they were also to arrest the chief leaders of the insurrection, John Hancock and Samuel Adams.

Gage had arrived at Boston about a month before Percy, and like

Percy quickly grasped the situation. Indeed, Gage, with the benefit of age and many years of experience in America, understood the situation better than Percy, and far better than the ministry in England. Gage knew, among other things, that the force he had in Boston was utterly inadequate for the mission London expected him to accomplish. In late 1774 Gage had requested of the American secretary in London, William Legge, the Second Earl of Dartmouth, an army of 20,000 men.

It was just a few weeks before the action at Lexington and Concord that Gage received an answer from Dartmouth. The violence committed in Massachusetts, Dartmouth informed Gage, "appeared to me as the acts of a rude rabble, without plan, without concert and without conduct." Dartmouth in London assured Gage in Boston that "a smaller force now, if put to the test, would be able to encounter them with a greater probability of success" than would a 20,000-man army once the rebels had organized.

The secret mission Gage planned for the 18th was in response to Dartmouth's letter. It was "the opinion of the King's servants," Dartmouth wrote, "in which His Majesty concurs, that the first and essential step to be taken towards reestablishing government would be to arrest and imprison the principal actors and abettors" of the insurrection. No local court would ever find them guilty, of course, but under the new laws governing the colony "the courts of justice are at present not permitted to be opened," and thus their imprisonment without trial was likely to be a long one.

Gage was also to "on no account suffer the inhabitants of at least the town of Boston to assemble themselves in arms on any pretense whatever either of town-guard or militia duty." Dartmouth added, pointedly, that "a report prevails that you have not only indulged them in having such a guard but have also allowed their militia to train and discipline in Faneuil Hall."

Under those suggestions and admonitions Gage gave orders for the troops to assemble on a deserted beach on Boston's Back Bay, where boats from the Royal Navy would carry them across the Charles River to the opposite shore. In command of the column was Lieutenant Colonel

Francis Smith, an old and experienced officer. Second was the very able Major John Pitcairn of the marines. The troops, about 800 in all, were the elite of Gage's army.

By the mid-eighteenth century, every British regiment had attached to it two distinct companies called "flank companies." One of these flank companies was the grenadiers, the biggest and strongest troops in the army, made more formidable looking by their distinctive tall beaver hats. Originally their function had been to hurl the crude hand grenades of the period. By the time of the Revolution they no longer sported grenades but rather served as the shock troops of the army, the unstoppable infantry wave.

The other flank company was the light infantry, and their inclusion as a regular part of the army was largely through the influence of William Howe. While rank-and-file troops were drilled in marching and firing in formation, the light infantry was trained in more irregular tactics such as open-order combat, woodland fighting, swimming, climbing, and marksmanship. Having come to appreciate the utility of light infantry during the French and Indian War, Howe persuaded the king to create such a company in every regiment. The light infantry was composed of the most active and intelligent troops. They were the forerunners of today's special forces, and their organization, training, and field tactics were largely Howe's doing.

For the mission to Concord, Gage chose to send only the flank companies. To keep the intended operation a secret, he issued general orders on April 15 that "the Grenadiers and Light Infantry in order to learn Grenadrs. Exercise and new evolutions are to be off all duties 'till further orders." This subterfuge did not fool many. Lieutenant John Barker commented in his diary, "This I suppose is by way of a blind. I dare say they have something for them to do."

Not only did the officers guess something was up, but Gage's secret leaked out to the general public with shocking speed. The first inkling that something was amiss came from the British sailors who had received orders to man the boats and bring them around to Back Bay, and who, in the way of sailors everywhere, could not keep their mouths shut.

This and other hints made their way to the Sons of Liberty and the leaders of the insurrection in Boston. Sam Adams and John Hancock had left town a few weeks before to attend a meeting of the Provincial Congress and had concluded that it would be healthier for them to remain out of town. The only man central to the revolutionary movement left in Boston was Dr. Joseph Warren.

Word of British movement reached Warren, but neither he nor anyone else knew what the target was. Warren had another source of information, however, an informant very close to General Gage. That person's identity was so secret no one but Warren ever knew who it was, though it was and still is strongly suspected that the informant was Gage's American wife, Margaret Kemble Gage.

Whoever it was, Warren tapped that source and received confirmation of the British plans to march on Concord and to arrest Hancock and Adams. He sent Richard Dawes, Paul Revere, and possibly another express rider to alarm the countryside, though their primary mission was to alert Hancock and Adams to the danger.

John Crozier, who was in command of the flotilla of boats carrying the troops across the river from Boston, recalled that, despite the secrecy, the people of the town guessed that something was afoot. "In consequence of this conception," he wrote, "a light was shown at the top of a church stiple directing those in the country to be on guard." That, of course, was Revere's famous "two if by sea" lanterns in the steeple of the Old North Church.

The result of all this activity was that the arrival of the "regulars," as the British troops were called, at Lexington Green was anything but a surprise. Most of the military stores had been moved to safety, and Hancock and Adams, along with other revolutionary leaders also in the path of the British column, such as Elbridge Gerry, Jeremiah Lee, and Azor Orne, managed to escape.

More ominously for the British troops, American militia had turned out in significant and ever increasing numbers. Lieutenant Colonel Smith sent word to Gage that the countryside was alarmed and reinforcements would be needed. Both British and American officers had admonished their men not to fire the first shot, but as British troops advanced on the American militia on the green, someone disobeyed that order. A gun went off, and when it did, the British regulars, acting without orders, fired a volley into the militia, and the militia fired back. Eight Americans were killed in the brief exchange, ten wounded; the remaining militia dispersed. One British private was injured slightly. The first blood of the war was spilled, the first fight between British and American troops begun.

Who fired the shot, whether British or American, is not clear. It was important to both sides, politically and morally, that it not be them, that they could lay the blame for bloodshed on their enemy. Many depositions were taken after the incident, but no consensus has ever emerged. Most British witnesses believed the Americans fired first, and, predictably, most Americans felt it was the British. It just as likely might have been a misfire, a nervous finger on the trigger, or the weak catch slipping on the flintlock of an ancient musket. Possibly more than one gun went off at the same time. It was one of the most momentous shots in history, and it will probably never be known who fired it.

Smith's column moved on to Concord, where they destroyed what war matériel they could find, which was not much. The Americans had hidden the most valuable stores, and the regulars found only some gun carriages, musket balls, a few iron cannons, and sundry tools. In fact, the Concord raid did more harm than good. The time spent searching the town gave the militia more chance to collect, and the smoke from two buildings that were burned—whether by accident or purposefully is not known—alerted more militia to the danger.

While Smith's men were searching the town for supplies, more and more American troops gathered nearby until they numbered around 400. With the smoke from the burning buildings rising in the early morning sky, it was obvious that the time for action had come. The militia marched off to Concord's North Bridge, "with as much order as the best disciplined Troops," a British officer noted, where three companies of Smith's infantry were posted.

The British were "drawn up in order to fire Street fireing," that is, in three ranks, one behind the other, while the Americans on the other side of the river deployed in a single line. The British fired, but the Americans stood their ground and, to the surprise and dismay of the British, returned fire with an intensity that drove the regulars back. Under the fusillade of American shot the unthinkable happened—the British formation broke, and the redcoats were put to flight, running back down the road toward the protection of the rest of their troops.

By noon Smith had restored order, and his column moved out, beginning the long march back to Boston. Smith sent companies out on the army's flanks to sweep the militia from the stone walls and stands of trees that bordered the road. For a mile or so they met with no resistance, but then, as the flankers rejoined the column, the firing began. The fighting grew heavier as more and more Yankee militia joined those already lying in wait for the redcoats. To the increasingly worried regulars it seemed as if "men had dropped from the clouds."

Soon Smith's column was badly outnumbered, with militia firing on either side and a large body of armed men following behind. Lieutenant Colonel Smith himself was shot in the leg and badly wounded. Lieutenant John Barker of the King's Own Regiment of Foot recalled, "The Country was an amazing strong one, full of Hills, Woods, stone Walls, &c., which the Rebels did not fail to take advantage of, for they were all lined with People who kept an incessant fire upon us, as we did too upon them but not with the same advantage, for they were so concealed there was hardly any seeing them."

As Smith's column began to take casualties, discipline began to break down. By the time Lexington was in sight the men were starting to run, driven by building panic and a desire to get away from the murderous fire of the militia. The officers tried to form the men into column, but they were beyond listening. "At last," wrote Ensign Henry De Berniere, "we got to Lexington and the officers got to the front and presented their bayonets, and told the men if they advanced they should die. Upon this they began to form under Heavy fire."

It was around 2:00 P.M., and Smith's column had been on the move since the evening before, having marched through the night and morning.

The men were exhausted, hungry, and thirsty. Many were wounded. They were surrounded by an enemy that they could not get at, and their ammunition was running low. Lieutenant Barker was staggering along with his troops; he later wrote, "Very few Men had any ammunition left, and so fatigued that we cou'd not keep flanking parties out, so that we must soon have laid down our Arms, or been picked off by the Rebels at their pleasure." Then the men in the van saw a sight that must have seemed like a gift from heaven itself, and they began to shout and cheer. "In this critical situation," Lieutenant Barker wrote, "we perceived the 1st Brigade coming to our assistance."

"A CLEVER LITTLE ARMY"

Even before Smith's request for reinforcements arrived, Gage was growing concerned for the safety of the flank companies. He was certainly aware that his secret was out. Percy had overheard civilians on Boston Common talking about the march to Concord, and he informed Gage of this. According to one British officer, "the town was a good deal agitated and alarmed" by the troops mustering on the beach. Gage may even have heard the clang of alarm bells rolling over the Charles River from the countryside beyond.

Not wanting to wait for word of a disaster, Gage gave orders for the 1st Brigade to muster under arms at 4:00 A.M. What followed was a staggering series of blunders that delayed the relief troops by hours and doubtless resulted in many more casualties than the British might otherwise have suffered.

Gage sent written orders to the brigade major of the 1st, an officer named Montcrieffe, who was responsible for seeing the men mustered. Major Montcrieffe was not at his quarters, and rather than hunt him down the messenger left the orders for him. When Montcrieffe finally returned, his servant neglected to mention the sealed note from the commander in chief. The major went to bed unaware that his men had been ordered into battle.

Four o'clock rolled around, and the brigade failed to muster. At 5:00 A.M. a breathless rider pounded into headquarters with a request from Smith for reinforcements. It was only then that Gage learned that the 1st Brigade was still in bed. At 6:00 Gage sent another order "for the 1st Brigade to assemble at ½ past 7 on the grand parade."

Two divisions of marines were also ordered to accompany the 1st Brigade, their orders sent at the same time as the first set of orders to Major Montcrieffe. In this case the orders were addressed to the commanding officer of the marines, Major John Pitcairn. The messenger did not find Pitcairn at his quarters because he was at that moment marching to Lexington with Smith's column. As was done with Montcrieffe's orders, Pitcairn's were left at his quarters to wait for his return.

The 1st Brigade was "on the parade at the hour appointed, with one days provisions," but the marines were nowhere to be found. The minutes ticked by as that mix-up was straightened out. Unknown to the assembled troops, about ten miles away their brothers in arms were just arriving in Concord after having marched all night and exchanged fire with the minutemen at Lexington Green. Soon those men, so far from their base of operations and reinforcements, would start taking serious casualties from the growing mob of armed colonials.

By 8:30 the marines, with their red coats and bright white cross belts, were assembled on the parade. It was then that the men learned their mission. "Here we understood that we were to march out of town to support the troops that went out last night," Lieutenant Frederick Mackenzie noted in his diary. No one seems to have been much worried about the hazards of the mission. The British army was one of the best trained, best equipped, and best led armies in the world. During the time those troops had been in Boston, the American militia had never attempted armed resistance, and it made the regulars contemptuous of Yankee courage and willingness to fight. They were not concerned about the danger posed by farmers with muskets. At 8:45 they moved out.

In the van of the column was an advance guard of a captain and fifty men. Behind them came the Royal Artillery in their blue coats, accompanying two six-pounder field guns drawn by teams of horses. After them the 4th and the 47th regiments, the battalion of marines, the Royal Welsh Fusiliers, and last a rear guard of fifty men. In all there were about 1,000 troops out of what Percy referred to as "a clever little Army."

The column marched through the narrow streets of Boston and across the neck of land that connected the city to the mainland at Roxbury. As they marched they played a fife and drum tune that had become a favorite of the British army in Boston, "Yankee Doodle." As Captain W. Glanville Evelyn of the 4th Regiment wrote, the brigade marched along in the morning sun, "little suspecting what was going on."

It was a lovely morning in a lovely country, one, in fact, that Percy very much admired. He wrote to his father:

It is most delightfully varied. The hills, rising from the valleys by gradual & gentle ascents, interspersed everywhere with trees, give it a most agreeable appearance. Nor do the small lakes of water with which the country abounds, contribute little towards the richness of the scene. In short, it has everywhere the appearance of a Park finely laid out.

The countryside around Boston was sparsely but evenly settled, or, as Captain Evelyn said, "This country is a continued village." Still, as the 1st Brigade marched down the road toward Lexington it was clear that something was not right. "In all the places we marched through, and in the houses on the road, few or no people were to be seen," Lieutenant Mackenzie wrote, "and the houses in general shut up."

The column continued its march to Lexington, but Percy could find no one to give him an idea of what was taking place to the northwest. It was not until he had marched through Menotomy (today called Arlington) that Percy "was informed that the Rebels had attacked His Majesty's Troops, who were retiring, overpowered by numbers, greatly exhausted & fatigued, & having expended almost all their ammunition."

Hearing that, Percy pushed the men on, "as fast as good order & not blowing the men would allow." The 1st Battalion and the marines marched up the Lexington Road toward the town where the fighting had begun. It was around 2:00 P.M., as the grenadiers and light infantry staggered into Lexington from the northwest, that Percy's column approached the town from the southeast. Mackenzie recalled, "We heard some straggling shots fired from about a mile in our front:—As we advanced we heard the firing plainer and more frequent."

As the battalion approached Lexington, they could at last see the remains of the flank companies now all but running down the Lexington Road, pursued by a great crowd of militia. The gunfire was nearly continuous, and a cloud of gray smoke hung in the air and trailed behind the advancing troops.

The extent of the disaster was immediately clear to Percy, and he wasted not a moment. He ordered the artillerymen to bring their six-pounders up to a high point at the south end of town called Munroe's Hill. "I immediately ordered the 2 field-pieces to fire at the Rebels," Percy reported, "and drew up the Brigade on a Height."

The six-pounders opened up at long range on the pursuing militia, and they had the desired effect. Barker wrote, "As soon as the Rebels saw this reinforcement, and tasted the field pieces, they retired." Practically speaking, muskets fired from the flank companies offered much greater danger to the militia than cannons fired from a distance at men in loose formation, but the psychological impact of the field pieces was much greater. For the first time since the fighting began, the Americans disengaged and dropped back.

Percy ordered his men to form in a line of battle on either side of the road, which they did with the speed and efficiency of highly trained troops, though "by reason of the Stone walls and other obstructions it was not formed in so regular a manner as it should have been." One of the key differences between trained, professional troops such as the British and the embattled farmers who opposed them was the ability to form and maneuver as a unit on the battlefield and to deliver volleys of fire against an enemy in tight formation. Training and discipline also allowed men to stand up to an enemy's volley without breaking and running in panic. This was the standard eighteenth-century mode of combat and the way the British would have expected to fight another European army. This was also the reason that the untrained Americans had no intention of meeting the British in an open field.

From the high ground on which they were formed, the 1st Brigade got a good look at what they were up against. "We could observe a Considerable number of the Rebels," Mackenzie wrote, "but they were very much scattered, and not above 50 of them could be seen in a body in any place. Many lay concealed behind the Stone walls and fences." The grenadiers and light infantry rushed through the gap made by the road in the 1st Brigade's line and collapsed to the ground in exhaustion, free at last from the deadly tormentors who had chased them nearly all the way from Concord.

Among those who came staggering through the line was twenty-two-year-old Ensign Jeremy Lister, a young officer of the 10th Regiment of Foot. He was not part of a flank company, and so had not been called up to go with the 2nd Brigade when they marched on April 18, but when one of the lieutenants of the 10th's grenadiers who lodged in the same house as Lister turned out for the secret mission, Lister accompanied him to the parade ground, "anxious to know the reason for this Order."

On the parade they met Captain Parsons of the light infantry. Parsons was waiting with mounting impatience for the arrival of one of his lieutenants, James Hamilton. When Hamilton at last sent word that he was sick, Lister volunteered to go in his place and rushed back to his lodging to get his gear. He met the company as they were marching through the dark streets toward the Back Bay and the waiting boats. Lieutenant Colonel Smith told Lister to go back to town "and not go into danger for others particularly Hamilton whose Illness was suppos'd by everybody to be feign'd which twas clearly prov'd to be the case afterwards." (Hamilton's name disappears from the Army List in 1776. This incident may have led to the loss of his commission.)

Lister argued that "it would be rather a disgrace for the Comp^y to March on an expedition, more especially it being the first, without its Compliment of Officers." At this Smith relented, and Lister joined the 2nd Brigade on its march and stood with the troops at Lexington Green and the Concord Bridge. As the column retreated toward Lexington, the ensign recalled, it "became a general Firing upon us from all Quarters, from behind hedges and Walls [and] we return'd the fire every opportunity."

As he and the others marched through that hail of musket fire, Lister "rec^d a shot through my Right Elbow joint," which shattered the joint and left the ball lodged in his arm. Clutching the agonizing wound, blood running over his hand, Lister hurried on, the firing growing more and more intense as the militia poured in from the surrounding communities. As Percy put it, "The rebels were in great no^s., the whole country having collected for 20 m around."

As they came into the town of Lexington, "We was then met by a Reinforcement of 4 Batalians under Lord percie," Lister wrote, "to our great joy our amunition being then nearly expended." Lister was less happy to learn that the cannons had only seven rounds each (he was mistaken; they actually had twenty-four). This he blamed on the commander of artillery, though in fact it was Percy who did not want to be slowed by an ammunition wagon and "did not imagine there would be any occasion for more than there was in the side-boxes" of the gun carriages. After the brigade had marched, Gage on his own accord sent two ammunition wagons after Percy, which were both ambushed and taken by militia en route.

Lieutenant John Barker wrote that he and the rest of the flank companies "rested ourselves a little while, which was extremely necessary for our Men who were almost exhausted with fatigue." Meanwhile the 1st Brigade continued to form a screen for the tired men, with a swampy area off to their left helping to keep the enemy back. Ensign Lister asked the surgeon's mate of the 43rd Regiment "to examine my Arme when he extracted the Ball it having gone through the Bone and lodg'd within the Skin."

After the few shots initially fired from the six-pounders to drive the militia off, the artillery seems to have remained quiet, perhaps to save ammunition, and slowly the Americans closed in again. Mackenzie wrote, "The Rebels endeavored to gain our flanks, and crept into the covered ground on either side, and as close as they could in front, firing now and then in perfect security." Both sides continued to exchange a brisk fire, and Percy ordered three nearby houses that offered shelter to the enemy put to the torch. Marksmen from the 1st Brigade were sent forward to take cover behind stone walls and try to pick off some of the militia. For all the lead that was flying, though, neither side was able to do much damage. It was not until the column continued on for Boston that the real slaughter began again.

Despite the danger of the march, the last thing that Percy wished to do was to remain stationary. The longer the column waited, the more the militia was augmented from the surrounding towns. Word was spreading fast as express riders raced out in every direction, and "numbers of armed men on foot and on horseback, were continually coming from all parts guided by the fire."

It was around this time that two men whose presence would have a profound impact on the rest of the fight joined the American militia. One was General William Heath, one of four men empowered to take command of the Massachusetts militia. The other was Dr. Joseph Warren, who was, from the British perspective, possibly the most dangerous man in America.

Chapter Two

DR. JOSEPH WARREN

When the first band of separatists from the Church of England clambered down the *Mayflower*'s side in 1620 and stepped ashore in Provincetown, Massachusetts, they were doing more than simply ending a miserable sea voyage. They were taking the first step in the long road that would lead ultimately to Lexington, Concord, and Bunker Hill. As Colonel Isaac Barré would thunder in Parliament in 1765, it was British "Oppressions planted 'em in America. They fled from your Tyranny to a then uncultivated and unhospitable Country."

The Pilgrims may have set the nascent country on that path, but there was no one more responsible for guiding the colonies along those last final steps from organized resistance to outright war for independence than Dr. Joseph Warren. He was not quite thirty-four years old at the time he showed up at Lexington to stand with the minutemen against Smith and Percy. He was handsome and respected, considered the finest physician in Boston. He was the widowed father to four children. For the past decade he had been at the epicenter of the revolution. One British officer referred to him as "the famous Doctor Warren, the greatest incendiary in all America."

Joseph Warren was born in Roxbury, which at the time was a small farming community southwest of Boston. It was situated at the base of the narrow strip of land called Roxbury Neck that tied the city of Boston to the mainland. The first Warren known to have settled there was Peter Warren, Joseph's great-grandfather. Peter is listed in the records as a "Mariner." He arrived in Roxbury in 1657 after working as a fisherman off the island of Monhegan in Maine. Joseph was born June 11, 1741, in the house that was built by his grandfather, also Joseph, in 1720.

The Warrens were of the hardworking, upwardly mobile class of Americans who were able to see each generation improve on the previous. Joseph's father was a successful farmer who took his place in local government, serving as a selectman for Roxbury. The elder Warren had a particular interest in cultivating fruit trees and gave the colonies an apple called the Warren Russet. He died in 1755 after falling from a ladder while tending his orchard. His son Joseph Warren III was fourteen, the oldest of four brothers.

As with many of the leaders of the Revolution, very little is known about Warren's childhood. His education began in the Roxbury Latin School, one of the best public schools in New England. Warren's father had accumulated enough of an estate that his death did not leave the family destitute, and soon after, Joseph entered Harvard College as a freshman. After graduation he taught grammar school for a year before deciding on a career in medicine.

The wealthiest Americans who wished to enter the medical field went to Europe for study. Warren was not one of those. To learn medicine in colonial America, one apprenticed to a practicing doctor. Fortunately for Warren, there was in Boston a London-trained physician named James Lloyd who was very active in training young men for the profession. Warren studied under Lloyd and was thus able to get a London education, once removed.

In 1764 Warren advanced his position in society in the traditional manner, the same route taken by George Washington and so many others: He married a woman of considerable fortune. In Warren's case it was Elizabeth Hooton, an eighteen-year-old beauty and the only heir to

Richard Hooton, a successful merchant. Now married and having completed his medical training, the twenty-three-year-old Warren set himself up in practice in Boston. By the outbreak of the Revolution, and with Lloyd's retirement, he was the most successful doctor in the city.

Joseph Warren was a unique man in a unique circumstance. He was well educated, urbane, and financially well-off, an excellent orator and a skilled writer. He came of age during the French and Indian War, when Massachusetts was on a military footing and many of his neighbors were marching off to fight. That war ended a year before he was married, and the repercussions from the Treaty of Paris of 1763 were just being felt as Warren was coming into his own as a professional and a man of consequence.

As Warren stepped out into the world, the restive discord in the colonies was growing, and Boston, where the young doctor settled, was at the hub of it. England found itself saddled with a national debt twice what it was before the war, and Parliament and the king looked to the colonies, who in their view were the chief beneficiaries of the conflict, for revenue by way of taxes. Primarily the British government expected the colonies to help bear the expense of the standing army that remained in America for the protection of that country.

At the same time, the elimination of the threat posed by the French in Canada suddenly made the British army seem less necessary to the colonies, its presence and cost an unwelcome and unneeded burden. Young men such as Ebenezer Fox, born the year the French and Indian War ended, came to believe the "colonies had born the foremost part in the conflict, with very slight assistance from the mother country . . . [T]heir men and money had been freely contributed, and every demand of the English government promptly complied with."

Needless to say, the British government did not see things the same way, and from that conflicting vision of history and a hundred others rose the spirit of rebellion on the one hand and the reflexive need to crush it on the other.

In 1761 Warren joined the Freemasons, a move that might be expected of a young professional looking to make connections. At the time there were two Masonic lodges in Boston, representing the two different branches of Freemasonry in America. One was the St. John's Lodge, part of what was known as the modern Freemasons, who affiliated themselves with the Grand Lodge established in England in 1717. The other, newly established when Warren joined, was known as St. Andrews and was part of the ancient society, which did not associate itself with the more modern organization.

The modern Freemasons such as those at St. John's Lodge tended to be more conservative and wealthy, and their ranks often included royal officials and military officers. Warren, however, joined St. Andrews. His fellow members included John Hancock and Paul Revere, which gives some indication of the political leanings of the ancient societies in America.

Initially, Warren was a lackluster Freemason at best, and seems to have dropped out of St. Andrews soon after joining. In 1765, however, he was readmitted, and from then until his death he was one of the most active Masons in the country, quickly rising to grand master of the lodge. St. Andrews had a particularly political bent to it. Not just Hancock and Revere but many of the lesser-known but still central figures in the revolutionary movement in Boston were members. The lodge met at the Green Dragon Tavern on Union Street in Boston's North End, a public house that soon gained a reputation as a hotbed of revolutionary activity.

It is not clear whether association with the members of St. Andrews led Warren to his radical politics or a growing radicalism in Warren led him to seek out men of a similar mind. Either way, by 1765 Boston had become the eye of a perfect storm of political unrest, and Warren would do as much as any, and far more than most, to whip that storm up into hurricane force.

THE POLITICS OF LIBERTY

The government of Massachusetts, prior to the colony's break with the crown, was comprised of an executive, in the form of a royal governor, and a bicameral legislature called the General Court, consisting of an upper house known as the Council and a lower house sometimes called the House of Representatives. In most other colonies this upper body was appointed by the crown, but Massachusetts's twenty-eight-man Council was elected by the General Court, subject to the governor's approval. The men who formed the Council tended to be those of influence and wealth in the colony. However, since they were elected by the lower house, and not appointed by the king, they were not necessarily those with the most allegiance to the crown. This quirk of Massachusetts politics would help hasten the rift between the local government and that in London.

The lower house, or House of Representatives, was made up of more than one hundred elected members from the various towns in the colony. In this way the Massachusetts government, like most other colonial governments in America, was modeled after that of England, with the governor and the upper and lower houses of the legislature analogous to the king, the House of Lords, and the House of Commons.

It was the governor's prerogative to distribute government jobs such as that of judge, justice of the peace, sheriff, and the like to whomever he chose, without the approval of the General Court. Since many of those men who sat on the General Court held these potentially lucrative posts and owed them to the governor, the executive was able to wield considerable influence over the legislature. Indeed, this question of prerogative was one of the hot-button issues of the day.

More central to the growing rift with England, however, was the question of who could tax whom, a debate that went far beyond monetary policy to the question of self-rule and the relationship of the colonies to the government in London. Each of the colonies had enjoyed, since its inception, its own charter and its own government. By the 1760s the more independence-minded Americans were beginning to see their colonies as largely independent states under the rule of the British king.

Most Americans were still willing to recognize Parliament's right to legislate for the colonies as it did for all of England. They would even admit to Parliament's right to impose external taxes such as duties on imports and exports (and many Americans made a career out of evading those duties—in other words, smuggling), but they did not recognize the right of Parliament to impose internal taxes. The colonial legislatures, they felt, and not Parliament, held the sole power of such taxation.

Once again, the king and Parliament begged to differ.

In 1765 the question was brought to a head by the Stamp Act, which levied a small tax on all printed paper. The colonies were outraged. Boston exploded in violence. A mob, led by men who would later form themselves into the Sons of Liberty, hanged in effigy Andrew Oliver, stamp distributor for the colony. Oliver's house was ransacked, as was that of Benjamin Hallowell, the comptroller of customs.

The town house of Thomas Hutchinson, lieutenant governor and chief justice—and Oliver's brother-in-law—was also sacked. As he and his children hid in a neighbor's house, his furniture was smashed, doors and wainscoting hacked up, portraits destroyed. The lieutenant governor had been working for years on a history of Massachusetts, but the mob, as Hutchinson wrote, "scattered or destroyed all the manuscript and other papers I had been collecting for 30 years together, besides a great number of Publick Papers in my custody." Hutchinson actually opposed the Stamp Act, but on the grounds that he thought it was unwise, not unconstitutional.

By this time Joseph Warren was deeply entrenched in the politics of resistance and had formed a close relationship with radicals such as Sam Adams and Paul Revere, and with more moderate leaders such as John Adams and John Hancock. Warren was younger than most of those men by five or ten years, but his energy, his natural gifts, and his enthusiasm for the cause propelled him to the forefront of the radical leadership. Perhaps it was the intemperance of youth, but Warren was often the one urging the older men to take bold action. John Adams would write in his autobiography, "I was solicited to go to the Town Meetings and harangue there. This I constantly refused. My Friend Dr. Warren the most frequently urged me to this: My Answer to him always was 'That way madness lies.'"

In 1766 Warren wrote to his friend Edmund Dana in London congratulating him on his marriage to "a lady of noble birth" and filling him in on the latest news from the colonies. The Stamp Act had just recently been enacted, and Warren wrote, "The whole continent is inflamed to the highest degree . . . [T]he strange project of levying a stamp duty . . . has roused their jealousy and resentment."

Warren went on for page after page with a reasoned and reasonable argument against the imposition of the Stamp Tax. "If the real and only motive of the minister was to raise money from the colonies," he wrote, "that method should undoubtedly been adopted which was least grievous to the people. Instead of this, the most unpopular that could be imagined is chosen." Warren finished with a request that Dana "pardon my prolixity upon so important a subject."

Joseph Warren's skill with a pen was one of the chief assets he brought to the Revolution, but his specialty was not calm and dispassionate argument. Rather, he soon became one of the chief propagandists for the cause, a fiery essayist who did not let a strict adherence to the truth interfere with his rabble-rousing. While Warren could write with reason and eloquence in private, he could also write scathing vitriol, as he did of Governor Francis Bernard in the *Boston Gazette:*

> When a diabolical thirst for mischief is the alone motive of your conduct, you must not wonder if you are treated with open dislike; for it is impossible, how much soever we endeavor it, to feel any esteem for a man like you.—Bad as the world may be, there is yet in every breast something which points out the good man as an object worthy of respect, and marks the guileful, treacherous man-hater for disgust and infamy.

Warren signed this vicious attack "A True Patriot."

As a doctor, Warren held a unique place in Boston society. His patients included people from every social stratum, from sailors and common laborers to government officials and merchants like John Hancock, the wealthiest man in the city. The nature of Warren's profession meant that his relationship with all those people was particularly intimate, and that the people who came to him would tend to regard him with respect and even admiration. Thus Warren had the ear and the confidence of everyone—the men of wealth and influence who could shape public policy and attitudes, and the working-class people who would form the backbone of the fight, who could be turned into mobs to dump tea into Boston Harbor or tar and feather royal officeholders or, later, take up a musket and do battle with the king's troops.

The early revolutionary movement in Boston was a loose coalition of radical groups more or less working toward a similar purpose. Historian David Hackett Fischer has compiled a list of seven groups representing the affiliations of many of Boston's revolutionaries. These groups include the St. Andrews Lodge and the Loyal Nine, which would form the nucleus of the Sons of Liberty, as well as the North Caucus and the Long Room Club. The other three groups included those men who were known to have participated in the Boston Tea Party, those on the Boston committee of correspondence, and those who made it onto a 1775 London enemies list. Of the 255 men associated with one or more of these groups, none belonged to all seven, and only two were members of as many as five. Those two were Paul Revere and Joseph Warren.

Warren's closest associate in revolutionary politics was Samuel Adams, cousin of John Adams and one of the few men as radical as Warren in his views. The two were an odd couple. They were both graduates of Harvard, and that, besides their politics, was just about all they had in common. Adams was nineteen years Warren's senior. In the mid-1760s, as the Stamp Act crisis was shaking colonial America, Warren was an up-and-coming physician who would rise to the top of his profession, while Adams had already failed at just about everything he had tried.

Sam Adams graduated from Harvard with his master's of arts two years after Warren was born. He studied law for a while, then dropped it, apparently at his mother's urging. He worked in a countinghouse for a few months before going into business for himself. For start-up capital he borrowed £1,000 from his father, a successful brewer and real estate investor. The younger Adams lent half the money to a friend, who never repaid it, and managed to lose the other half on his own. He worked for a while at his father's brewery, a business for which he also showed no particular enthusiasm or skill.

On the death of his parents, Adams inherited a third of their estate and the brewery, all of which he managed to lose bit by bit until nothing was left. He served, ironically, as tax collector for the town of Boston for eight years, but even with that sinecure, profitable since the time of Jesus, Adams managed to end up owing the Town of Boston £8,000. It was not until the Parliament in England passed the Sugar Act and the Stamp Act that Sam Adams found the only career for which he showed a genuine aptitude: political organizer and rabble-rouser.

From the mid-1760s on, Warren and Adams were the principal leaders of the most radical wing of the revolutionary movement in Massachusetts, their names frequently mentioned in the same breath. When the Stamp Act was repealed in 1766, due largely to the objections of London merchants whose trade was being stifled, and the flames of rebellion seemed to cool, it was chiefly Warren and Adams who kept the fight alive until the Tea Tax sparked the revolutionary spirit back into life.

Joseph Warren differed from the other political leaders of the Revolution in another significant way: When the shooting began, he was the only one to pick up a musket and take his place in the deadly fighting his political activity had brought about. Men such as John and Sam Adams, John Hancock, and others gravitated toward Congress and continued their work in the political sphere. (Hancock, to be sure, would later propose himself as commander in chief of the army, and while he likely relished the way he would look in a splendid uniform with gold braid, he showed little interest in joining the bloody fighting going on at Lexington.)

Others, such as William Heath, Artemas Ward, and George Washington, who had more of a military bent, took up the fight in the field, though they had little involvement with the political movement that ultimately led to the shooting war.

Joseph Warren, politician though he was, was not shy about putting himself in harm's way. It is one of the reasons that he was the only movement leader left in Boston on April 18 as Gage's men gathered for their march on Concord. As such, it was Warren who sent his old compatriot

Paul Revere off on his midnight ride to warn Sam Adams and John Hancock of the pending danger in order that they might get clear of it, while he himself rode to the sound of the guns.

"A NEW AND MORE TERRIFIC SCENE"

It was around 3:15 on the afternoon of April 19 that Percy made the decision to continue the retreat to Boston. He could wait no longer. Every minute they remained in Lexington the enemy grew more numerous, and their chances of making it back to safety more remote.

The flank companies had managed to rest in the relative safety of the 1st Brigade's battle line and had quenched their thirst from the canteens of their fellow redcoats. Neither the original expedition nor Percy's relief column had much in the way of supplies. Ensign Lister, who was growing faint from the "long fateagueing March and loss of Blood," had not eaten in nearly twenty-four hours. Seeing "a Soldier eating a little Bisquet and Beef I beg'd to partake with him he generously comply'd and gave me half what he had which was about a Mouth full of each," the ensign wrote. Lister asked a grenadier to fill his hat with water "out of a Horse pond which he did and refresh'd me a good deal."

Hugh Percy now had close to 2,000 men under his command. The Royal Welsh Fusiliers were ordered to serve as rear guard as the men formed up into marching order. The fusiliers set marksmen out along a nearby wall to cover them as they organized the column, then "retired from the right of Companies by files to the high ground a Small distance in our rear, where we again formed in line." Once again the drill and discipline instilled in the British troops made the complicated maneuvers of large bodies of men nearly routine, even while under fire.

The rear guard remained posted while the rest of the troops formed up. "I ordered the Gren[adiers]s & L[ight] I[nfantry] to move off, covering them with my Brig[ade]," Percy wrote. The flank companies had done all the fighting they were going to do that day. Percy formed the 1st Brigade in a square around the exhausted men to shield them from the militia. Smith's men had already commandeered any wagon they came across to carry the wounded, and every available horse was pressed into service. Jeremy Lister wrote, "Seeing Lt Col^l Smith borrow a horse from an Officer of Marines, he having been wounded some time before in the Leg, I apply'd to him to lend me his Horse which he did."

Earlier in the day, Major Pitcairn's horse had been shot out from under him, and in the course of abandoning the animal he left his pair of silver-mounted and engraved pistols behind. They would fall into American hands and eventually become a gift to General Israel Putnam, who would carry them through the war.

As Percy was organizing the combined columns for the march back to Boston, Heath and Warren were organizing the American regiments to resist them.

Major General William Heath was a farmer from Roxbury and likely knew Warren and his family all his life. He was thirty-eight years old in 1775, four years older than Warren. He described himself as "middling stature, light complexion, very corpulent and bald-headed," not exactly the Washingtonesque model of military bearing. Heath had had an impressive career as an officer of local militia units but had never seen real combat before. Like his fellow Revolutionary War generals Henry Knox and Nathanael Greene, "he was remarkably fond of military exercises, which . . . led him to procure, and attentively to study, every military treatise in the English language, which was obtainable."

As the likelihood of fighting increased in Massachusetts, Heath was appointed one of five general officers to command the militia. On the morning of April 18 Heath had attended a meeting of the Massachusetts committee of safety, on which he served. On his way home he "met eight or nine British officers on horseback, with their swords and pistols, riding up the road towards Lexington." These men were one of the patrols Gage had sent out to reconnoiter the countryside prior to Smith's column marching to Lexington. They were supposed to help the Concord raid go more smoothly, but their presence aroused the suspicion of everyone who saw them, including William Heath.

At dawn the following day, General Heath was woken with news of the British column marching on Concord. He hurried off to find the committee of safety, with whom he met briefly. No record of the proceedings remains, but when they were finished Heath made his way toward the fighting. Knowing that the British were in possession of the Lexington Road, he went by way of Watertown. There he encountered some militiamen who were on their way to the fighting and who now applied to him for orders. Heath sent them to Cambridge to tear up the planks of the bridge over the Charles River and to position themselves on the south side to prevent Percy from returning the way he had come. That done, Heath pushed on to Lexington and the scene of the action. It was at a crossroads leading toward Lexington that Heath met up with Joseph Warren.

Like Heath, Warren had received word in the early morning hours of the fighting taking place on the Lexington Road. He directed one of his apprentices to care for his patients that day and rode off to the Charlestown ferry. At the ferry landing he ran into a friend named Adan, with whom he discussed the fighting and its implications. "Keep up a brave heart!" Warren told Adan as he boarded the ferry. "They have begun it,—that either party can do; and we will end it,—that only one can do."

Jacob Rogers, a resident of Charlestown, recalled the confusion and fear that the conflicting reports filtering into town were causing. "About ten in the morning, I met Dr. Warren, riding hastily out of town, and asked him if the news was true of the men being killed in Lexington. He assured me it was. He rode on." Warren's confirmation led to a rapid exodus from Charlestown, with some men fleeing with their families and their valuables, and others grabbing up muskets to join the fight. Later in the day Gage tried to prevent this reinforcement of the American militia by sending word to Charlestown that, according to Rogers, "if one single more man went out armed, we might expect the most disagreeable consequences." The people of Charlestown likely took that to mean that the British would shell or burn the town.

As Warren rode for Lexington, he ran into a colleague, a Dr. Welch,

who joined him for part of the ride. Near Watson's Corner they encountered two British soldiers trying to steal a horse from an old man, "the
old man, with his cat and hat, pulling one way, the soldiers the other."
Warren, with his typical boldness, charged in and drove the soldiers off,
saving both horse and cat, before continuing on his way.

It was not long afterward that Warren came up with the end of Percy's
column on its march to relieve Smith. With a genuine reckless daring
Warren tried to pass the redcoats (even Heath had taken another route
to avoid them), but he was brought up short at the end of the infantry-
men's bayonets. Two officers who fortunately did not recognize Warren
approached and asked the doctor, "Where are the troops?" Warren answered truthfully that he did not know, and the officers sent him on his
way. Before long he met up with Heath, and the two men found their
way to the American lines.

The Americans were in need of some leadership. Heath found that
the former organization "had been broken by the shot from the British
field-pieces, (for the discharge of these, together with the flames and
smoke of several buildings . . . opened up a new and more terrific scene)."
What's more, hundreds of new militiamen had joined the fight in the
hours that Percy had allowed the flank companies to rest, and they had
to be integrated into the rolling battle.

As the two British columns continued their weary trek back to Boston, Heath and Warren began to organize the American troops into
regiments. The parklike countryside that Percy so admired was looking
considerably more ominous with the many features of the landscape now
hiding musket-wielding militia. Percy knew he could not simply march
his men down the road and through the gauntlet of enemy fire; he had
to flush the enemy out and drive them away. He did that, or tried to, by
"detaching strong flanking parties wh[ich] was absolutely nec'y, as the
whole country we had to retire thro' was cov^d with stone walls, & besides
a very hilly, stony country."

Percy sent five companies of the King's Own to sweep the south side
of the road, and part of the 47th Regiment to the north. Mackenzie and
the Royal Welsh Fusiliers made up the rear guard as the British column

rolled forward. For the first two miles or so they encountered little opposition from the Americans. Then the hail of lead set in again.

THE LONG RETREAT

The firing came from the houses that lined the road and every makeshift breastwork along the way. Lister, who was nearly done in by hunger and loss of blood, was jolting along on his borrowed horse when he "found the Balls whistled so smartly around my Ears I thought it more prudent to dismount and as the Balls came thicker from one side or the other so I went from one side of the Horse to the other." Near Lister in the marching column, another horse had one wounded man on its back and three more clinging to it for support. When that horse was shot dead, Lister gave the men the use of his and resumed his march on foot and without his equine shield.

The British troops returned fire as best they could, but it was ineffectual. Mackenzie pointed out that "our men had very few opportunities for getting good shots at the Rebels, and they hardly ever fired but under cover of a Stone wall, from behind a tree, or out of a house; and the moment they had fired they lay down out of sight until they had loaded again, or the Column had passed."

The militia were firing from sheltered positions, but that was not the only reason that their fire was more effective than that of the British. Indeed, the militia who followed behind the British column, attacking the rear guard, marched in the road and "came on pretty close, frequently calling out, *'King Hancock forever'*" (which would have done much for John Hancock's ego, had he heard it, but was hardly in keeping with the growing republican ideal).

British troops of that period were not trained in firing on individual targets. The order "aim" was not even in the manual of arms. There was only the word "present," which meant the musket was leveled at the enemy before firing. The intention was for the troops to stand shoulder to shoulder and hit the enemy with a wall of bullets. It was not a subtle tactic, and it was meant to be used against an enemy who was also standing shoulder to shoulder. In such a case the ability to load and fire fast was more important than marksmanship. The troops who would have been most effective against the irregular tactics employed by the militia were the light infantry, but they were essentially out of the fight. The rank-and-file redcoats were not trained for that kind of fighting.

The British soldiers would likely have had no experience with guns save that they gained in the army. The same was not true of the Americans, who were often raised with guns and taught to shoot from an early age. Eight months before the fighting at Lexington, Percy had complained to his father, "What makes an insurrection here always more formidable than in other places, is that there is a law of this Province wh[ich] obliges every inhabitant to be furnished with a firelock." Men who were expected to serve in the militia were often issued muskets purchased by their towns, a practice unimaginable in Europe, where the ruling classes were more concerned about popular uprisings, which had to be stamped out on occasion.

Also, for all the training the regulars had received, they had youth and inexperience working against them. Lexington and Concord was the first significant battle the British army had seen for more than a decade, and for most of the troops this was their first time in combat. One officer credited the wasted fire to "the too great eagerness of the Soldiers in the first Action of the War. Most of them were young Soldiers who had never been in Action, and had been taught that everything was to be effected by a quick firing."

Again, this was a weakness that the Americans did not suffer. The militias tended to be made up of older, settled heads of households. Almost 60 percent of the Lexington militia, for example, were over the age of thirty. Many had seen service in the French and Indian War. Many, in fact, had more military experience than the regulars they were facing. Percy, for one, discovered a determination in the "country people" he would not have imagined. "Nor are several of their men void of enthusiasm, as we experienced yesterday," he wrote, "for many of them concealed themselves in houses, & advanced within 10 yds. to fire at me &

other officers, tho' they were morally certain of being put to death themselves in an instant."

With each passing mile the number of militia opposing the column
grew greater, to the point where Lieutenant Colonel Smith no longer believed that they had mustered that morning, but rather was convinced
they had been gathering for several days. Heath and Warren continued to
exert control over the American troops. Despite a lack of any real combat
experience, Heath proved an able leader and kept the militia hanging on
to the marching British column. Warren moved between functioning as
a field officer and as a doctor, one moment directing troops, the next
attending as best he could to the wounded.

The two brigades under Lord Percy now found themselves attacked
on both flanks and from a large column that followed behind. Other
militiamen came to the fight mounted and were able to keep ahead of
the British troops, firing at the front of the approaching column, then
remounting and racing up the road ahead to take up another firing position. Soon Smith's exhausted men and Percy's relief brigade found themselves "under an incessant fire" from the American militia units, "wh[ich]
like a moving circle surrounded & fol^d us wherever we went."

This method of fighting angered many in the rank and file, who viewed
it as essentially unfair. Lord Percy did not entertain any such nonsensical
notions. He understood what the Americans were doing and why. He
later reported to Gage, "They have men amongst them who know very
well what they are about, having been employed as Rangers ag[ain]st the
Indians & Canadians, & this country being much cov^d w. wood, and hilly,
is very advantageous for their method of fighting." He explained that the
Americans did not "dare to form into any regular body," but, professional
that he was, he did not look on that as cowardice. "Indeed," he added,
"they knew too well what was proper, to do so."

It has become part of the mythology of the American Revolution that
throughout the course of the war the Americans fired from behind stone
walls and other barriers while the British foolishly stood in straight lines
in the open. That is not at all the case, of course. In nearly every major
battle the Americans employed the same European-style tactics as the

British. The fighting from Concord to Boston was one of the few exceptions, and it was there that the myth was born.

The young British foot soldiers who were enduring the worst of the American fire were not so understanding as Hugh Percy. As they continued to be tormented by an often invisible enemy, as they began to take more and more casualties, and as hunger and exhaustion set in, the regulars became increasingly enraged. One soldier complained to his veteran father, "We did not fight as you did in Germany, as we could not see above ten in a body." Another wrote, "They did not fight us like a regular army, only like savages."

As the British approached Menotomy, the fighting grew hotter and discipline began to break down. The Americans were taking shelter in the houses along the way and firing on the column as it passed. Often they would conceal themselves so that the flanking companies who searched the house could not find them, only to emerge and fire on the British after they had left. "If we had had time to set fire to those houses," Mackenzie wrote, "many Rebels must have perished in them."

The British were not the only ones to take casualties. William Heath recalled that at Watson's Corner, where Warren had earlier driven off the British soldiers, a number of militia "imprudently posted themselves behind some dry casks." They were too close to the road, within reach of "the enemy's flank-guard, which came in behind them, and killed every one of them dead on the spot."

Because of the threat from the buildings along the road, every house was swept by the troops ahead of the column. The rebels "suffer'd for their temerity," Lieutenant Barker wrote, "for all that were found in the houses were put to death." Most of the Americans killed were under arms, but not all. As the column pushed on and the officers continued to lose control, the British troops began plundering the houses they were searching. The redcoats stole "anything of value that could be taken away." What could not be stolen was smashed in an orgy of rage and destruction; "looking-glasses, pots, pans, &c. were broke all to pieces." Mackenzie admitted that "many houses were plundered by the Soldiers, notwithstanding the efforts of the Officers to prevent it." As one American wrote, "The people say the soldiers are worse than the *Indians.*"

William Heath wrote, "On descending from the high grounds in Arlington [Menotomy], on to the plain, the fire was brisk." A British musket ball buzzed so close by Warren's head that it knocked out the pin that was holding his hair in a fashionable earlock. The British artillery again unlimbered their guns and fired at the rebels, but the sound of the six-pounders was "now more familiar than before" and did not scatter the attackers as it had at Lexington. Heath recalled that "here the militia were so close on the rear of the British that Dr. *Downer,* an active and enterprizing man, came to single combat with a British soldier, whom he killed with his bayonet."

The battle rolled southeast toward Cambridge and Roxbury. Percy ordered the artillery to continue firing at the rebels to give the column some relief, but soon the ammunition in the side boxes began to run low. The Royal Welsh Fusiliers, serving as rear guard, were also low on ammunition, and Percy shifted the marines into the rearguard position and gave the battered fusiliers some relief.

The route from Cambridge to Roxbury involved crossing a bridge that spanned the Charles River, which Percy understood was a potentially deadly bottleneck. Realizing that the bridge "might either be broken down, [or] required to be forced," the young officer made a bold decision. As he approached, Percy swung his column off to the left, heading for Charlestown rather than returning the way he had come, by way of Roxbury. It was a brilliant stroke and likely saved the remains of the army from complete destruction. William Heath had, of course, ordered the bridge torn down, and a large contingent of rebel militia was waiting for the British brigades to run headlong into the impassable river.

The moving circle of fire continued to envelop Percy's soldiers as they trudged for Charlestown. The marines in the rearguard were in turn relieved by the 47th Regiment, which was later relieved by the 4th. The grenadiers and light infantry who had first gone out with Smith, "being exceedingly fatigued by their long march, kept at the head of the Column." There, it was thought, they would be more protected from the enemy's guns, but in fact "the fire was nearly as severe as in the rear." No one was safe. Even a few Americans who had been taken prisoner were killed by what we would today call "friendly fire."

It was around sunset, the muzzle flash from the muskets distinct in the fading light, when the remnants of the two brigades came stumbling across Charlestown Neck. The rebel militia had pursued them every inch of the way from Concord, but now they dared go no farther. Moored in the narrow stretch of water between the neck and Boston lay the powerful sixty-eight-gun ship of the line *Somerset,* her heavy guns trained on the neck and ready to pour fire into anyone who tried to cross without her blessing. Admiral Samuel Graves, commander of the North American fleet, wrote, "It was the *Somerset* alone that preserved the detachment from Ruin. The vicinity of the formidable Ship to Charles Town so intimidated its Inhabitants that they (tho' reluctantly) suffered the King's Troops to come in and pass over to Boston, who would otherwise have been undoubtedly attacked."

"We then March'd upon Buncars Hill and was ordered to draw up," Ensign Lister recalled. He was on the verge of passing out from exhaustion and loss of blood, but Percy wanted the high ground secure. Unlike Graves, he was not certain that the man-of-war's guns would absolutely dissuade the rebels from following.

Percy understood that Bunker Hill was crucial to the defense of Charlestown, a fact that the Americans would not entirely appreciate when they later fortified the peninsula. "When the troops had drawn up on the heights above Charlestown neck, and had remained there about half an hour," Mackenzie wrote, "Lord Percy ordered the Grenadiers and Light Infantry to march down to Charlestown." There boats were waiting to ferry them across the water to Boston. The wounded went first, then the flank companies. When the boats returned, they brought troops from the 2nd, 3rd, 10th, and 64th regiments "to take possession of Charlestown, and the heights Commanding the Neck."

Heath, meanwhile, gathered the militia officers to him at the foot of Prospect Hill, the high ground opposite Bunker Hill on the mainland side of Charlestown Neck. He "ordered a guard to be formed, and posted near that place, sentinels to be planted down the neck, and patrols to be vigilant in moving during the night, and an immediate report to him, in case the enemy made any movements."

The Battle of Lexington and Concord was over. The Americans had 50 men killed outright or who would die of their wounds, 39 wounded, and 5 missing. The casualties came from 23 different towns, indicative of how the entire countryside was alarmed and turned out for the fight. The British lost 65 killed, 180 wounded, and 27 missing, around three times the number of American casualties. One British officer, as the story goes, asked another, after the brigades returned to Boston, how he liked the tune "Yankee Doodle" now. "Damn them," the officer replied, "they made us dance to it till we were tired."

Some learned a hard truth from the brutal fighting. Hugh Percy was one of them. Ten months earlier he had written, "I am still convinced that nothing but either drunkenness or madness can force them to molest us." Now he wrote to Gage, "Whoever looks upon them as an irregular mob, will find himself much mistaken . . . You may depend upon it, that as the Rebels have now had time to prepare, they are determined to go thro' with it, nor will the insurrection here turn out so despicable as it is perhaps imagined at home. For my part, I never believed, I confess, that they wd have attacked the King's troops, or have had the perseverance I found in them yesterday."

It was an important lesson, and one Percy learned well. However, the men who most needed to learn it, the generals who would lead the fighting in America for the next three years, were not at Lexington and Concord. As Percy and Smith were fighting their way along the Lexington Road, those men were on board a ship in the mid-Atlantic, bound for Boston. They would have to learn the lesson for themselves, and for them, and for the troops under their command, it would come at an even higher price.

Chapter Three

"THE BUTCHERING HANDS OF AN INHUMAN SOLDIERY"

The dam had burst with the fighting at Lexington and Concord, and the flood of rebellion had been let loose. There would be no easing of tensions, as had happened with earlier crises. This was not a brief moment of outrage like the Boston Tea Party or a minor skirmish like the Boston Massacre. This was a real bloodletting. This was war.

It was the moment that Warren and the other radical leaders had been waiting for. Sam Adams, on hearing the sound of the muskets along the Lexington Road and recognizing that it represented the final step on the path to rebellion, supposedly exclaimed, "Oh! what a glorious morning is this!"

Joseph Warren certainly understood that the world had changed on April 19, and by the next day he had given up command in the field and returned to his former role of political organizer. For Warren and the other leaders of the revolutionary movement, there was no going back to Boston where they would certainly have been arrested. Instead, the committee of safety met in Cambridge, which would become the headquarters for the military as well. Their first task was to control the military and political fallout that would stem from the fighting and the public perception of events. This was what they were good at.

From those meetings of the committee of safety came a circular letter to be sent to the other towns in Massachusetts from which the committee hoped to draw troops. It was written by Warren in the doctor's most inflammatory style. "The barbarous murders committed on our innocent brethren, on Wednesday the 19th instant, have made it absolutely necessary that we immediately raise an army to defend our wives and our children from the butchering hands of an inhuman soldiery" who would, he wrote, "take the first opportunity in their power to ravage this devoted country with fire and sword."

Warren urged the towns to immediately enlist men and send them on to Cambridge. Speed was urgent. "Death and devastation are the instant consequences of delay. Every moment is infinitely precious. An hour lost may deluge your country in blood, and entail perpetual slavery upon the few of your posterity who may survive the carnage."

In fact, Warren did not really believe any of the wild hyperbole that was flowing from his pen. The commander of the "inhuman soldiery," Thomas Gage, was a man he knew personally and had met with on several occasions. Joseph Warren may have looked on Gage as his enemy, but he knew full well that Gage was not going to deluge the country in blood. Indeed, far from it; Gage's biggest fear was that the violence at Lexington and Concord would continue, and he worried that the rebel leaders were actually promoting it. A few weeks after the fighting on the 19th, Gage wrote to Dartmouth, the American secretary:

If they proceed in their Movements, it seems impossible to be long before we come again to Blows, and from the Beginning I have perceived that it was the wish and Design of the Leaders here to bring Affairs to the Crisis; but so to manage it as to bring the rest of the Colonies to Support them. It is astonishing how they have duped the whole Continent.

Gage certainly was not giving the rest of the colonies enough credit for independent thought, suggesting they had been taken in by Massachusetts (in several instances Virginia had taken the lead in resisting the crown and Parliament). He was not wrong, though, about the designs of Warren, Adams, and the rest. Indeed, Bunker Hill would prove him exactly right in his belief that some leaders wished to continue provoking the British army into action and to escalate the fighting into a war that would not be easily negotiated away.

On the day that Warren wrote his inflammatory circular calling for more troops, he also wrote a very reasonable letter to Gage asking the general how many days he would allow for people to remove their personal effects from Boston if they decided to abandon the city. "I think it of the utmost importance to us," he wrote to Gage, "that our conduct be such as that the contending parties may entirely rely upon the honor and integrity of each other for the punctual performance of any agreement that shall be made between them."

General Thomas Gage, governor of Massachusetts and commander in chief of His Majesty's armed forces in America, was arguably the most powerful man on the continent, but he was not about to ravage the countryside, which Warren well knew. Gage had spent a great deal of his career in America and generally liked Americans, though the year prior to Lexington and Concord had strained that affection. He was married to an American, which, of course, may have been his greatest security breach.

In 1775, when the American Revolution began, Gage was around fifty-five years old. He was the second son of an aristocratic family that had its seat at Firle Place in Sussex. The family traced its lineage to a Norman nobleman who had emigrated to England with William the Conqueror. Since then, the Gages had shown an amazing propensity for always being on the wrong side of every major political conflict. They had stood with King John against the Magna Carta and with Charles I, the deposed and later beheaded king, against Parliament.

The Gage family remained Roman Catholic after the Reformation and Henry VIII's break with the church and sided with Queen Mary against the future Queen Elizabeth. Sir John Gage actually served as Elizabeth's jailer during part of the time she was imprisoned in the Tower of London by her half sister, Mary. Roman Catholic writers described

Gage as a kind man, Protestants as cruel. Either way, he had the good sense to die two years before Elizabeth assumed the throne.

In 1715 the Catholic son of the deposed James II invaded Scotland, and once again papists, who had been more or less suspect since the days of Elizabeth, were viewed as enemies of the state. Thomas Gage's grandfather Sir William Gage apparently had had enough. Catholics were ostracized, forbidden from public service and even from the use of horses, so William left the Roman church and joined the Church of England. This allowed him to stand for Parliament, which he did, successfully, and for his grandson Thomas to pursue a military career, a thing that would have been denied him had he still been Catholic.

Gage did not attend Eton like many of his peers but rather the equally prestigious Royal College of St. Peter in Westminster, known as the Westminster School. Among his classmates were many of the men who would be central to the British effort in the American Revolution, including John Burgoyne, Richard Howe, Francis Bernard, who would serve as governor of Massachusetts, and Lord George Sackville, who later changed his name to George Germain and, following Dartmouth's tenure, served as American secretary for most of the war.

Like many of his fellow general officers, Gage was a good student but not a brilliant one. The second son of the aristocracy, Thomas would inherit neither wealth nor title and so needed to settle on a career of some sort. There were not too many options available; the usual choices were the army, the navy, the church, politics, or the law. Young Thomas probably did not wrestle long with his decision.

By the time Thomas Gage took command in Boston in 1774, he had likely seen more hard and bloody warfare than any other man in America at the time, or any who would fight in the American Revolution over the next eight years. He entered the army as a teenager with the rank of ensign, then purchased a lieutenancy in 1741. By 1743 he had advanced to the rank of captain when he saw action in the War of the Austrian Succession, which included taking part in the disastrous Battle of Fontenoy. In that massive set-piece battle, which pitted an army of 50,000 British, Dutch, Hanoverian, and Austrian troops against 48,000 Frenchmen, the combined army suffered over 10,000 casualties. There were few men in the American theater on either side who had seen that kind of carnage.

With war in Europe still raging, Gage's regiment was sent to Scotland to help put down an uprising that had coalesced around Bonnie Prince Charles, grandson of James II, who had returned from exile in France, inspired in part by the British defeat at Fontenoy. Earlier generations of Gages would likely have been supporters of the Catholic Charles, but Thomas was not. He and his regiment helped drive the Young Pretender from Britain in fighting that culminated in the bloodbath that was the Battle of Culloden. With the uprising over, Gage returned to the war in Europe.

In 1755, after some years of peace, Gage was once again sent into harm's way, now as a lieutenant colonel of the 55th Regiment. This time his orders took him to America for the war that would be known as the French and Indian War in that country and as the Seven Years' War in Europe. The 55th was part of the column under the command of Major General Edward Braddock that was so disastrously ambushed at the Monongahela River. Braddock was killed during the fighting, but the bold leadership displayed by Gage and the American volunteer George Washington did much to mitigate the slaughter of the British troops and enhance the reputation of both men. For the next few years they maintained a friendly correspondence.

In 1757 Gage received permission to organize a regiment of light infantry, the first of its kind in the British army, with himself as colonel. His regiment took part in the failed attack against the French at Fort Ticonderoga under Major General James Abercrombie, the action in which the Howes' older brother, George, was killed. Gage made the step to brigadier general soon after, and for the next few years took part in the campaigning in New York and Canada. In 1760 he accepted the post of military governor of Montreal, which he held until the end of the war in 1763.

With peace signed, Gage was eager to return to England, or at least escape the tedium of administering the frozen backwoods of Canada. In the fall of 1763, however, a better opportunity arrived. Sir Jeffery Amherst, commander in chief of the British army in North America, had been granted leave to return home. Gage was made commander in chief in his place, and he quickly traded dreary Montreal for his new post in New York City. He would hold the post of commander of British troops in North America for the next twelve years, until that, too, became a casualty of Bunker Hill.

COMMANDER IN CHIEF

Gage's years in New York were mostly happy ones. He and his wife, Margaret Kemble, whom he had married in 1757, were much liked and admired in New York society.

Thomas Gage's father had a reputation for drinking and gambling and ignoring his family, and perhaps for that reason both Thomas and his older brother William were sober and reliable men. Thomas developed a reputation in the army for his steadiness, his honesty, and his good nature. Charles Lee, who served under him for a while and would go on to become a major general under George Washington, was enormously fond of Gage. Gage also enjoyed the affection of General James Wolfe, the hero of Quebec, which undoubtedly was of greater importance to him.

Gage in his years in New York was near the pinnacle of his profession, in command of an army that consisted of fifteen regiments stretched over half a continent, from Nova Scotia to the Illinois country down to Florida. He and his wife entertained often and enjoyed the many amusements of the second-largest city in the American colonies. Then, in 1764, Parliament passed the Sugar Act, followed the next year by the Stamp Act, and soon Gage's largely peaceful administration began to take on a much darker aspect.

It was not long after word of the Stamp Act reached the colonies that Gage reported trouble in the offing. The House of Burgesses in Williamsburg was the first to take official action, issuing the Virginia Resolves, which outlined the colony's stance on the issue of taxation. The fourth resolution read:

Resolved, that his Majesty's liege People of this his most ancient and loyal Colony have without Interruption enjoyed the inestimable Right of being governed by such Laws, respecting their internal Polity and Taxation, as are derived from their own Consent.

Parliament, in other words, had no right to levy taxes on the people of Virginia. Historically, they claimed, only Virginians themselves could do that, and that was still the case. The sentiment was certainly in line with anything that Sam Adams or Joseph Warren might have written, even if the language was more polite than would have come from the Bostonians' pens.

Massachusetts could not be far behind in the matter of protest, and the reaction in that colony would not be as civilized as that of Virginia. In September of 1765 Gage wrote from New York to Sir Henry Conway, then the secretary of state, that "the Populace of Boston took the Lead in the Riots, and by an assault upon the House of [the] Stamp Officer, forced him to a Resignation."

Other colonies followed suit. In Rhode Island, New York, Pennsylvania, Maryland, and the Carolinas, unprecedented mob violence led to the destruction of the homes of government officials connected to the hated stamps. Any man who had taken the post of stamp distributor quickly renounced his position, and no one else dared to take his place.

Once the violence had cooled, both government officials and leaders of the insurrection seemed stunned by what had happened. Mob actions were certainly not new to the colonies, particularly in Boston, but never before had there been such a continent-wide uprising of such explosive fury. In its wake, America seemed to take a deep breath. By the end of September 1765, Gage could write to Conway, "Every thing is quiet at present, and a calm seems to have succeeded the Storm. People talk and Reason more cooly."

After the mobs stood down, the political leaders began to address the issue of the Stamp Act. The Virginia Resolves were published in newspapers in every colony, and a number of colonial legislatures passed similar resolutions. The Massachusetts legislature proposed a Stamp Act

Congress to be held in New York with delegates from each of the colonies. Perceptive men such as Gage understood that such organized political action was far more dangerous to British interests than any street gang that could be disbanded with bayonets.

The Congress met on October 7, 1765, and though it is little remembered today, it was a turning point in the affairs of America. Not once, since the first settlers had come ashore in Jamestown or the first Pilgrims at Plymouth, had the colonies ever done anything in concert. It had always been assumed in England that the American colonies, each with its separate government, charter, character, and interests, would never find common cause. Divide and conquer was never a strategy because no one ever thought the colonies would be united enough to need dividing. Now the Stamp Act was doing the unimaginable—it was bringing the colonies together.

Gage kept a close eye on the proceedings but did not try to interfere in any overt way. He even entertained the Massachusetts delegation for dinner, where he likely tried to influence their thinking on the matter of taxation, though apparently to no end. Writing to Conway concerning the delegates at the Congress, Gage observed, "They are of various Characters and opinions, but it's to be feared in general, that the Spirit of Democracy, is strong among them."

Neither the cost nor the inconvenience of the stamp tax was particularly onerous to the Americans. Gage recognized that "the Question is not of the inexpediency of the Stamp Act, or of the inability of the Colonys to pay the Tax," but rather that it was "contrary to their rights." The Americans, who had until that point enjoyed unprecedented liberty, viewed it as the camel's nose under the tent, a minor usurpation of what they considered their traditional prerogative that would lead ultimately to their total subjugation. The Stamp Act was, as John Adams put it, an "enormous Engine, fabricated by the british Parliament, for battering down all the Rights and Liberties of America."

The Stamp Act was destined to be short-lived. George Grenville, the prime minister who had created the act, found himself out of office even before it went into effect. The new prime minister, Charles, Lord Rockingham, was more sympathetic to the American cause.

Of greater influence than the prime minister was the merchant class of England, whose financial power gave them great sway over the workings of government. Americans, as a means of protesting the sugar and stamp taxes, were refusing to buy English goods, and that was crippling the British merchants' business. As the economic slump spread, Americans who owed money to English merchants could no longer pay their debts, which exacerbated the situation. The merchants made their displeasure known, and Parliament took note.

In March 1766 Parliament repealed the Stamp Act. It did so for purely pragmatic reasons. "If we enforce the Stamp Act," Secretary of State Conway declared, "we shall have a war in America, and the Bourbon league [France and Spain] will take this advantage." The other concern, of course, beyond war, was the economic catastrophe that was about to sweep England and the colonies as a result of the Americans' nonconsumption.

The king and Parliament knew it was essential for the Americans to understand that England's willingness to cave on the Stamp Act in no way amounted to a concession on the issue of taxes in general, or weakness in the face of colonial opposition. On the same day that the Stamp Act was repealed, the Declaratory Act was passed by the Parliament and approved by the king. The act declared that the colonists erroneously "claimed to themselves, or to the general assemblies of the same, the sole and exclusive right of imposing duties and taxes upon his majesty's subjects." It went on to correct that notion, stating that in fact the colonies "are, and of right ought to be, subordinate unto, and dependent upon the imperial crown and parliament of Great Britain" and that the king and Parliament have "full power and authority to make laws and statutes of sufficient force and validity to bind the colonies and people of America, subjects of the crown of Great Britain, *in all cases whatsoever.*"

The Declaratory Act was largely ignored in America, while the repeal of the Stamp Act was celebrated with unabashed jubilation. Gage wrote, "Rejoicings on this Occasion have been remarkably great, beyond what Many Moderate People wished to see." Few appreciated that far from resolving the issue, Parliament had only kicked it down the road a bit.

Gage's problems were certainly not over. Increasingly, the colonies,

New York in particular, were refusing to comply with the Quartering Act of 1765. The act specified that if no barracks were available for His Majesty's troops, then the colonists were

> to quarter and billet the residue of such officers and soldiers, for whom there shall not be room in such barracks, in inns, livery stables, ale-houses, victualling-houses, and the houses of sellers of wine by retail to be drank in their own houses or places thereunto belonging, and all houses of persons selling of rum, brandy, strong water, cyder or metheglin, by retail, to be drank in houses.

The act, a lengthy bit of legalese, went on to clarify in considerable detail how the troops were to be quartered and supplied (troops were to be furnished with "fire, candles, vinegar, and salt, bedding, utensils for dressing their victuals, and small beer or cyder, not exceeding five pints, or half a pint of rum mixed with a quart of water").

For all the specifics of the act, Gage still found it filled with loop-holes. He informed Conway that it would not serve its purpose as writ-ten, as it "depends too much upon the temper and whim of an Assembly, One may perhaps grant, the Next not, One province consent, Another refuse."

With passage of the Sugar Act, Stamp Act, and Quartering Act, the cycle of political action and reaction was well established. Parliament would pass a set of regulations it viewed as reasonable, designed in part to assert its authority over the colonies. The Americans would view the act as an imminent threat to their liberty and rise up in protest. For almost a decade after the repeal of the Stamp Act, that political loop would play again and again, until at last blood was spilled.

GAGE IN BOSTON

The next act in the escalating drama was introduced in 1767 by Charles Townshend, the forty-one-year-old recently appointed chancellor of the exchequer. As overseer of the British government's finances, he was concerned about the ongoing cost of supporting the army in America. This became an even greater concern after Parliament approved a reduction in the land tax paid by English landowners, which left a £500,000 gap in the country's budget.

Townshend also worried about the Americans. Specifically, he worried that the Americans still felt Parliament had no right to tax them.

During the Stamp Act crisis, Americans had argued that Parliament could not impose internal taxation on the colonies, though they had explicitly agreed that Parliament had the right to impose external taxes. Townshend now hoped to give the Americans a chance to prove their sincerity, which he himself doubted, by proposing an external taxation in the form of import duties on lead, glass, paper, painters' colors, and tea.

Along with import duties, the Townshend Acts called for suspending the New York Assembly until the citizens of that colony would comply with the Quartering Act, and establishing an American Board of Customs Commissioners so that duties already imposed, as well as the new ones, would actually be collected. The money would be used in part to pay judges and other government officials in the colonies, rather than having their pay come by way of the colonial legislatures, thus depriving the colonies of the leverage they enjoyed over those men.

Predictably, the American colonies exploded in outrage, none more so than Massachusetts, with Boston again the epicenter of the anger. Joseph Warren had by then taken a central role in the opposition leadership, and his articles written for the *Boston Gazette* under the nom de plume "True Patriot" helped fan the flames. In June of 1768 the customs officials in Boston seized a sloop named *Liberty* that belonged to John Hancock and was suspected of being used for smuggling. A mob gathered, and the customs officials fled to the man-of-war *Romney,* which had earlier been sent by the admiralty to Boston as the threats of violence mounted.

The situation was growing increasingly dangerous. The governor of Massachusetts, Francis Bernard, wanted British troops sent to the city, but he dared not ask for them. A request for troops would have to go through the General Court, and Bernard, who was already enormously unpopular, was certain that such a request coming from him would be the spark in the powder keg.

Gage also wanted to send troops to Boston. He favored taking a firm stand against the civil unrest that was growing in the colonies. "Quash this spirit at a blow," he wrote to the secretary at war, William Barrington, "without too much regard to the expence and it will prove an œconomy in the end . . . If the principles of moderation and forbearance are again adopted . . . there will be an end to these provinces as British colonies." However, Gage did not feel he could send troops on his own accord without a request from the civil authorities or orders from London.

What he did not know, even as he wrote those words to Barrington, was that orders were on their way from the ministry for him to send one or more regiments to Boston to put an end to the uprising there. In this way both he and Bernard would get what they wanted, but neither would be on the hook for the decision.

On receiving the instructions from London, Gage decided to send to Boston the 14th and 29th regiments, then stationed in Halifax. Soon after, the ministry decided to augment those troops with the 64th and 65th from Ireland. The men from Halifax arrived on September 28, their transports dropping anchor in Boston Harbor along with a naval escort consisting of one ship of the line and seven frigates. No one, least of all the redcoats, knew what would happen when they went ashore.

Violence was a distinct possibility, and the British were ready. Each man was issued sixteen rounds of powder and ball. The men-of-war cleared for action, their great guns loaded and directed at the close-packed wood and brick buildings of Boston. Each ship had a spring rigged to its cable, that is, a heavy line run from the stern of the ship forward and attached to the anchor cable. By hauling on that line, or spring, the ship could be swung in almost any direction, its guns brought to bear on the town even if the wind or tide were running counter.

On October 1 the troops were landed at Long Wharf, the great pier that jutted out nearly half a mile into the harbor. They marched into the beleaguered city, where they met no resistance at all. Lieutenant Governor Thomas Hutchinson wrote, "The red-coats make a formidable appearance and there is a profound silence among the Sons of Liberty."

Rioting was one thing, but taking on regular troops was something else, and the Bostonians were not ready, either politically or militarily, to take that step. Nor was the spirit of rebellion so universal throughout America that Adams, Warren, Hancock, and the rest could have hoped for the other colonies to rise up in support. Resistance and protest were still the watchwords. It would be some years yet before anyone was ready for armed rebellion.

On October 15 Gage himself and members of his staff arrived in Boston, having traveled overland from New York. Bernard, not surprisingly, was having trouble finding anyone in Boston to rent space to house the troops, and Gage made the trip to help facilitate the negotiations. That done, he returned to New York by mid-November.

For seventeen months the redcoats and the people of Boston lived under a strained truce. "Broils soon commenced between the townsmen, ready to insult the military," Gage later wrote, "and the soldiers, as ready to chastise an insult." The people of Boston were resentful of the army's presence, antagonized by them with renditions of "Yankee Doodle," and were harassed by British sentinels as they walked the streets.

The Bostonians, in turn, retaliated at every chance. "Every straggling soldier, and some sentinels on duty, were beat, and the guards threatened and pelted." The presence of the troops did not prove to be the comfort that Governor Bernard and Lt. Governor Thomas Hutchinson, who became acting governor in July of 1769 and was appointed governor in 1771, had hoped. In fact, the regulars were of little use, since no one dared call on them to quell mob violence for fear that the whole thing would escalate out of control.

On March 5, 1770, things escalated anyway. Confrontations between the regulars and the civilian population had grown increasingly ugly. Finally the audacity of the mob, the fear and anger of the regulars, and a miscommunication in the face of an angry and threatening crowd led soldiers of the 29th Regiment to open fire, killing five.

As with the first Stamp Act riots, the violence of the Battle of King

Street, as it was known, or later the Boston Massacre, seemed to stun people on both sides. The night of the shooting, a mob patrolled the streets of Boston but did no damage. Hutchinson, to appease the civilians, jailed the troops responsible for the shooting and sent the rest of the soldiers to Castle William, a fortification in Boston Harbor. Tensions began to ease. Later the soldiers would be successfully represented at trial by John Adams and Josiah Quincy.

Soon after the Boston Massacre, word reached the colonies of the repeal of four of the five duties imposed by the Townshend Acts. The government in London had changed once again, and now Frederick, Lord North, was prime minister, an office he would hold throughout the American Revolution. North was not much interested in tangling in colonial politics, and the Townshend duties and the subsequent nonimportation agreements in the colonies were once again hurting British trade. It was the old pattern playing out anew. North and Parliament wished to eliminate the Townshend duties, but again they did not want to appear to be giving in to American demands. The colonies were already expanding the list of areas in which they felt Parliament had no right to interfere, from purely internal taxes to all taxes and beyond. The Declaratory Act was still in effect, but the ministry wanted a more forceful reminder of who was in charge. To achieve this, they eliminated all of the Townshend duties save for the one on tea. Thus, as with the Declaratory Act, the colonists were made to understand that Parliament's actions were economically based, and in no way reflected an acceptance of the Americans' vision of limited parliamentary authority.

The remaining tax on tea caused few ripples in the colonial pond. Indeed, the years from 1770 to 1773 were markedly calm. The economy was good, and it is difficult to incite people to rebellion when they are making money. No great outrages from Parliament followed the repeal of the Townshend Acts. Even the redoubtable John Adams was ready for peace, writing in his diary that he was done with sacrificing for the cause and would from then on "become more retired and cautious; I will certainly mind my own farm and my own office."

In November of 1772 Sam Adams, Joseph Warren, and the other

leading radicals in Boston established a Boston committee of correspondence, which would be key to paving the way to open rebellion. They drafted a statement of colonial rights and grievances that was circulated to other towns. In this and other ways they struggled to keep the flames of rebellion burning during a time when American thoughts, and Parliament's focus, had turned to other issues.

In October of 1772 Gage wrote to the Earl of Hillsborough, secretary of state for the colonies, for "your Lordship's friendly Assistance to obtain His Majesty's Grant of a Leave of Absence." Gage had been in America for seventeen years without once having returned to England. In that time he had married, fathered six children, and risen from lieutenant commander to commander in chief. There were affairs in England that required his attention, and the situation in the colonies seemed calm enough. In June of 1773 he boarded a ship and stood out past Sandy Hook for England. His leave would not last long.

Chapter Four

WEED OF SLAVERY

I n the end, it would take three tubby, innocuous merchant ships and the 342 crates of tea stowed down in their holds to break the decade-long cycle of parliamentary taxation, colonial protest, and qualified ministerial retreat.

With the repeal of the Townshend duties on everything but tea, Americans found themselves in an awkward situation. Indeed, though it was not calculated to have that effect, the partial repeal served to create fissures in the colonies' political unity. The merchants who had been suffering from the nonimportation agreements were quite ready to say that Parliament's actions constituted a real concession on the part of the British government and were good enough. The fire-breathing Patriots of the Adams and Warren stripe, which included others in New York, Philadelphia, and beyond, felt that accepting any tax imposed by Parliament was an invitation to slavery.

Eventually, one by one, the various seaports yielded to fiscal temptation and voted to allow importation of British goods. Soon British imports were once again flowing into the warehouses of American merchants, including tea from England, on which colonists paid the three pence per pound

Townshend duty, as well as tea smuggled from Holland, on which they did not.

By the summer of 1770 Boston alone still clung to the policy of importing nothing at all. Eventually even the Bostonians began to waver. They liked English goods, particularly tea, and they really liked the profit to be made from importing them. Soon they, too, were willing to swallow the last of the Townshend duties. In 1771, 265,000 pounds of tea were imported into Boston. Merchant John Hancock alone paid £1,350 in duties on imported tea.

Despite the veneer of peace that marked the first years of the 1770s, the spirit of revolution was never far from the surface, kept alive in Boston by the core radical element. In January of 1773 the *Boston Gazette* would write of this smoldering anger, "It must afford the greatest pleasure to the friends of liberty and the constitution, to perceive the country so thoroughly awakened to a sense of their danger." A few months later the same paper, a mouthpiece for the most ardent Patriots in Boston, would write, "The UNION of the colonies, which now is the grand object the Americans are pursuing, will fix their rights and liberties upon an immovable basis."

Clearly the colonies in general, and Massachusetts in particular, were primed for the spark that would blow the powder keg, for the catalyst that would lead to the impromptu violence of Lexington and Concord and to the first real battle of the war, Bunker Hill. There were any number of political conflicts that might have provided that spark. Had General Gage been more aggressive in quashing the spirit of revolt, had he begun arresting the leaders as his superiors in London wanted, that might have done it. Another incident like the Boston Massacre, if less adroitly handled, could have pushed things to the next level. In the end, the explosion came with the Tea Act of 1773.

The United Company of Merchants Trading to the East Indies, more commonly known as the East India Company, was, along with the Bank of England, one of Britain's most powerful financial institutions, but by 1773 it was in serious trouble. Mismanagement and a series of national financial crises had shaken the stability of that bedrock of the British mercantile system. The company was spiraling down into bankruptcy, with 18 million pounds of unsold tea stacked in warehouses.

The East India Company was, in today's parlance, too big to fail. To rescue the troubled company, Parliament passed the Tea Act, which gave the East India Company a monopoly on importing tea to America. Prior to that, tea imported into England was subject to the same duty of three pence per pound as that imported into the colonies. The Tea Act, however, eliminated the duty on tea coming into England while retaining the Townshend duty on tea coming into America.

To handle the distribution of tea once it was landed in the colonies, the East India Company selected colonial merchants who would serve as their consignees. Needless to say, the company chose those who had displayed loyalty to the king, Parliament, and the mother country and not rabble-rousing "patriots." In Boston, two of the five consignees chosen were sons of Governor Thomas Hutchinson.

Governor Hutchinson, a descendant of Anne Hutchinson, the seventeenth-century Puritan dissenter, had an American pedigree as solid as anyone's. He was born in Massachusetts in 1711 and first entered politics at the age of twenty-six. As lieutenant governor and later governor, Hutchinson was initially popular. He had opposed the Stamp Act (though not as vigorously as some might have liked), but as the spirit of rebellion swept through Massachusetts he was forced by his Loyalist convictions to oppose the popular uprising. By the time of the Tea Act he was quite despised.

In London, Benjamin Franklin served as the agent for the colony of Massachusetts. It was he who represented the interests of Massachusetts and spoke for that rebellious colony before the Parliament. Given how pivotal Massachusetts was to the political situation in America, and how tricky the politics were, it was fortunate for the colony that it had an agent of Franklin's skill on its side. It was an important post, and a difficult one.

In this instance, however, it was Franklin who fanned the flames. The Massachusetts agent had managed to get his hands on some of Hutchinson's correspondence, letters in which the governor urged that harsh measures be used to put down the Boston mob. Franklin sent the letters to friends in Boston, suggesting that, inflammatory as they were, they only be shown to a few people. Instead, Sam Adams had them printed and sent to every town in the colony.

As Josiah Quincy Jr. wrote of the letters, "Their effect was convulsive." Hutchinson was pilloried in the newspapers. Several towns burned him in effigy. A petition for his removal was circulated. Quincy observed, "From being a man of the greatest influence and popularity, he became the most obnoxious of all the tools of the British ministry."

It was in the middle of that brouhaha, in the fall of 1773, that word of the Tea Act arrived.

The bear of rebellion might have been sleeping for the past few years, but the Tea Act was a hard poke in its side. If the chief purpose of the act had been to incite rebellion, it could hardly have been better written. American merchants, who were making a good profit off importing tea, and who for that reason had been instrumental in setting aside the non-importation agreements, were now looking at being cut out of the lucrative trade. One of the consignees wrote to a friend in London, "What difficulties may arise from the disaffection of the merchants and importers of tea to this measure of the East India Company, I am not yet able to say." He did feel that "no small opposition will be made thereto."

The Tea Act also served as a reminder that the question of taxation had never been settled. For years Americans had tacitly acquiesced to the hated Townshend duty, and now Parliament was reminding them of that fact. Even worse, the duty no longer applied to tea coming into England, only that coming into America. It had been suggested by some that both duties be abolished, but in the end Parliament had retained the duty in the colonies specifically to reinforce its right to tax.

With Boston still obsessed with the Hutchinson letters, New York and Philadelphia took the lead in resistance. Long before any ships bearing tea sailed from London, the Sons of Liberty in those cities had, through threats of violence, dissuaded the consignees from continuing in their assigned duties. In Boston, Governor Hutchinson was willing to go to greater lengths than other governors to support the Tea Act. His sons were agents of the East India Company, and Hutchinson had four regiments of British troops and a significant naval presence at his disposal.

What's more, since the advent of the Stamp Act, Hutchinson had been knocked around by Adams, Warren, and the Sons of Liberty. He had stood up to them then, and he was too stubborn to give in now. He had been attacked in the press, grossly insulted, and thwarted in his attempts to govern; his house had even been ransacked. Hutchinson had actually asked to be relieved of duty and had received permission just before the Tea Act crisis erupted. Though he was ready to leave, Hutchinson remained in Boston. He would not give the Sons of Liberty the satisfaction of thinking they had driven him out.

As a result, the five consignees in Boston could not be intimidated into renouncing their positions as those in other cities had done. The Sons of Liberty gave notice that, on November 3, the East India Company men were ordered to attend a public meeting at the Liberty Tree, an old elm just west of Boston Common, where they were expected to resign. When the consignees understandably refused to appear, a delegation, which included Warren and a number of other leading Patriots, hunted them down at the warehouse of one of their number, Richard Clarke. A large and worked-up mob trailed behind the delegation.

William Molineux, who along with Warren, Adams, Dr. Benjamin Church, and others was a leader of the radical movement, was chosen head of the delegation. As the delegates, with the mob behind, approached the warehouse, Molineux announced their presence to the men inside.

"From whom are you a committee?" Richard Clarke asked, tacitly pointing out the extralegal nature of this gathering.

"From the whole people," Molineux replied.

Clarke then asked who else made up the delegation, and Molineux told him. "What is your request?" Clarke demanded.

"That you give us your word to sell none of the teas in your charge," Molineux replied, "but return them to London in the same bottoms in which they were shipped. Will you comply?"

"I shall have nothing to do with you" was Clarke's response.

Molineux read the resolves passed at the Liberty Tree and declared the consignees would be considered enemies to their country. When the consignees still would not agree to the people's demands, the mob stormed the warehouse, pulling the doors off the hinges and ransacking the place while the consignees took shelter in a locked room on the second floor. Still they would not resign.

All of the wrangling was academic, of course, since no East India Company tea had actually made it to American shores. That situation changed on November 28 when the merchant ship *Dartmouth* stood in from the open sea and worked its way through the scattering of islands to anchor in Boston's sheltered harbor. In her hold were 114 chests of what Abigail Adams called the "weed of slavery."

THE BOSTON TEA PARTY

The ship's arrival created an immediate standoff. The Patriots of Boston had already decided that under no circumstances would the tea be landed. They maintained that it must be sent back to England, but the law forbade tea to be reimported, which meant the cargo would be seized and confiscated if it was sent back. The law also said that if it was not landed in America, and the duty paid within twenty days of the ship's arrival, it would be seized by colonial customs inspectors, who would have the backing of Hutchinson and the troops at his disposal.

The owner of the ship, Francis Rotch, wanted the tea landed. He had other cargo on board to come ashore, and a shipment of whale oil he wished to send back to England aboard *Dartmouth*. Governor Hutchinson also wanted the tea to come ashore, as that would get it one step closer to being officially imported.

The Sons of Liberty, as Hutchinson knew, did not want the tea to come ashore. They feared that if it did, the duties would be paid and the tea would find its way to market, thus frustrating their attempts to prevent that. For the sake of political symbolism, they vowed that no British tea would come ashore in America.

The night of the *Dartmouth*'s arrival, the Patriots posted notices calling the people of Boston to an emergency meeting the next day. The notices may have been written by Warren—they certainly carried his signature hyperbole and use of dashes, along with a passing knowledge of Shakespeare's *Julius Caesar:* "Friends! Brethren! Countrymen!—That worst of plagues, the detested tea, shipped for this port by the East India Company is now arrived in this harbour—the Hour of Destruction or Manly Opposition to the Machinations of Tyranny stares you in the Face." More than five thousand people responded to the call.

The meeting began at Faneuil Hall but was moved to the larger Old South Meeting House. There it was again unanimously resolved that the tea should be sent back to England. A guard of twenty-five men was sent to "protect" the *Dartmouth,* tied up at Griffin's Wharf on the waterfront southeast of town and about half a mile from the meetinghouse. Paul Revere took a watch as part of the guard, as did a local bookseller, a hulking man who had long been a student of military matters and who served in the local militia, named Henry Knox.

Hutchinson and the consignees were beginning to fear for their personal safety. Hutchinson asked the legislature for permission to call up troops or justices of the peace for their protection, but the legislature would not consent. With no options left, most of the consignees fled to the protection of Castle William.

For twenty days, the time allowed for the master of the *Dartmouth* to clear customs and pay the duties on the tea, the city of Boston was a swirl of tension and frantic negotiations. The consignees offered to land the tea and store it while they waited for instructions from the East India Company, but the Patriots would not allow it. When it became clear that the tea was not coming ashore, owner Francis Rotch offered to send the ship out to sea again, but this time Hutchinson would not allow it and refused to give her clearance to sail. Even the young painter John Singleton Copley, son-in-law of consignee Richard Clarke, became embroiled in the negotiations, pleading with Warren, Adams, and the other leaders to avoid violence over the issue. Abigail Adams, writing to her friend Mercy Otis Warren (sister of the Patriot leader James Otis but not related to Joseph Warren), gave a sense of the tension that prevailed; "My Heart beats at every Whistle I hear," she wrote, "and I dare not openly express half my fears."

Though it was still a year and a half before the bloodshed at Lexington and Concord, it was increasingly clear to everyone, Abigail Adams included, that the course of events would ultimately lead to violence. Abigail wrote to Mercy:

> Altho the mind is Shocked at the thought of Sheding Humane Blood, more especially the Blood of our Countrymen and a civil war is of all wars the most dreadfull, Such is the present spirit that prevails, that if once they are made desperate Many, very Many of our Heroes will Spend their lives in the cause with the Speach of Cato in their Mouths, "what a pitty it is, that we can dye but once to save our Country."

On December 2 a second tea ship, the *Eleanor,* arrived in Boston and was ordered to join the *Dartmouth* at Griffin's Wharf. Five days later the brig *Beaver* made landfall, but she carried smallpox on board and was made to wait at anchor in quarantine before joining the others at the wharf on December 15. A fourth brig, the *William,* owned by Richard Clarke, whose warehouse had been torn apart by the mob, was driven ashore on Cape Cod by a storm and wrecked.

Despite the vigorous negotiations, threats, and resolves, the stalemate continued. Francis Rotch was forced by the ad hoc committee of the people to make the rounds from the governor to the customs collectors to the committee trying to secure clearance for his ship to leave port, but to no avail.

A cold rain was falling on the morning of December 16, when a crowd of five thousand people once again assembled at the Old South Meeting House. Around two thousand of them had come in from the countryside, as not just Boston but all the towns of Massachusetts had been swept up in the crisis. In less than twelve hours the customs officials would be free to seize the tea on board the three vessels, at which point the consignees could pay the duty and sell it. Rotch was sent off to find Hutchinson and once again ask for permission to sail.

It was around 6:00 P.M., the town of Boston plunged into winter darkness, when the weary Rotch returned to the Old South, now dimly lit by candles and still crowded with an anxious mob waiting to hear what the ship owner would say. With time running short, Rotch's request of Hutchinson was considered the final option. Even before they heard from Rotch, merchant John Rowe, anticipating how things would end up, had posed the question to those around him, "Who knows how tea will mingle with salt water?"

Rotch reported that the governor would not relent, that the tea ships could not sail. The crowd began to jeer and threatened to turn on Rotch before they were calmed. Rotch was asked if he would, on his own volition, send his ship to sea, but he replied that he could not, that doing so "would prove his ruin." With just hours to go before the deadline, the Patriots had only one option left. Sam Adams stood and announced, "This meeting can do nothing more to save the country."

That did not mean there was nothing more that the Sons of Liberty could do. Indeed, that pronouncement was apparently a prearranged signal, and as soon as it left Adams's lips, "a number of brave and resolute men, dressed in the Indian manner, approached near the door of the assembly, and gave a war-whoop, which rang through the house." This was followed by shouts from the gallery of "Boston Harbor a tea-pot tonight!" and "Hurrah for Griffin's wharf!"

None of this was spontaneous. Adams and the others had made arrangements for a gang to disguise themselves as Indians for the purpose of tossing the tea into Boston Harbor. The "Indians" were young, working-class men, mostly apprentices or journeymen, who had blackened their skin with grease and soot and lamp black, dressed in old blankets, and armed themselves with tomahawks and axes. It's not clear how many there were, but their numbers were likely somewhere between twenty and fifty. If they were not enough, there were plenty of other willing hands to pitch in and help.

As the meeting turned into a frenzied rally, the leaders declared it

adjourned, and the thousands of people in attendance flooded out of the
Old South. John Andrews, who lived nearby, had, ironically, been enjoy-
ing a cup of tea when he heard the shouting, and out of curiosity headed
off to the meetinghouse. He arrived just as the gathering was letting out.
"I found the moderator was just declaring the meeting to be dissolved,"
he wrote to a friend, "which caused another general shout, out-doors and
in, and three cheers. What with that and the consequent noise of breaking up the meeting, you'd thought the inhabitants of the infernal regions
had broke loose."

Andrews headed home and "finished my tea," but the bulk of the
mob, led by the Indians, shouting and whooping, headed down Milk
Street and then Hutchinson Street for Griffin's Wharf. The crowd carried lanterns and torches that lit the scene with a stark, flickering light so
that, as one participant wrote, "everything was as light as day . . . [A] pin
might be seen laying on the wharf."

Captain James Bruce, master of the *Eleanor,* was a Boston Loyalist
and was not pleased to find himself in the center of an anti-Parliament
protest. In a deposition taken soon afterward he wrote, "about the hours
of 6 or 7 o'clock in the same evening, about one thousand unknown
people came down the said wharf, and a number of them came on board
the said ship, some being dressed like Indians."

Most of the people had come from the meeting at Old South, while
others had joined the parade as it wound its way to the docks. The Indians
were divided into three groups, one for each ship, and one man appointed
"captain" and another "boatswain" to oversee the work (one participant
named Hewes, locally famous for his whistling talent, was made boatswain of the gang boarding the *Beaver* because of it).

The *Dartmouth* and *Eleanor,* which had been some time at the dock,
had nothing on board but tea, having discharged their other cargo. The
captain's log of the *Dartmouth* records that a number of people "dressed
like whooping Indians . . . came on board the ship, and after warning
myself and the custom-house officers to get out of the way, they undid
the hatches, and went down the hold, where was eight whole, and thirty-
four half chests, of tea."

The *Beaver,* quarantined for smallpox, had only come alongside the dock the day before, and all of her cargo, including the tea, was still on board. The ship's master, Captain Hezekiah Coffin, argued that the tea was stowed beneath other cargo owned by various Boston merchants. The Indians informed him that "the tea they wanted and the tea they would have," but if he would go to his cabin and not interfere, nothing would be hurt. The *Beaver's* mate handed over the keys.

Indeed, it was universally understood that this was to be a controlled mob action, that the tea alone was to be destroyed and nothing else hurt. Despite the fact that at least half the men on board the ships were not part of the original planning and had joined at the last minute, that stricture was strictly obeyed. After a small padlock belonging to one of the captains was accidentally broken, another was sent a few days later to replace it.

The one person who tried to take advantage of the situation was an Irishman named Charles Conner or some variation of that name, who rented horses in Boston. Conner had ripped the lining under the arms of his coat and waistcoat (he was apparently not one of those dressed as an Indian) and was caught stuffing tea into the space between the lining and the coat. According to John Andrews, who had finished his tea and come down to the dock to watch the activity, Conner "was handled pretty roughly. They not only stripped him of his clothes, but gave him a coat of mud, and a severe bruising into the bargain."

As the thousand or more spectators watched from the dock, the Indians and those who had joined with them pulled open hatches and swayed the chests of tea up from below using the ship's stay tackles. The ships' officers and crews remained below and did not interfere, though in a few instances the sailors helped the Indians sway the tea up. The crates were hacked open with axes, and tea and crates dumped into Boston Harbor. John Andrews reported to his friend, "They say the actors were Indians from Narragansett; whether they were or not, to a transient observer they appeared as such, being clothed in blankets, with their heads muffled, and copper-colored countenances, each being armed with a hatchet or ax, or pair of pistols." They even spoke in what Boston Yankees thought an Indian dialect might sound like.

Even with all the hands that were available to help, the task was not a small one. The *Massachusetts Gazette* reported, with a touch of pride, "They applied themselves so dexterously to the destruction of this commodity, that in the space of three hours they broke up three hundred and forty-two chests, which was the whole number in these vessels." As the rising tide carried the tea and broken chests off, the surface of the harbor was all but covered with tea and shattered wood from the South End of Boston all the way to Dorchester Neck. The Indians took brooms and swept up any remaining mess off the ships' decks, returned everything to its rightful place, and departed.

Admiral John Montagu was visiting a friend's house at the head of Griffin's Wharf and watched the action from a window. According to one account, as the Sons of Liberty headed back toward the city, Montagu leaned out the window and called to Lendall Pitts, who had headed up the destruction of the *Beaver*'s tea, "Well, boys, you have had a fine pleasant evening for your Indian caper, haven't you? But mind, you have got to pay the fiddler yet!"

To that Pitts replied, "Oh, never mind! Never mind, squire! Just come out here, if you please, and we'll settle the bill in two minutes!" Montagu slammed the window down. He did not take Pitts up on the offer.

That night, and the next day and night, Boston remained calm. The Sons of Liberty and the radical leaders had solved the tea crisis in a way that was deeply satisfying to them, and to most of the citizens of Massachusetts. The example they set in destroying the offending tea created a precedent for other cities to follow when the tea ships arrived in their harbors. More than one participant noted the general good cheer that ran throughout the city, a sharp contrast to the days of anxiety that had proceeded the Tea Party. Sam Adams observed, "You cannot imagine the height of joy that sparkles in the eyes and animates the countenances as well as the hearts of all we meet on this occasion."

Governor Thomas Hutchinson called the Boston Tea Party "the boldest stroke that had been struck in America." John Adams wrote in his diary, "This destruction of the tea is so bold, so daring, so firm, so intrepid and inflexible, and it must have so important consequences, and so lasting, that I cannot but consider it as an epoch in history."

In that he was absolutely right. Thirty young men dressed as Indians and a thousand supportive onlookers had just set the country on the path to war.

INTOLERABLE ACTS

Thomas Hutchinson was taken aback by news of the destruction of the East India Company's tea. He genuinely thought that he had outmaneuvered the Patriots, that once the twenty-day waiting period was up they would have allowed his customs officers to seize the tea. He certainly knew that the mob was capable of violence—years earlier during the Stamp Act crisis they had sacked his house—but he did not think that the men of influence such as Hancock, Sam Adams, and Dr. Joseph Warren who were running the show would make themselves liable for such an act. The tea thrown into Boston Harbor was valued at £9,659, and someone was going to have to pay for it.

Hutchinson understood that the people who had urged the destruction of the tea and who were now delighting in the aftermath were the same people who had been trying all along to escalate the conflict with England. "To engage the people in some desperate measure had long been their plan," he wrote in his *History of Massachusetts-Bay* (which he did manage to complete despite the destruction of his documents and manuscript by the mob in 1765). "They never discovered more concern than when the people were quiet upon the repeal of an act of Parliament, or upon concessions made or assurances given."

The governor was dead-on with that assessment. The radical leaders and the Sons of Liberty had been searching for years for some issue, some manner of protest, that would do irreparable damage to the union of the colonies and the mother country. The Sugar Act, the Stamp Act, and the Townshend duties had all come and gone without creating a major rift. Now, with the confluence of taxes, parliamentary authority, corporate interest, and the destruction of private property, it was pretty universally understood that they had found it.

Individual reactions to the Tea Party—joy, anger, trepidation—were almost entirely a reflection of the individual's attitude toward Parliament. John Rowe, a Boston merchant, political moderate, and owner of the tea ship *Eleanor,* dreaded the consequences. On December 18 he wrote in his diary:

> The affair of Destroying the Tea makes Great Noise in the Town. Tis a Disastrous Affair & some People are much Alarmed. I can truly say I know nothing of the Matter nor who were concerned in it. I would rather have lost Five Hundred Guineas than Bruce [*Eleanor*'s captain] should have taken any of this Tea on board his Ship.

News of the Tea Party reached London on January 20, 1774, aboard John Hancock's ship *Hayley,* which sailed from Boston on December 22. The news did not cause any great stir at first, in part because the incident was downplayed in American versions of the event. It was only as other accounts filtered in, including Hutchinson's official report on January 27, and word of tea protests in other cities arrived, that the king and his ministers understood they had a serious problem on their hands.

The first focus of the government's anger was Benjamin Franklin. A petition from Massachusetts had been sent to the ministry asking for the removal of Hutchinson and Lieutenant Governor Andrew Oliver from office. Two days after official word of the Tea Party arrived, Franklin, as agent for the colony of Massachusetts, was called to appear before the Privy Council, a group of the king's closest advisers. He was ostensibly there to answer questions with regard to the petitions. In actuality, the government used this opportunity to excoriate Franklin for his part in releasing the Hutchinson letters, his character in general, and the breakdown in the king's authority over the colonies.

For an hour Franklin stood in silence as his character was shredded in front of the central figures in British government. In the end, he was stripped of his post as deputy postmaster general of North America, and his salary as agent for various colonies was stopped. General Thomas Gage, who was in the audience, wrote to a friend, "The Doctor was so abused, his conduct and character so cut and mangled I wonder he had the confidence to stand it."

Franklin had never been a radical in the mold of Sam Adams or even John Adams. Indeed, he had been living in Europe for most of the past seventeen years and had always longed for status and position within the British Empire. No more. By 1775 he was back in America. Soon it would become clear that the Privy Council had managed to create Great Britain's most dangerous enemy.

To the king and ministry, humiliating Franklin was just the beginning. The violent protests throughout the colonies against the Tea Act were intolerable, but the bright center of that rebellious activity was Boston. Various schemes for punishing the city were discussed, and evidence was collected. In mid-February half a dozen witnesses to the Tea Party, including Francis Rotch and Captain James Hall of the *Dartmouth,* were called before the Privy Council to testify, and other relevant documents were gathered.

Lord Dartmouth requested that the attorney general and solicitor general offer their opinion as to whether or not those responsible for the Tea Party could be brought to trial on an accusation of high treason. After some deliberation the legal officers replied that in their opinion the actions taken in Boston "do amount to the crime of high treason, namely to the levying of war against His Majesty." They specifically named Hancock, Adams, Molineux, and Warren, among others, as men liable to that charge, giving those men the distinction of being the first in the American Revolution to be thus accused. No warrants, however, were issued for their arrest, in part because it was deemed impractical to try them in England and unlikely they would be found guilty in America.

Initially the king and ministry intended to deal with the matter themselves, but they soon decided the necessary steps could not "be completely effected by the sole authority of the Crown." Parliament was asked to review the matter and decide on a just punishment. On March 7 Lord North read a message from the king to the House of Commons:

His Majesty, upon information of the unwarrantable practices which have lately been concerted and carried on in *North America,* and particularly of the violent and outrageous proceedings of the town of Boston . . . with a view of obstructing the commerce of this Kingdom, and upon grounds and pretenses immediately subversive to the constitution thereof, have thought to lay the whole matter before his two Houses of Parliament.

By way of punishment, the ministry proposed closing Boston Harbor to all commerce until such time as the people of Massachusetts reimbursed the East India Company for the tea that was destroyed. Only coasting vessels carrying fuel and supplies would be allowed into port, and they would have to clear through Marblehead first. The customhouse would be moved to Plymouth, and Salem would become the seat of government for the colony. It was an act well designed to inflict maximum economic pain on the city.

Days of debate followed. One MP pointed out that "the *Americans* were a strange set of People, and that it was in vain to expect any degree of reasoning from them; that instead of making their claim by argument they always chose to decide the matter by tarring and feathering." A majority in Parliament, including those who were traditional friends of America, were in favor of the bill, feeling it was a just punishment. One claimed "the town of Boston ought to be knocked about their ears and destroyed . . . [Y]ou will never meet with that proper obedience to the laws of this country until you have destroyed that nest of locusts."

Others thought the bill ridiculous and overly broad, punishing the entire city for the actions of the mob. One particularly prescient member rose to object that "instead of quieting the disturbances in *Boston,* it will promote them still further . . . which may be productive of mutual hostilities, and most probably will end in a GENERAL REVOLT." Finally, on March 25, the Boston Port Bill was passed by the Commons.

The following day it went to the House of Lords and soon passed there, with even greater support.

Over the next three months Parliament passed four more acts, which, with the Boston Port Bill, came to be known collectively in the colonies as the Intolerable Acts. The acts altered the charter of the colony of Massachusetts to give the crown vastly greater control over the local government. The members of the Council, formerly elected by the legislature, would now consist of councilors chosen by the king and serving for as long as he wished. Judges would be selected by the governor, and towns would be limited to one town meeting per year, and that only for electing officials and making any needed rules for local administration. The new laws allowed for royal officials accused of capital crimes to be sent to England for trial. They established new regulations for quartering troops. They were, in short, the boldest attempt yet by Parliament to rein in the growing spirit of rebellion and independence in Boston and send a message to the other colonies.

The impasse reached by the Americans and Great Britain in the spring of 1774 formed a classic political standoff, of a type seen many times before and since. The British government could not ignore the extraordinary affront that was the Boston Tea Party. The leniency shown in the past had done no good as far as anyone could see. The unreasonable and ungrateful attitude of the colonists was generating considerable anger in England, leading Parliament and the king to take a hard line with their increasingly rebellious subjects. Yet taking a hard line would only solidify colonial opposition and turn even more Americans against the crown's authority. It was a downward spiral, and it was spinning faster and faster.

Chapter Five

GAGE'S RETURN

Governor Thomas Hutchinson had at his disposal an overwhelming military and naval force, but that was not as helpful in the Tea Act crisis as might be imagined. Hutchinson was unwilling to unilaterally call out the army, be it the regulars or the militia, and there was some question as to whether he even had the legal authority to do so. What's more, Hutchinson understood that if the military were called out, the situation might quickly spin out of control.

For backing on the military question he looked to the Council, the upper body of the General Court. In most colonies, members of the Council were appointed by the governor, and the governor could thus count on them for support. In Massachusetts, however, they were elected by the General Court and were of a more patriotic bent than in other colonies. As a result, Hutchinson could never find a majority who were willing to back him up. Writing to the American secretary, Dartmouth, with regard to the use of military force, Hutchinson explained, "I have not one magistrate in the province who would venture upon such a measure." As to calling up the Company of Cadets, who served as a personal guard for the governor, their lieutenant colonel (appointed by Hutchinson in 1772) was John Hancock, and he had little inclination to use force against the protesters.

Hutchinson, of course, had already asked for leave, a request that had been granted, and someone was needed to take his place. In the spring of 1774, King George realized that he had the perfect man for that embattled office. On April 9 Dartmouth wrote to General Thomas Gage, still on leave in England, saying:

> The King having thought fit that you should return immediately to your command in North America and that you should proceed directly to Boston on board His Majesty's ship *Lively,* now lying at Plymouth ready to sail with the first fair wind, I send you herewith . . . a commission . . . appointing you Captain-General and Governor-in-Chief of His Majesty's province of Massachusetts Bay.

On a number of levels Gage was a brilliant choice. Having spent seventeen years in America in various positions of authority, and being married to an American, he knew the country as well as any nonnative might, and certainly understood the political situation better than anyone in the ministry or Parliament. Gage was already known and respected by most Americans. As someone with a generally positive attitude toward the colonies, he could at least understand the colonial point of view, while there was no question of his being completely devoted to enforcing the will of king and Parliament.

To that end, Gage believed as the king did that it was time to take uncompromising measures with the rebellious Americans. Nevertheless, Gage was not an unreasonable or overly aggressive sort, not the kind who might claim that Bostonians "ought to be knocked about their ears and destroyed." He knew far more about war than any civilian governor, and he was not about to blunder thoughtlessly into bloodshed.

Naming Gage as governor in chief also went far toward solving the issue of calling up the military, since Gage was also still commander in chief of the army in North America. Should Gage meet with opposition in enacting the new parliamentary acts, Dartmouth wrote, "your authority as the first magistrate combined with your command over the King's troops will it is hoped enable you to meet every opposition and fully to preserve the public peace by employing those troops with effect."

Use of the military, however, was to be a last resort. Dartmouth reminded Gage "it will be your duty to use every endeavour to avoid it, to quiet the minds of the people, to remove their prejudices, and by mild and gentle persuasion" induce them to obey the law. Gage had the right temperament to fulfill such a directive, if indeed it were still possible. He would certainly look to the military only when all other options were expended. Given the buildup of men and arms on both sides during the years 1774 and 1775, the terrific violence that broke out under Gage's watch, and the years of fighting that followed, it's easy to forget how long and hard both sides sincerely worked to avoid bloodshed—and how eager each was to blame the other when it came.

Dartmouth's orders to Gage were many pages long and included a copy of the Boston Port Bill, which closed the port of Boston and Gage, as his primary mission, was expected to enforce. Since the ministry could not predict what sort of political climate Gage would find when he arrived in Boston, he was instructed to meet with the military and civilian leaders "at the town or within the Castle (as circumstances shall point out)" and determine what steps should be taken to enforce the will of Parliament and the king.

Boston, "where so much anarchy and confusion have prevailed," was no longer to be the seat of government; Gage and the General Court were to relocate to Salem. Gage was also instructed to prosecute "in the ordinary courts of justice within the colony" those individuals whom the attorney general and solicitor general had determined might be tried for high treason. The king considered the punishment of those offenders "as a very necessary and essential example to others," but he also understood that a guilty verdict might not be easy to come by in America. Gage was warned that if "the prejudices of the people should appear to you to be such as would in all probability prevent a conviction," he was to give up the prosecution. An "ineffectual attempt," Dartmouth wrote, "would only be a triumph to the faction and disgraceful to the government."

For all of the unwarranted optimism so often displayed by the minis-try, Dartmouth, in this instance at least, seemed to have a healthy under-standing of the problems that Gage would face. "The last advices from Boston," he wrote, "are of a nature to leave but little room to hope that order and obedience are soon likely to take [the] place of anarchy and usurpation."

In that Dartmouth was certainly right, and Gage certainly knew it. Since the Tea Party, the situation in Boston had been largely a stalemate as everyone waited for the reaction from London. The Patriots took the opportunity to further solidify their position, making plans for the cre-ation of a purely colonial postal system and forming new committees of correspondence in various towns. Hutchinson understood the threat that such activities posed, and he informed the Patriot leaders that their plans were "unconstitutional and unwarrantable upon any principles of the English government."

On March 6 the brig *Fortune* arrived in Boston with thirty chests of tea aboard. If there was any thought that Bostonians were feeling remorse for their actions of the previous December, it was answered the next day when sixty men in Indian guise went aboard the brig and dumped her cargo of tea into Boston Harbor. "The owners of the tea are very silent," Hutchinson reported to Dartmouth, and would probably not press charges even if they knew who perpetrated the crime. The original consignees of the tea destroyed in the first Tea Party were still hiding out in Castle William, and the current owners did not care to join them.

This second Boston Tea Party may have lacked the drama of the first, but it served as proof that colonial attitudes had hardened, just as the Parliament in London was deciding what to do about it. Rumors were crossing the Atlantic with regard to the punishment Parliament would mete out to the Bostonians, and tensions were escalating. Sam Adams and the other radical leaders in Boston had been actively promoting an-other nonimportation agreement with the merchants of Massachusetts and the other colonies, though distrust among the merchants based on the failures of the last such agreement were making things more diffi-cult. Hutchinson and the General Court had come to such an impasse that on March 9 he prorogued the legislature, that is, dismissed them without actually dissolving the body, though there was considerable business still to be decided.

On May 10 a ship arrived from London carrying the official version of the Boston Port Bill, and the reaction in Massachusetts and the other colonies was as intense as it was unsurprising. Sam Adams wrote to Arthur Lee in London with his usual understatement, "For flagrant injustice and barbarity, one might search in vain among the archives of *Constantinople* to find a match for it . . . For us to reason against *such* an Act, would be idleness. Our business is to find means to evade its malignant design."

As word spread, the other colonies moved to support Boston, even if the merchants of those colonies were not entirely on board with non-importation. A town meeting in Providence, Rhode Island, proclaimed, "We are of opinion that an universal stoppage of all trade with *Great Britain* . . . until such time as the port of *Boston* shall be reinstated in its former privileges, &c., will be the best expedient." A committee in Chestertown, Maryland, voted a series of resolves "thus to baffle the designs of a corrupt and despotic Ministry" (most Americans still felt it was Parliament, not the king, that was behind the repression). From Philadelphia came a broadside reading (with a nod to Ben Franklin, the city's most famous resident), "An union of the colonies, like an electric rod, will render harmless the storms of *British* vengeance and tyranny."

It was right in the middle of all this that His Majesty's Ship *Lively* of twenty guns dropped anchor in Boston. Her primary passenger, General Thomas Gage, was no doubt relieved to disembark from the cramped sloop-of-war with her tiny cabin and 130-man crew. The day was Friday, the 13th of May, and if Gage did not think that date an unlucky one at the time, he soon would.

"I CANNOT GET A WORSE COUNCIL"

General, now Governor, Gage anticipated trouble in Boston. He had urged his wife to stay behind in England, but she refused. Instead, she sailed three weeks after her husband, going first to New York, where she remained with old friends until September before joining her husband.

The general was probably not encouraged to find that former governor Hutchinson, the chief justice, the customs commissioners, and the consignees of the East India Company's tea were all either hiding out at Castle William or off in the countryside, "not daring to reside in Boston." On the same day that *Lively* came to anchor in the harbor, a town meeting was taking place in Faneuil Hall "to determine upon proper measures to be taken by the town," in reaction to the Boston Port Bill. Sam Adams was elected moderator, and the bill itself was read and its implications explained to the people, with, one would imagine, a heavy anti-Parliament slant.

After some debate it was voted, as the opinion of the town, that if the other colonies were to stop all imports and exports to Great Britain until the port bill was repealed, "the same will prove the salvation of *North America* and her liberties." If, however, the other colonies continued to trade with England, "there is high reason to fear that fraud, power, and the most odious oppression, will rise triumphant over right, justice, social happyness and freedom." The choices seemed pretty clear-cut.

A committee consisting of Sam and John Adams, Joseph Warren, John Rowe, Josiah Quincy, William Molineux, and others was elected to compile the various suggestions offered at the town meeting and report back. Another committee was selected to go to Marblehead and Salem with word of what the Boston town meeting had decided.

From Castle William, Gage sent word ashore of his arrival. He remained at the garrison until Tuesday, May 17, when arrangements could be made for his formal reception. He may have feared that his arrival would be seen as an opportunity for further protest. When he stepped off the boat and onto Long Wharf, however, he was met with all the pomp appropriate for an official of his stature. A number of the members of the General Court were there to greet him, along with Hancock's Company of Cadets, under arms, and "many of the principal gentlemen of the town."

Long Wharf ran into King Street, where the Troop of Horse, the

Company of Artillery, the Company of Grenadiers, and several militia companies, all under arms, were arrayed along Gage's route and saluted him as he passed. The Town House, in which the Council Chamber was located, stood at the end of King Street. There Gage's commission was read by the secretary, and "after the usual ceremonies" he was sworn in as governor and vice admiral of the province. The high sheriff then read Gage's proclamation that all officers and officials would remain in their places until further orders. This was "answered with three huzzas, firing of cannon from the battery and artillery company, and three vollies of small arms."

Gage reviewed the militia and received the compliments of the gentlemen present; then the entire party retired to Faneuil Hall, "where an elegant entertainment was provided at the expense of the Province." Only those who were professed friends of the government were invited, with the result that, according to one attendee, "there were but very few Gentlemen of the Town asked to Dine there."

The welcome that Gage received in Boston was dignified and restrained. The general was a known and respected figure in America, and certainly anyone coming to replace the despised Hutchinson would have been looked on with favor, at least initially. The Boston Port Bill had only just arrived, the rest of the Intolerable Acts were not yet known in Boston, and no one knew what parliamentary orders Gage carried with him. Merchant John Rowe, who was part of the Patriot movement but not at all the radical that Sam Adams or Joseph Warren was, wrote in his diary, "The Lively, Man of Warr . . . has Brought out Genl Gage, our New Governour. God Grant his Instructions be not severe and I think him to be a Very Good Man."

Sam Adams and others recognized the potential threat inherent in having the office of military commander and civilian leader invested in one man. Adams wrote to Arthur Lee, "We expect studied insult in the appointment of the person who is Commander-in-chief of the troops in *America* to be our Governour." With this sense of wariness on both sides, Gage launched into the business of governing the rebellious colony. Once he did that, once the welcomes were over and the business begun, the goodwill broke down with astonishing speed and was replaced by bitter animosity. The only surprise, in retrospect, was that it still took eleven months before people started shooting at one another.

Soon after Gage's arrival, Boston Harbor was shut down, per the Boston Port Bill, while a draft of the act altering the charter of Massachusetts, which was still being debated in Parliament, found its way into print in the colonies. "I am afraid of the Consequences that this Act will Produce," wrote merchant Rowe, again taking a moderate and considered position. "I wish for Harmony & Peace between Great Britain Our Mother Country & the Colonies—but the Time is far off. The People have done amiss and no sober man can vindicate their Conduct but the Revenge of the Ministry is too severe."

On May 25 the General Court met and elected a new Council. Gage, who now had the authority to appoint all the councilors, immediately overturned the election of twelve of them who were considered particular enemies of the crown. On June 7 the General Court met again at Salem, where the Port Bill specified they were to meet, and things continued to unravel. Several bills were passed that made the colony, not the crown, responsible for the salaries of the governor and the agents for Massachusetts in London, thus giving the colonial legislature greater influence over them. This was long a point of contention, and Gage refused to sign the bills into law.

Around that same time, the many committees of correspondence, which had been created throughout the colonies as a response to the crisis of the past years, now began to show their worth. Letters moved up and down the coast as various colonial governments, reacting to the latest parliamentary outrage in Boston, called for a congress of representatives from all the colonies. The consensus was that the people of Massachusetts should name the time and place for such a meeting.

On June 17 a town meeting was held at Faneuil Hall, not to discuss the planned Continental Congress, which was something of an open secret, but to discuss the current crisis and the manner in which the city of Boston would meet it. Letters from the various committees of correspondence were presented to the people, and votes taken on how to respond to them. It was exactly the sort of local, popular government that Parliament expected Gage to put a stop to.

On the same day, June 17, a committee of the House of Representatives, which had been considering the question of the Continental Congress, was ready to report to the House as a whole. The committee had been meeting for days, and its deliberations were strictly secret. To throw Gage off, the members spread the rumor that their discussions "were upon moderate and conciliating measures." Now, as the House met to consider the question, committee member Sam Adams ordered the door to the meeting hall locked, and he personally pocketed the key. Despite the precautions, one of the members, pleading illness, was allowed to leave, and he immediately reported the goings-on to Gage.

On hearing that the House was voting on delegates to the Continental Congress, Gage dispatched the secretary of the province, a man with the unfortunate name of Thomas Flucker (who also happened to be the father-in-law of future Revolutionary War general Henry Knox), with a proclamation dissolving the General Court. Adams, however, would not unlock the door, so Flucker stood on the stairs outside the hall and read the proclamation to the people assembled there while on the other side of the door the General Court carried on with the vote.

It was decided that the first meeting of the first Continental Congress would take place in Philadelphia on September 1. Five delegates from Massachusetts were chosen. Among them were Sam Adams and his cousin John Adams, who, in agreeing to the post, was taking his first real step into politics. The House then voted a tax to be paid by the local communities to raise £500 for the support of the delegates. That done, Adams unlocked the doors, and the Court allowed itself to be dissolved.

A week later Thomas Gage wrote to the Earl of Dartmouth with a report on the proceedings:

> If the dissolution will be productive of good or not remains to be known, but from what I could learn or see I cannot get a worse Council or a worse Assembly who with exceptions . . . appeared little more than echoes of the contrivers of all the mischief in the

town of Boston. Those demagogues I am informed are now spirit-
ing up the people throughout the province to resistance.

It had been just six weeks since his celebratory arrival at Faneuil Hall.

MEN AND ARMS

As the summer wore on, the troops began to arrive. The transport
carrying the 4th Regiment, the King's Own, anchored in Boston on
June 10, just around the time Gage was starting to lock horns with the
General Court, and the men came ashore on the 14th. They made camp
on Boston Common, "notwithstanding the violent threat denounced
against us."

The next day the 43rd joined them on the Common, and soon after
that the 5th and the 38th arrived from Ireland. Before long the sprawling
green fields were covered with lines of sharp white tents, officers' mar-
quees, bright regimental colors snapping in the breeze, men in scarlet
uniforms marching in precise order, stacked muskets, and lines of field
guns. Captain Evelyn of the King's Own noted that the troops "with a
small park of artillery, of six pieces of cannon and two cohorns, make a
formidable appearance." The commons, symbol of communal welfare,
that part of the city reserved for the people, had became a garrison, over-
run by the hated redcoats.

The people of Boston did not fail to notice the formidable appearance
of the soldiers, and they resented it deeply. A classic and inevitable conflict was once again setting up in Boston. Gage needed troops to maintain
order. The presence of the troops inflamed the Americans, who made
their anger known at every opportunity. This in turn created a loathing
for the Americans on the part of the soldiers. Evelyn explained to his
father in a letter written soon after his arrival that the friends of the king
"are distinguished here by the name of Tories, as the Liberty Boys, the
tarring-and-feathering gentlemen, are by the title of Whigs."

Evelyn did not think the troops were in any danger of being attacked, despite the undisguised animosity toward them. The Bostonians, he felt, "upon paper . . . are the bravest fellows in the world, yet in reality I believe there does not exist so great a set of rascals and poltroons."

On July 1, John Rowe noted in his diary, "The Preston Man of Warr with Admirall Graves came into this harbour this day, as did several Transport Ships with the Remainder of the 5th and 38th Regiments on board. Lord Percy is with them." With the seat of government moved to Salem, Gage as governor was obliged to live there, and not Boston, so Percy found himself with "the honour of commanding the Troops encamped" on the commons.

Like Evelyn, Percy quickly developed a dislike for the locals. "The people here are a set of sly, artful, hypocritical rascalls, cruel, & cowards," he wrote to a relative back in England. "I must own I cannot but despise them compleately." Soon journals were reporting confrontations between soldiers and the people of Boston.

As the summer grew hotter ("We have days here full as hot as Spain," Percy wrote), so, too, did the political and military machinations. With the closing of the Port of Boston, which prevented any sort of supplies from reaching the city by water, the other colonies began to send relief: rice from the South landed at Marblehead, as stipulated by the Port Bill, and transported overland; sheep and cattle driven to Boston from nearby communities or shipped like the rice and landed elsewhere. A Boston paper noted, "Yesterday arrived at *Marblehead,* Captain *Perkins,* from *Baltimore,* with three thousand barrels of *Indian* corn, twenty barrels of rye, and twenty-one barrels of bread, sent by the inhabitants of that place for the benefit of the poor of *Boston,* together with one thousand bushels of corn from *Annapolis,* sent in the same vessel and for the same benevolent purpose."

One of those who brought supplies was Israel Putnam, a fifty-six-year-old former soldier who arrived in Boston with 130 sheep from his hometown of Brooklyn, Connecticut. Putnam was a Massachusetts native by birth, descended from a family that had settled in Salem in 1640. In his twenties, Israel had moved with his young bride to Connecticut, where he farmed his land and soon became one of the leading men in his community.

At the outbreak of the French and Indian War, Putnam joined a Connecticut regiment and received a commission as second lieutenant. Soon after, he joined the ranger unit commanded by Robert Rogers, with whom he remained throughout the war. Roger's Rangers were famous for some of the hardest fighting in the most brutal conditions. They operated in the area of Lake George and Lake Champlain, specializing in woodland-style tactics and small-unit guerrilla actions against the enemy.

By 1758 Putnam had advanced to the rank of major. He was at the side of General George Howe in the skirmish during which Howe was killed. At one point Putnam was captured by Indians, and when his fellow rangers came to his rescue they found him tied to a tree with preparations under way to burn him alive. Four years later Putnam was shipwrecked in Cuba while sailing on an expedition to capture Havana.

With the end of the French and Indian War, Putnam continued his military career, fighting against the Indians in an uprising known as Pontiac's Rebellion. Finally, in 1764, after a decade of tough military service, he retired into civilian life. He had reached the rank of colonel.

Israel Putnam's exploits during the French and Indian War made him famous, and a second marriage to a wealthy widow, after the death of his first wife, improved his fortune and his social standing. As the conflict with Great Britain heated up, Putnam stood solidly with the Patriot cause, serving as chairman of his local committee of correspondence. When he arrived in Boston at the head of his regiment of sheep, the people were delighted to see him. "The old hero, Putnam, arrived in town on Monday . . . ," one of the Boston Patriots wrote. "He cannot get away, he is so much caressed, both by the officers and the citizens." Putnam did eventually return to Connecticut. The next time he marched for Massachusetts, he would not be leading sheep.

While in Boston, Putnam stayed at the home of Joseph Warren. With Sam Adams off to Philadelphia, Warren now assumed an even larger role in the organized resistance to parliamentary authority. Between his medical practice and the increasing burden of his political activities, the young doctor was constantly on the run. In August he wrote to Sam Adams in Philadelphia, assuring him he would soon send all the news and intelligence from Boston. "Haste now prevents it," he pleaded, "as I am constantly busied in helping forward the political machines in all parts of this province."

It was in August that the next two acts of Parliament "for regulating the government of Massachusetts Bay" arrived at Gage's office in Salem. One of the new rules called for the Council to be made up of councilors selected by the king, not elected by the House. Gage had already dissolved the old Massachusetts legislature in frustration. Now he moved quicky to assemble a new one that would be friendly to the Crown. "No time was lost in forming the new Council," he assured Dartmouth. Unfortunately, being a king's appointee in Revolutionary Boston was not an entirely safe proposition, and some of the new councilors, Gage reported, "refused to accept the nomination or are wavering."

Lord Percy, for one, was disgusted. "Such a set of timid creatures I never did see," he wrote to a friend. "Those of the new Council that live at any distance from town have remained here [Boston] ever since they took the oaths, & are, I am told, afraid to go home again." Such accusations were easier to make when, like Percy, you were surrounded by British troops day and night.

Another clause in the new act banned the calling of town meetings without the governor's consent, which he was unlikely to give. Once again Gage found nothing but frustration in trying to enforce this provision. Anticipating this order of Parliament, the participants in a town meeting in July, rather than ending the meeting, had simply adjourned it. Thus when the meeting was assembled in August they were not actually calling a new meeting, just continuing the old one. Gage assembled the selectmen of Boston and read the clause to them. They protested "they had *called* no meeting, that a former meeting had only adjourned themselves." Gage pointed out that "by such means they might keep their meetings alive these ten years."

In other communities the people were careful to obey the ban on town meetings. Instead, they held their meetings in the countryside, at which point they became county meetings, which were still permissible according to their reading of the act.

By one means or another the people of Boston and the surrounding communities continued to meet, and the results of their meetings were increasingly radical. Hoping for more coordinated action, a committee from the town of Worcester requested a meeting with that of Boston to agree on a general plan to resist new parliamentary acts. Ultimately, representatives from the counties of Suffolk (which included Boston), Essex, Middlesex, and Worcester met at Faneuil Hall. Joseph Warren was elected to chair.

The result of the meeting was some of the strongest statements yet with regard to the steps to be taken to resist Gage and the Parliament. It was voted that the seating of all officials named under the new act was unconstitutional. Another resolve called for the thorough defeat of the new measures for regulating the government of Massachusetts and said that courts held under the act ought to be opposed. Most significantly, it called for a Provincial Congress, that is, a new government for the colony of Massachusetts completely divorced from Gage, the General Court, and the Parliament in London.

On August 30 the county of Middlesex held a convention to consider the resolutions of the Faneuil Hall meeting. The results of that meeting, voted on the following day, perfectly delineated the state of mind among most members of the Patriot factions in Massachusetts and most other colonies as well. They began with the resolution, based on the still widely held belief that it was the Parliament, not the king, that was oppressing them, "that as true and loyal subjects of our gracious Sovereign *George* the Third, King of *Great Britain,* &c. we, by no means, intend to withdraw our allegiance from him." For all the upheaval, most Americans were still a long way from contemplating independence.

Questions of Parliament's right to tax were now small beer compared to the issues raised in the Intolerable Acts, which allowed the king to stack the Council and the courts with his men, stop town meetings, and close down the port of Boston. The resolves made the now familiar arguments that Parliament had no authority to alter the charter of the colonies and, in words that would find their echo in the First Amendment of the Constitution, that "every people have an absolute right of meeting together to consult upon common grievances, and to petition, remonstrate, and use every legal method of their removal."

As with the Faneuil Hall meeting, perhaps the most significant result of the Middlesex Resolutions was the resolve that read, "It is the opinion of this body of Delegates, that a Provincial Congress is absolutely necessary in our present unhappy situation." This was the first time a county as a whole had called for the establishment of a colonial legislature separate from the existing government. Others would follow. Soon Massachusetts would essentially have two governments: that approved by Parliament and headed by General Gage, and that approved—and adhered to—by the people.

The Middlesex Resolutions closed with the following words:

No danger shall affright, no difficulties intimidate us; and if in support of our rights, we are called to encounter even death, we are yet undaunted, sensible that he can never die too soon, who lays down his life in support of the laws and liberties of his country.

The British troops encamped on Boston Common would have scoffed at such a statement, and considered it more of the Americans' courage on paper. Even so, they also understood, as did the Americans, that the time was not far off when that proposition would be put to the test.

Chapter Six

THE LOYAL AND
ORDERLY PEOPLE

The playwright George Bernard Shaw observed, "The reasonable man adapts himself to the world; the unreasonable one persists in trying to adapt the world to himself. Therefore all progress depends on the unreasonable man." So it was in Massachusetts in the fall of 1774.

General Thomas Gage was a reasonable man trying to obey his orders in the context of the political situation he found. John Andrews, no great friend of government, admitted that "the Governor is dispos'd to preserve peace among us, and that he intends to observe a strict and impartial administration of justice, so far as he is permitted to act himself."

Those whom Gage was up against—Sam Adams, Joseph Warren, Paul Revere, William Molineux, and the other radical leaders in Boston—were not reasonable men. There was no hyperbole too great for their propaganda, no conspiracy too wild for them to promote in the cause of American liberty. No act of intimidation was too extreme unless in its extremity it risked backfiring. The very idea of colonial self-rule was nearly unprecedented in the history of the world, and the Patriots were committed to that goal with a fervor that no hired soldier or government official (and Gage was both) could ever match. Passion, in those men, quite eclipsed reason.

The task set for Thomas Gage was to bring the colony of Massachusetts back to its former relationship with the crown, but that could never happen. The French and Indian War had permanently shifted the tectonic plates of Anglo-American politics. Gage was one man alone, his civilian allies in Massachusetts too afraid to do anything in his support. Arrayed against him were many smart, highly motivated men and women who had resources far greater than he could muster. Gage's one advantage—a theoretically superior military—was also the one tool he dared not use, at least not to its full capacity. When he finally did, he would learn that in truth it was not so great an advantage as he had thought.

Three and a half months after Thomas Gage was sworn in as governor, his entire administration had come apart at the seams, and his effectiveness as a political leader was at an end. Gage probably did as well as anyone could have, tasked as he was with an all but impossible job and shackled by the dictates of the king and Parliament, the Boston Port Bill, and the other Intolerable Acts. In hindsight one can see he was doomed from the start.

Gage could hardly be blamed for that situation, though he probably guessed that he would be. Even if he had wanted to appease the Americans (which he did not), there was nothing he could have done. Had Gage ignored all of his instructions from Dartmouth and the king, and the recent acts of Parliament as well, there was still the unresolved issue of the Tea Act. By the fall of 1774, any peaceful resolution would have required serious compromise on the part of the Boston radicals on the one hand and the king and Parliament on the other, and neither side was in the least interested in compromise.

On September 2 Gage wrote to Dartmouth with a thorough description of how far things had deteriorated. He had given up on Salem as the seat of government and returned to Boston, despite having spent "near, or quite two thousand sterling in building hospitals, hutts, &ca," for the use of the troops stationed there, all of which the locals had torn down, "save the chimnies, and brought entirely away."

The new councilors, chosen by the king, were afraid "they would be watched, stopped and insulted on the road to Salem" and so asked to meet in Boston instead. Lieutenant Colonel Stephen Kemble recorded in his journal that the people of Massachusetts were "obliging every Man who had shown any disposition towards upholding the Authority of Government to swear not to Act in their several stations, or to quit their habitations, and retire into Boston for Security, the Governor not excepted, whose residence in Danvers was not thought [any] longer safe."

As a result of the threats and rough handling, many of the councilors had already resigned their positions. For those who were left, and for the British military and the Loyalist population, Boston was rapidly becoming both a safe haven and a land of exile. Gage acknowledged as much in his letter to Dartmouth, informing the secretary that he and the Council felt that the "only step now to take was to secure the friends of government in Boston and to reinforce the troops here with as many more as could possibly be collected and to act as opportunities and exigencies shall offer." In other words, Gage was all but out of options and could do no more than hunker down in Boston and see what the Americans would do next.

The situation in Massachusetts, as Gage presented it to Dartmouth, was about as bad as it could be, short of open warfare. To make matters worse, it was becoming clear that many of the other colonies were also being swept up in the revolutionary fervor, the people there, according to Gage, "as furious as they are in this province."

Gage had come to realize that he was no longer dealing with a local insurrection but rather a continent-wide revolution. It would be many more months before the king, the ministry, and Parliament understood this as well. Indeed, throughout the course of the war in America, the officials in London would always be months or years behind the field commanders in their understanding of the situation. In many instances they never did get it. This was due in part to the slow communications of the day, of course, but it was also the result of a failure to appreciate the nature of the war and the people they were fighting, as well as a constant, unwarranted optimism with regard to British strength, American weakness, and Loyalist sentiments among the population.

Gage understood all too well the nature of the situation, and he did not suffer from an excess of optimism. "Civil government is near its end," he wrote, "the courts of justice expiring one after another . . . I mean, my lord, to secure all I can by degrees, to avoid any bloody crisis as long as possible, unless forced into it by themselves, which may happen."

He had eight more months before it did.

Finding it impossible to govern, Gage began to turn his attention from political to military matters. He ordered General Frederick Haldimand in New York to come to Boston with all the troops he had available and sent transports to Quebec to fetch the 10th and 52nd regiments. He sent a column of 250 troops to Cambridge to remove the gunpowder from the provincial powder house there and carry it to Castle William. Thousands of Americans grabbed up arms and turned out, but the work was done by the time any significant force mustered, and no violence ensued.

Anticipating a need to regulate the people coming in and out of the city, Gage ordered fortifications to be strengthened and expanded on Boston Neck, the narrow strip of land that connected Boston to the mainland over which anyone traveling by land had to pass. A rumor spread that Gage intended to "cut a canal across and break off the communication with the country other than by a bridge." Anything that Gage might have done to fortify Boston would have set off an uproar, and building works on the neck, and the stories that went with it, certainly did that.

On September 5 a group of selectmen from the city called on Gage for an explanation. Gage replied that he had no intention of halting the flow of traffic or digging a canal but was building the works "to protect his Majesty's subjects, and his Majesty's troops in this town."

Unsatisfied with this answer, and reacting to a growing concern and outrage among the people of Boston and the outlying towns, the selectmen called on Gage again a few days later. Guards posted at the works, they told the governor, had been "assaulting and forcibly detaining" innocent citizens "who were peaceably passing in and out of the town." If that kept up, the market people would no longer bring their produce to the city, which would force those living in Boston to abandon the place. They asked Gage to stop construction of the fortifications, as these might "produce miseries which may hurry the Province into acts of desperation." For some time both sides had feared the spark that would turn the volatile situation violent. Now the Boston radicals were using that real possibility as a threat and a lever in their negotiations with Gage.

Gage would have none of it. He once again assured the selectmen that he had no intention of interfering with the free movement of people in and out of Boston, and he would not tolerate his troops harassing civilians, but he did not agree to stop fortifying the neck. He gave no explanation for that decision, but the reason was obvious enough. Gage was preparing for the day when he would have to defend the city against an armed and mobilized countryside.

At a meeting of delegates from the towns and districts of Suffolk County (not a town meeting, which was contrary to the new laws, but a county meeting), a committee of fifteen was elected to call on Gage to once again express the people's concern over the fortifications. The leader of the committee was Dr. Joseph Warren, and the address prepared by the committee to be presented to Gage was likely penned by him.

Warren was now responsible for quite a bit of the writing done in support of the Patriot cause, and the address was certainly couched in his rhetorical style. It began with a description of the alarm felt by the people of Suffolk County "at the formidable appearance of hostility now threatening his Majesty's good subjects . . . of the town of *Boston,* the loyal and faithful capital of this Province." If that description did not make Gage grit his teeth, it must have made him laugh out loud.

The fears expressed in the address were pure Warren. The letter claimed that the works, when complete, would allow Gage "to aggravate the miseries of that already impoverished and distressed city, by intercepting the wonted and necessary intercourse between the town and country, and compel the wretched inhabitants to the most ignominious state of humiliation and vassalage." The committee members were "at a loss to guess, may it please your Excellency, from whence your want of confidence in the loyal and orderly people of this county could originate." They asked that work on the fortifications cease, that the cannons that had been placed at the new earthworks—a formidable battery of two twenty-four-pounders and eight nine-pounders—be removed, and the entrance to Boston be returned to its former state.

Warren's address to Gage, in particular his reference to the "loyal and orderly people," was utterly disingenuous. Both Gage and Warren knew full well that the Americans had been as active as the British regulars in preparing for war. Just as Gage was securing all the gunpowder he could lay his hands on for the use of his troops, so the Patriots were snatching up whatever public stores of powder they could get to keep it out of British hands and secure it for their own use. Muskets were quickly disappearing from the armories in Boston, and a group of Americans had whisked away the cannons from a battery in Charlestown. Every day armed men were passing back and forth through the new works on Boston Neck. General Gage did not feel the Americans held the moral high ground, and his answer to the committee reflected that.

The governor pointed out again that he had no intention of stopping commerce by land in and out of Boston, that in fact it was his duty to encourage it. Nor did he think that civilians were regularly abused by soldiers, though he was willing to admit it might have happened on occasion. Then he had questions of his own: What was the reason for "such numbers going armed in and out of the town, and through the countryside, in an hostile manner? Or why were the guns removed privately in the night from the battery at *Charlestown*?"

The committeemen had no answers for Gage, and they did not find the governor's latest response to be particularly satisfying. They wrote him once again, this time putting the blame for all the troubles on Parliament and hoping that Gage would "refuse to be an actor in the tragical scene" that was playing out. Not only did Gage not reply, he refused to even accept their petition. The two parties had said everything that could be said on the matter, and neither side was going to give. As with so many issues roiling through Massachusetts and the colonies, further talk was pointless.

THE SUFFOLK RESOLVES

The Patriot faction was just about done with talking as well. Through intimidation and noncooperation they had managed to render Gage's government impotent. As Gage himself explained to Dartmouth, "The new Council [upper house of the legislature] appointed by the King who have taken refuge in this town dare not attend at Salem . . . The Assembly [the lower house] will not act with them and I cannot act with the old Council so that nothing but confusion can arise from a meeting of the General Court."

With the royal government neutralized, the Massachusetts Whigs began to take steps to form their own government. Representatives from each of the towns in Suffolk County met in Dedham to draft a series of resolves outlining their positions with regard to the latest troubles. Not surprisingly, the committee turned to Joseph Warren to pen the primary draft of the document.

On September 9 the delegates met again in Milton, where Warren introduced his most famous literary achievement, the Suffolk Resolves. There were nineteen points, as succinct as any such list was likely to be in the eighteenth century. They outlined the grievances, resolutions, and positions of the revolutionary people of Suffolk County in Massachusetts and, to a large degree, those in all of the colonies.

The preamble started with a historic note, reminding the reader of how Great Britain's power and vengeance "persecuted, scourged and excited our fugitive parents from their native shores," and how those same forces now pursued "their guiltless children." If the people of Massachusetts were to "basely yield to voluntary slavery," then they would be excoriated by future generations. If, however, they "disarm the parricide which points the dagger to our bosums," then "the torrents of panegyrists will roll our reputations to the latest period, when the streams of time shall be absorbed in the abyss of eternity." The preamble piled metaphor upon metaphor, each more excruciating than the last. Like the address to Gage, the Suffolk Resolves were classic Warren prose.

The first of the resolves acknowledged George III as the colony's rightful sovereign. This was a sentiment commonly expressed by a people not ready to go so far as to declare independence, and who did not clearly understand the views of king and Parliament, any more than king and Parliament understood the growing radicalization of the colonies. The second resolve made the point that it was the duty of the people to uphold the rights for which their forefathers fought, and the third that the late acts of Parliament were a clear violation of those rights. The fourth resolve claimed that the province owed no obedience to those acts of Parliament, as they were "the attempts of a wicked Administration to enslave *America*."

The fifth resolve announced that all judges in all courts not appointed under the original charter were unconstitutional, and since there were no longer any legal courts, the sixth resolve urged those with legal disputes to settle them through arbitration. It concluded with the statement that anyone refusing to do so would be considered "as co-operating with the enemies of this country."

Resolve number seven urged anyone, such as tax collectors, who had public money in his possession to hold on to it until a constitutional government was reestablished in Massachusetts. Number eight called for anyone who had accepted a seat on the Council through the king's appointment to resign that seat by September 20. Those who did not would "be considered by this county as obstinate and incorrigible enemies to this country." In the wake of the violence that the Sons of Liberty and sundry other mobs had inflicted on Massachusetts Loyalists, the implied threat, like that of the sixth resolve, would ring clear as a gunshot.

The Suffolk Resolves went on to condemn the fortifications on Boston Neck and the encouragement of Roman Catholicism in Canada. They called for all communities to revoke the commissions of their militia officers and in their stead elect new officers with military experience "who have evidenced themselves the inflexible friends to the rights of the people." The militia of each town was to begin military training and appear under arms at least once per week. The next resolve, number twelve, stated that the people were "determined to act merely upon the defensive, so long as such conduct may be vindicated by reason and the principles of self-preservation, but no longer." This was another subtle but significant step. The colonies had always insisted on the right to self-defense, and insisted further that they meant no more than that. Now the people of Suffolk County were making it clear that if pushed they would move their military posture beyond the merely defensive. They were ready to fight.

The Suffolk committee understood that resolve thirteen said that the ministry had called for the arrest of the leaders of the revolutionary movement. In that event, the resolution called for the arrest and detention, in turn, of "every servant of the present tyrannical and unconstitutional government throughout the county and province," to be held until the Patriot leaders were released.

The resolves went on to call for a halt to importing or exporting from Great Britain or her possessions, to encourage American manufacturing, and to discourage "any routs, riots, or licentious attacks" against Tories, as they tended to undermine the legitimacy of the Patriot cause. A system of couriers was called for, to spread the alarm quickly throughout the county if the enemy threatened action.

Perhaps most significantly, the Suffolk Resolves called for the establishment of a Provincial Congress to act as a local government, and for the county to look to the Continental Congress, then in session, for further guidance. This was a major step for the Patriots, away from merely resisting the royal government and toward self-government. Deny it as they might, they had passed a milestone on the road to independence.

The Suffolk Resolves were the most radical declaration of rights and determined resistence yet generated in the colonies. The entire document was read several times to the committee; then each paragraph in turn was voted on. The votes, in favor of the resolves, were unanimous.

That done, Warren turned to his friend and frequent co-conspirator Paul Revere to carry the resolves, along with copies of the correspondence with Gage regarding the works on Boston Neck, to the Continental Congress in Philadelphia. Revere reached Philadelphia on September 16, seven days after the resolves were approved in Milton. They were read to a Congress that was considerably divided as to how far the spirit of rebellion should be carried. Some, such as Patrick Henry, considered the rupture with England a foregone conclusion. Others were still looking toward some sort of peaceful reconciliation.

Despite these differences the Suffolk Resolves were "read with great applause," according to Sam Adams, and approved unanimously. John Adams called it "one of the happiest days of my life." To Abigail he wrote:

> These votes were passed in full Congress with perfect unanimity. The esteem, the affection, the admiration for the people of Boston and the Massachusetts [*sic*], which were expressed yesterday, and the fixed determination that they should be supported, were enough to melt a heart of stone. I saw the tears gush into the eyes of the old, grave, pacific Quakers of Pennsylvania.

While most in Congress applauded the Suffolk Resolves, others viewed them as a tacit and unwelcome declaration of independence and a call to arms. Pennsylvania delegate Joseph Galloway, leader of the Loyalist faction in the Continental Congress, wrote, "By this treasonable vote [on the Suffolk Resolves] the foundation of military resistance throughout America was effectually laid." Of greatest concern to Congress was the establishment of a provincial government and the resolution to take armed resistance beyond mere defense if necessary.

In a letter to Joseph Palmer, a Braintree neighbor and one of the political leaders in Massachusetts, John Adams explained that while the Congress approved of the resolves, they feared the result of any action that might be taken. Adams wrote, "When you ask the Question what is to be done? they answer Stand Still, bear, with Patience, if you come to a Rupture with the Troops all is lost." Most in Congress felt that the people of Massachusetts should "live wholly without a Legislature and Courts of Justice as long as it will be necessary to obtain relief." As to military concerns, "the commencement of Hostilities," Adams explained, "is exceedingly dreaded here." The delegates felt, correctly, that any attack on the British troops would quickly draw the entire continent into war.

Around the time Adams was writing to Palmer, Sam Adams was writing to Dr. Joseph Warren, taking particular note of the Congress's approval of the resolve calling for military action "merely upon the defensive," for as long as they reasonably could, "but no longer." Adams saw the day coming fast that the people of Massachusetts would be pushed beyond the defensive. He assured Warren that the Congress had great faith in the "tried patience and fortitude" of the people of Massachusetts and understood that they intended to defend themselves and their "civil constitution."

Adams had been assured privately that if it did come to fighting, the delegates in Congress would support the people of Massachusetts "by all the means in their power." Like his cousin John, Sam doubted Congress would "think it necessary for you to set up another form of government." As much as Sam Adams would have liked to forge ahead, he saw the need for unity. "It is of the greatest importance, that the American opposition should be united," he wrote.

By November, word of the Suffolk Resolves had reached London. The significance of the measures were not lost on the ministry. Former Massachusetts governor Thomas Hutchinson, now an expatriate in England, having yielded his office to Gage, recalled a discussion he had with American Secretary Dartmouth on the subject. "I saw Ld Dartmouth yesterday," he wrote in his diary. "'Why Mr H.,' says his Lordship, 'if these Resolves of your people are to be depended on, they have declared War against us: they will not suffer any sort of treaty.'"

Chapter Seven

A WELL-DIGESTED PLAN

Soon after the Suffolk Resolves were written and adopted, Gage reported to Dartmouth that the people of Massachusetts "talk of fixing a plan of government on their own." Indeed they did. Not only did the resolves lay that down as a goal, but they actually set the place and the date, "at Concord, on the second Tuesday of October," when the first meeting would be held.

Gage had already scheduled a session of the General Court to take place in Salem in the first week of October. By late September he could see that the time for such orderly government meetings was long past, and he published a proclamation explaining that with "the present disordered and unhappy state of the Province, it appears to me highly inexpedient that a Great and General Court should be convened," and suspending the meeting until further notice.

The Loyalists on the General Court had by then either resigned or made it clear they would not be leaving the safety of Boston to travel to Salem. The members who were aligned with the Patriot cause met anyway, despite Gage's proclamation. Since they were of a like mind, they had no trouble passing resolutions declaring Gage's reasons for canceling the General Court inadequate and voting "to resolve themselves into a

Provincial Congress . . . to take into consideration the dangerous and alarming situation of publick affairs in this Province."

Their task, as they saw it, was to "promote the true interests of his Majesty, in the peace, welfare, and prosperity of the Province." It is hard to imagine that such a statement could be anything but disingenuous, but if it was sincere, it demonstrates how completely the representatives misunderstood King George's role in the issues roiling the colonies. Even as this Congress sat in session, the king wrote to Prime Minister North, "The New England governments are in a state of rebellion, blows must decide whether they are to be subject to this country or independent."

The men assembled in Salem proceeded to vote themselves in as members of a Provincial Congress. The roll included the usual suspects: Sam Adams, John Hancock, Joseph Warren, and Benjamin Church, among others from Boston; William Heath from Roxbury, who would fight beside Warren at Lexington; John Adams and Joseph Palmer from Braintree; and more than 250 others who had been more or less active in the cause. They represented over two hundred towns throughout Massachusetts and Maine. John Hancock was elected president of the body.

For a week the new Congress met at Salem. They drafted a message to Gage reiterating the usual points concerning their alarm at the military buildup in Boston, while insisting they did not have "the least intention to do any injury to his Majesty's Troops." Then they adjourned, to meet the following week in Cambridge.

Gage received the message from the Provincial Congress but had "some difficulty in contriving" an answer. He knew that the radicals would make political hay of any refusal on his part to accept it, but he also did not want to give the Congress a veneer of legitimacy by negotiating with it. In the end he replied to the message and let his annoyance show: "It is surely highly exasperating, as well as ungenerous, even to hint that the lives liberties and properties of any persons, except avowed enemies, are in danger from *Britons*."

He went on to assure them, again, that he had no wicked designs on their freedom. He also pointed out that while they complained about Parliament altering their charter, they were themselves subverting the charter by creating an illicit council. He ended his reply by insisting they "desist from such illegal and unconstitutional proceedings."

Tensions continued to mount, and they moved from political squabbling to minor acts of sabotage. Gage complained to Dartmouth that his "moderation and forbearance has been put to the test by burning the straw and sinking boats with bricks coming for the use of the troops and overturning our wood carts."

As the autumn progressed, Gage knew he would need barracks to house his growing army. Despite the mass unemployment brought about by the Boston Port Bill, however, no workers would hire on for the job, nor, he found, could he import any from New York. Captain Evelyn was still camping on Boston Common in late October when he wrote to a friend, "The good people of this place have done everything in their power to prevent our getting quarters, and to distress us by forbidding all labourers and artificers to work for us." The locals were likewise stopping any merchant from selling blankets, tools, or materials of any kind to the British army.

In the face of escalating confrontations between soldiers and civilians, Gage struggled to keep the peace, and to prevent an explosion. In November, to the disgust of many of the troops, he forbade soldiers to carry sidearms in the streets. "Is this not encouraging the Inhabitants in their licentious and riotous disposition?" wondered Lieutenant Barker of the King's Own. Gage also instructed the guards to seize any soldiers caught in a disturbance and secure them until the matter could be looked into.

That rule would be put to use when a group of officers, out carousing, were confronted by the city's night watch. A fight ensued, with the officers' swords against the watch's clubs and watch crooks, and injuries were sustained, including the loss of fingers and a nose. Gage's quick action in placing the officers under arrest saved the incident from blowing the city apart. The officers received mild punishment, but from the wildly conflicting accounts it is hard to know who was actually at fault.

The Provincial Congress continued to meet and to expand their sphere of influence. They voted to support nonimportation agreements and to set aside days of thanksgiving. Of more consequence, they approved the acquisition of military supplies, including sixteen three-pounder guns with carriages, four six-pounders, four mortars, twenty tons of grape and round shot, ten tons of bomb shells, five tons of lead for bullets, a thousand barrels of powder, and five thousand muskets and bayonets. It was an impressive, if wishful, list, and it indicated a government that now saw military confrontation as all but inevitable.

The next day the Provincial Congress took another step toward war. They agreed to appoint a Committee of Safety to oversee military matters and direct the militia, and every town was urged to pick officers and equip and train local troops. Another committee was appointed to prepare "a well digested Plan for the Regulating and Disciplining the Militia."

Nine men were selected to serve on the Committee of Safety, by design three from Boston and six from the other towns. The three men from Boston were John Hancock, Dr. Benjamin Church, and Dr. Joseph Warren. Three general officers to command the militia were also chosen: Jedediah Preble, Artemas Ward, and Seth Pomeroy. John Thomas and William Heath would later be added to that list.

Near the end of October the Provincial Congress adjourned for a month. The members of the various committees had their marching orders. They were laying the groundwork for a revolution, and there was a lot to do.

As the stalemate continued, the inevitability of conflict grew more clear to Americans and British alike. Gage's works on Boston Neck had been built up into a substantial redoubt, complete with blockhouse, and troops continued to arrive from New York, Canada, and England. "Nothing of any consequence has happened," Captain Evelyn wrote at the end of October, "but great preparations making for hostilities on both sides."

Evelyn, like all of the other British troops, was well aware of the Yankees' preparations:

The good people of these Provinces . . . are all provided with arms
and ammunition, and every man who is able to use them is obliged
to repair at stated times to the place of exercise in order to train;
in short, the frenzy with which the people are seized is now got to
such a pitch, that it can go but little farther.

Far from fearing the coming conflict, Evelyn looked forward to it,
as apparently did his fellow officers. "We only fear they will avail themselves of the clemency and generosity of the English," he wrote, "and by
some abject submission evade the chastisement due to unexampled vil-
lainy, and which we are so impatiently waiting to inflict." He need not
have worried.

On November 23 the Provincial Congress met again. In advance of
this meeting Gage issued a proclamation denouncing the "persons unlawfully assembled in *Cambridge* in the month of *October* last, calling
themselves a Provincial Congress," who assumed the powers of government "independent of, and repugnant to his Majesty's Government."
Gage ordered that no one attend the next Congress, and that all sheriffs
and justices of the peace do their utmost to prevent any such unlawful
assembly.

Gage's proclamation was, of course, ignored. The Provincial Congress
met again in Cambridge, where they sat until December 10. They passed
various resolutions of thanks, established recommendations for militia
training and organization, called for an increase in manufacturing, and
did sundry other business. They elected five delegates to the Second Continental Congress, slated to meet in Philadelphia on May 10, 1775.

A WINTER OF DISCONTENT

Boston remained quiet, or at least relatively so, through the start of the
new year. In mid-February Barker complained in his diary, "Nothing
has happened lately, this Town amazingly dull notwithstanding there

are so many Regts. in it." The waterfront was all but deserted, shops closed down, ships idle at the wharf. The Boston Port Bill remained in effect, strangling commerce and putting a big hurt on the city. The warehouses would have been empty as well, and the distilleries shut up, had they not been taken over as barracks after the British army found itself unable to procure workmen to build proper housing.

Ensign Jeremy Lister of the 10th Regiment of Foot wrote in his journal that winter was when he "experienc'd the chief part of my difficulties and distresses." His regiment had only recently arrived from Quebec, and he was perhaps not prepared for the blatant hostility of the people of Boston. Now he found himself "in eminent danger every Evening of being insulted by the Inhabitants the worst of Language was continually in our Ears often dirt thrown at us." At one point he and his fellow officers had to "sally out to the rescue" of a lieutenant of the 38th Regiment who was set on by a mob.

Drunkenness was an ongoing problem among the troops, with rum cheap and plentiful and many men with wives who were able to procure it for them. This was one item the Americans were happy to sell to the regulars, as it created discipline problems and made the soldiers more prone to desert. British redcoats even died from overindulging in cheap rum or from falls while drunk.

In February a soldier of the 4th Regiment of Foot received five hundred lashes for "disposing of Arms to the towns people." Americans in search of weapons were often able to find British soldiers willing to sell a whole musket or just the firing mechanism, or "lock." The lock was the most complicated part of the musket and the most difficult to manufacture, but with it the rest of the gun could be easily produced. Mackenzie wrote in his diary that the Americans "are particularly desirous of procuring the Locks of firelocks, which are easily conveyed out of town without being discovered by the Guards."

On days when the weather permitted, Gage allowed some of the regiments to march out of Boston "with their Arms, Accouterments, and knapsacks . . . and march three four or five miles into the country." It was exercise for the men, and it got the "country people" accustomed to the sight of the redcoats marching past on peaceable business so they would not be alarmed when the time came for the troops to march out with more aggressive intentions. The people were never so sanguine about this activity, however, and according to Lieutenant Mackenzie there were always "some persons appointed to Watch the motions and directions of the Troops."

As spring came on and the weather grew warmer, so, too, did the exchanges between British soldiers and the people of Boston. Gage, hoping to keep order and being naturally scrupulous about enforcing the law, did not hesitate to arrest his own men as they stepped up their harassment of the locals. This in turn led to resentment from the officers. According to John Andrews, "The officers and soldiers are a good deal disaffected towards the Governor, thinking, I suppose, that he is partial to the inhabitants, many of the latter have made no scruples to call him an Old Woman."

March 5 marked the fifth anniversary of the Boston Massacre, an event that was memorialized each year both to keep alive the memory of those who had been killed and for the propaganda value, which was still high.

Since March 5 was a Sunday, the memorial was scheduled for the following day at the Old South Meeting House, the place from which the Boston Tea Party had been launched. The meetinghouse was crowded with many hundreds in attendance, including the selectmen of Boston, Hancock, the two Adamses, Benjamin Church, and the other radical leaders, whom Mackenzie called "the most violent fellows in town."

There were also about forty British officers in attendance. They had got wind of the commemoration and, assuming it would be a derogatory harangue, showed up to "take notice of, and resent any expressions made use of by The Orator, reflecting on the Military."

The orator was Dr. Joseph Warren. It was the second time he had presented the memorial oration on the anniversary of the Boston Massacre, the first being in 1772. It was late morning when he stepped up to the black-draped pulpit and spoke before a silent audience. As he often did, he evoked the history of the founding of New England and the memory of the forefathers who "threw themselves on the bosom of the Ocean, determined to find a place in which they might enjoy their freedom, or perish in the glorious attempt." He went on at some length about the evolution of American and British relations, then described in stark terms how that relationship had been torn apart.

Warren's prose, as he described the massacre itself, was as melodramatic as one might expect ("Take heed, ye orphan babes, lest while your streaming eyes are fixed upon the ghastly corpse, your feet slide on the stones bespattered with your father's brains"). From there he went on, of course, to enjoin his listeners to "maintain your rights, or perish in the generous struggle," and ended with a great flourish, assuring the Patriots that when the glorious work was done they could "drop the mantle to some young *Elisha,* and take your seats with kindred spirits in your native skies."

Mackenzie thought that the speech, though obviously meant to disparage the troops and rouse sentiment against them, "contained nothing so violent as was expected." Barker considered it "a most seditious, inflammatory harangue." Nonetheless, the officers confined themselves to a little hissing during the course of the oration.

It was after Warren was done that the trouble began. Sam Adams, standing near the pulpit, called for the thanks of the town to be presented to Warren, and "that another Oration should be delivered on the 5th of March next, to commemorate *the Bloody Massacre* of the 5th of March 1770." This was too much for the British officers, who had been mostly holding their tongues. Some hissed, and others called out "Oh! Fie! Oh! Fie!" Unfortunately, in the bustle of people leaving the meetinghouse, the cries sounded like "Fire! Fire!" Panic struck.

"As there were numbers of Women in the Meeting," Mackenzie recalled, "their cries increased the confusion." People began pushing for the doors. To make matters worse, the 43rd Regiment was just returning from a march through the countryside and now passed the meetinghouse with fifes and drums sounding, adding to the noise and confusion. Those who could not get out the doors began to leap out of the lower windows. From the pulpit, Adams, Hancock, Warren, and the rest struggled to restore order.

For a moment the confusion seemed to hang on the edge of becoming a riot, and if either the officers or the Patriots had made any violent move the entire place would have erupted. Eventually the selectmen managed to calm those still inside the Old South Meeting House and the gathering broke up, but the spirit of pending violence still hung in the air. "The town's people certainly expected a Riot," wrote Mackenzie, "as almost every man had a short stick, or bludgeon, in his hand."

That evening the people of Boston had planned "a grand exhibition," as Lister wrote in his diary, "representing the Massacre in the year 1769 by the 29th Reg^t as the Boston people termed it" (Lister had the year of the Massacre wrong). With tensions running high, Gage was not about to allow so incendiary an event. He called the selectmen together and ordered them to cancel the exhibition. For once the people of Boston complied, and the night passed without incident.

Just days later, another confrontation took place that ratcheted up tensions and stoked the anger of the Patriot faction. With Warren's oration still fresh in everyone's mind, a "Country Fellow," apparently not the brightest of the lot, came to the British encampment hoping to buy a musket. The soldiers, seeing an easy mark, apparently set him up. One agreed to sell the would-be rebel an old gun without a lock, but once the deal was made, half a dozen others seized him "for breach of the Act against trading with the Soldiers."

The poor fellow was held overnight, and rather than being taken before a judge, who most likely would have fined him and let him go, he was sentenced by the army officers to be tarred and feathered. That sentence was carried out immediately. The man was then mounted on a cart, and twenty soldiers with fixed bayonets, along with a number of officers and sailors, accompanied the tarred man as he was paraded through the streets. On his back was a sign that read "AMERICAN *Liberty, or a specimen of Democracy.*" A fife and drum corps played "Yankee Doodle" as they marched.

The situation was nearing the breaking point, and it was clear that the violence would only escalate. The civilian population, Whig and Tory, began to desert Boston, hoping to get clear before the eruption came. One Boston merchant wrote, "The streets and Neck [are] lin'd with wagons carrying off the effects of the inhabitants, who are either afraid, mad, crazy or infatuated . . . imagining to themselves that they shall be liable to every evil that can be enumerated, if they tarry in town." Events would soon show that those who chose to leave then had made a wise choice.

The British troops, after enduring a full winter of abuse from the people of Boston, seemed no longer able to control themselves. "The officers," John Andrews wrote, "in general behave more like a parcell of children, of late, than men." On March 16, the day Warren's oration was published, a number of officers decided to stage an oration of their own. Out of a great crowd of officers, seven were chosen to portray the selectmen. Wearing ridiculous robes and wigs, they stood on the balcony of a coffeehouse owned by a woman named Cordis and delivered a mock harangue to the crowd of fellow officers watching below.

The British found it very funny, but the Americans were not amused. "It contained the most mischievous abuse upon the principal patriots here," one observer wrote, "wholly made up of the most vile, profane, blackguard language that ever was expressed." John Rowe wrote in his diary that "many Characters were Unfairly Represented & much abused & mine among the rest."

RESISTANCE TO REBELLION

As the weather warmed and the animosity between Whigs and Tories and the British troops grew hotter, Gage had no illusions as to what he faced. The Massachusetts militia had been training all winter, the Provincial Congress gathering military stores. Gage had already made various attempts to disarm the people, and for his trouble received only a stark foreshadowing of what would come.

On February 26 a few weeks before Warren's oration on the anniversary of the Boston Massacre, Gage sent a detachment of a little more than two hundred men on a secret mission under the command of Colonel Alexander Leslie to impound a dozen brass cannon and other guns stored at Salem. To avoid the inevitable alarm that would be raised by marching troops overland, Leslie's column boarded a ship in Boston and made the short trip to Marblehead by sea. There they landed, formed up, and headed off for Salem.

It being Sunday, Leslie had planned to swoop in and snatch the cannon while the people were in church, but his troops were observed nonetheless, and word of their advance quickly spread (the regulars could not resist playing "Yankee Doodle" as they marched, which did not help the cause of secrecy). Still, the advance was unopposed until the British reached a drawbridge at the north end of Salem, that the militia, about thirty or forty strong and gathered on the far side, had raised. While Leslie pulled up short at this impasse, others in Salem whisked the cannon away.

The minutes ticked by as more and more of the militia gathered, including the tough, disciplined troops of Marblehead, most of whom were sailors and many veterans of the French and Indian War. The armed Americans took up defensive positions along the road and pressed in on Leslie's troops, who no longer looked so formidable or numerous.

Leslie could see the makings of a disaster in the deteriorating situation. Finally a Salem minister with whom Leslie had been negotiating offered a compromise. The two men agreed that if the bridge were lowered the British "would march but thirty rods over it & return without doing any Thing further." The bridge was let down, the militia cleared the way, and true to his word Leslie made his face-saving march and then led his men back to the docks at Marblehead.

The Americans grew more organized and belligerent with each excursion made by British troops out into the countryside. On March 30 Lord Percy marched his brigade out of Boston on one of their regular training exercises. They had no baggage or artillery with them, an indication that they were not out on any serious business, but the militia took it seriously nonetheless. The Provincial Congress was meeting in Concord, and most of the militia's military stores were kept in that town. Either might have been a target for the redcoats.

The militia in "great numbers, completely armed, collected in the neighbouring Towns," Joseph Warren wrote to Arthur Lee in London. The Provincial Congress and the Committee of Safety, as part of their preparations, had developed systems for turning out the minutemen and the militia and for spreading the alarm. These were all in place, and they had already been tested and found to work to good effect.

"Expresses were sent to every town near," wrote Lieutenant Barker; "at Watertown about 9 miles off, they got 2 pieces of Cannon to the Bridge and loaded 'em but nobody wou'd stay to fire them." It may well have been that the volunteer artillerymen manning the guns ran at the sight of the orderly rows of regular troops, but Barker failed to appreciate that the militia would not have fired in any case, unless fired upon. High as the tensions were, each side was waiting for the other to make the first fatal move.

Nothing happened during Percy's exercise of March 30. For about five hours the 1st Brigade marched past lines of armed and watching Americans and then returned to Boston without incident. Still, each encounter between redcoats and militia only brought both sides closer to the moment when the situation would explode. "Things now every day begin to grow more & more serious," Percy wrote not long after the training march, and just days before he would have to go out again to rescue the flank companies at Lexington. The Americans, he observed, "have therefore begun seriously to form their Army & have already appointed all the Staff."

Thomas Gage had no illusions about how things stood. He had reports from his officers on which to rely and his own observations. He had another source as well, one well placed to provide him with information regarding American preparations for war, a spy high up in the rebel leadership—Dr. Benjamin Church.

From the early days of the Patriot movement, Church had been a close associate of Sam Adams, Joseph Warren, and the others, as trusted a member of the inner circle as any. As a member of both the Provincial Congress and the Committee of Safety, Church was privy to the Americans' most profound military and political secrets. Church also had close ties to England (his wife was English) and other Tories in Boston, however, and apparently came to feel he was backing the wrong horse. Money was also an issue, and Gage paid him well. For more than a year, beginning in 1774, Church earned his pay by feeding Gage excellent intelligence.

By September 1775 the doctor's correspondence with the enemy had been discovered, and he was tried by a court-martial. Church claimed that his intent had been to deceive the enemy with regard to American strength. Years later an examination of the Gage papers would reveal the true depth of his treason, but at the time he was found guilty of criminal correspondence, rather than treason, and instead of hanging was sentenced to life in prison. In 1778 he was permitted to emigrate to the West Indies due to ill health, but the ship on which he sailed was lost at sea.

During the crucial months of the spring of 1775, however, as American militia and redcoats teetered on the brink, Church kept General Gage well informed of all Patriot activities, and Gage was beginning to get a sense for how this would all play out. In early March he sent a letter to the Earl of Dartmouth, the American secretary, with his latest intelligence on the military situation and a startlingly prescient analysis, one that perfectly anticipated the Lexington and Concord fight. In it he told Dartmouth, "The most natural and most eligible mode of attack on the part of the people is that of detached parties of bushmen who from their adroitness in the habitual use of the firelock suppose themselves sure of their mark at a distance of 200 rods."

Gage had spent much of the French and Indian War fighting in the wilderness alongside Americans, and he knew that many of those veterans were now part of the militia in Massachusetts. He believed that the first fight would be "irregular, impetuous and incessant from the numerous bodies that would swarm to the place of action, and all actuated by an enthusiasm wild and ungovernable." He was right.

On April 14 the sloop-of-war *Nautilus* arrived in Boston from London. She had on board correspondence from the ministry, including a long letter from Dartmouth to General Gage. This letter, which Dartmouth surely viewed as just another attempt to goad Gage into action, would in fact profoundly alter the course of events in America. It would prove to be the flint and steel that sparked the Revolution.

Gage's life was a constant struggle between the reality he faced in Massachusetts and the orders he was receiving from his superiors in England who failed to appreciate that reality. As early as October of 1774, when the first Provincial Congress was organizing the militia and voting money to buy arms, Gage wrote to Dartmouth explaining that his army of 3,000 was inadequate, and because of its weakness "rather encourages resistance" among the Americans, "rather than terrifies." Instead, Gage felt "an army twenty thousand strong will in the end save Great Britain both blood and treasure."

Dartmouth, making policy from the comforts of London, thought this was unnecessary, and in the letter that *Nautilus* carried he addressed the governor general's concerns.

The American secretary knew about the Continental Congress meeting in Philadelphia, and he knew about the Provincial Congress in Cambridge. He knew that the men organizing the resistance were among America's leading citizens, many of them, such as John Adams, Thomas Jefferson, George Washington, Stephen Hopkins of Rhode Island, and Peyton Randolph of Virginia, professionally and intellectually accomplished men. Nonetheless, Dartmouth insisted that the troubles were "the acts of a tumultuous rabble without any appearance of general concert or without any head to advise or leader to conduct that could render them formidable to a regular force led forth in support of law and government."

Dartmouth's lengthy and often contradictory letter was intended as a mild rebuke of Gage and a means of nudging him into action. Dartmouth clearly felt, as did many in London, and even many military officers in Boston, that one good, unequivocal show of force would cow the Americans into submission. "The King's dignity and honour and safety of the empire require that in such a situation force should be repelled by force," he wrote Gage.

The British army of 1774 was still a peacetime army. To send 20,000 men to North America would require putting it on a war establishment, which meant greatly increasing the number of troops in the army as a whole, with all the expense that went with it. Dartmouth was "unwilling to believe that matters are as yet come to that issue." Instead he told Gage that a large detachment of marines was being sent out from England and with the other reinforcements should bring Gage's army up to around 4,000. "It is hoped . . . that this large reinforcement to your army will enable you to take a more active and determined part," Dartmouth prodded, suggesting that the seat of government be reestablished in Salem and that the other acts of Parliament be enforced.

Dartmouth reiterated his belief that the acts of rebellion were those of "a rude rabble, without plan, without concert and without conduct." The American secretary then informed Gage that in the opinion of the king and his ministers "the first and essential step to be taken towards reestablishing government would be to arrest and imprison the principal actors and abettors in the Provincial Congress (whose proceedings appear in every light to be acts of treason and rebellion)."

Essentially, the king and Dartmouth wanted Gage to arrest the leaders of what they considered a leaderless rebellion. Since the courts of justice were not permitted to open by act of Parliament, Gage would be able to hold the men indefinitely without trial. Dartmouth and the others thought this was a good idea and felt it would "become a test of the people's resolution to resist."

General Gage no doubt agreed it would test the people, and he knew how they would answer.

Gage had never tried to arrest the radical leaders, having a good idea that doing so would trigger a war. Indeed, soon after Gage's arrival in Boston, John Andrews wrote of "the talk of Government's taking up and sending home [to England for trial] a number from this town . . . which caus'd much uneasiness among the most thinking part of the community least such a step should cause commotions that would prove fatal to the town."

Now, a year later, tensions were much higher, the possible consequences much more dire. Reading Dartmouth's letter, Gage found himself trapped between Scylla and Charybdis, between instructions from home— instructions that carried the whiff of disapproval of his performance— and what he strongly suspected would happen if he employed real force against the Massachusetts militia.

Gage was a soldier though, and he was not shy about using force. Nor did he have any sympathy for the Americans, his wife and his former affection for the people with whom he had lived for seventeen years notwithstanding. It was Gage, after all, who had been looking for a 20,000-man army to roll over the rebellious factions of Massachusetts, Connecticut, and Rhode Island.

The Provincial Congress, Gage knew, was meeting in Concord, which meant Sam Adams, John Hancock, Joseph Warren, William Molineux, the whole rebellious lot of them were gathered together in one place. Intelligence from Benjamin Church informed him of "a large quantity of military stores being collected at Concord." Gage had his instructions, and he had in front of him an opportunity to carry them out.

The fuse was burning on both ends. James Warren, a member of the Provincial Congress from Plymouth (and no relation to Joseph), was the husband of Mercy Otis Warren, who was a famed playwright and later author of a three-volume history of the American Revolution. While attending the April session, James wrote to Mercy:

All things wear a warlike appearance here. This Town is full of Cannon, ammunition, stores, etc., and the [British] Army long for them and they want nothing but strength to Induce an attempt on them. The people are ready and determine to defend this Country Inch by Inch.

The next day Thomas Gage gave orders for the grenadier and light infantry companies to be taken off regular duty for the immediate future. He let out that they would be learning new tactics. In fact, they were heading for Lexington and Concord.

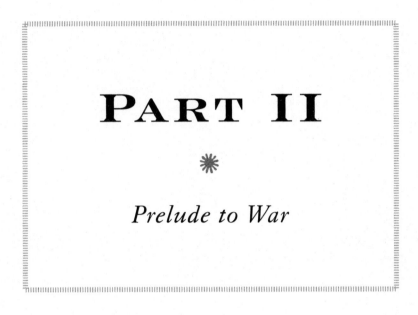

PART II

*

Prelude to War

Chapter Eight

FROM THE PENN
TO THE SWORD

A s the sun rose over Massachusetts Bay on April 20, its light touched first the high hills—Beacon, Copp's, Bunker, Prospect, Winter—and then the scattered islands in Boston Harbor, and finally the narrow streets and alleys of Boston, the wood-frame houses of Charlestown and Roxbury. It put an end to a hellish night during which men slept with their muskets held close and women and children in Charlestown huddled in the clay pits behind Breed's Hill, terrified by rumors that the British regulars were massacring the innocent. The wounded cried out in pain and the dead lay scattered for miles along the roads from Charlestown to Concord.

There had been little rest in the immediate aftermath of the Battle of Concord and Lexington. The journal of the fifty-gun flagship *Preston* recorded, "All the Boats of the Fleet Employed Transporting the troops who had been out, over to Boston." The wounded went over first, hundreds of men with bloody, makeshift bandages, some, like Lister, cradling shattered arms, some limping. Some, who were too hurt to walk, had been bounced along for hours on horseback. Many more lay groaning on the sides of the roads, left to be cared for by the Americans.

It took hours to bring the wounded over, and when that was done it was the turn of the exhausted men of the flank companies. The grenadiers and light infantry, by the time they were ferried back to Boston, had not slept in thirty-six hours, had marched forty miles in that time, and had been under near constant fire from a little after noon until 7:00 P.M. The people remaining in Charlestown had been ordered to provide the men some refreshment, while the officers had descended on the local tavern, calling out for drink to quench a wicked thirst and to drown memories of an unthinkable disaster.

General Gage was not convinced that the Americans were done fighting, and basic military prudence demanded that he prepare for an assault on his vulnerable men. He sent reinforcements over to Charlestown in the boats that were returning for more wounded. The fresh troops included marines and 200 men from the 64th Regiment stationed at Castle William who had been retrieved for that duty. Under the command of Brigadier General Robert Pigot, the men "were ordered to take possession of Charlestown, and the heights Commanding the Neck," that is, Bunker Hill. The fresh troops "threw up a work to secure themselves." That temporary redoubt took the form of a flèche, a V-shaped earthwork perhaps forty feet in length with the apex of the V pointed out at the neck of land connecting Charlestown to the mainland, the direction over which an attack would come, if it did.

Out on the water, on Back Bay and the Mystic River, Boston Harbor, and Massachusetts Bay, the British navy was also braced for any continuation of the violence. All of the men-of-war were cleared for action. The temporary bulkheads that made up officers' quarters were taken down, all extraneous gear stowed away, decks sanded to soak up the anticipated blood, the great guns loaded, and the slow match for igniting the powder in the cannon's vents lit and glowing. Beside each vessel was one of the ship's boats, armed with swivel guns and ready to be manned and sent into action at a moment's notice.

Admiral Graves, known mostly as inept, corrupt, and unwilling, showed more activity than was his wont, or at least that was how he recorded it in his memoirs. "The number of Guard Boats was doubled," he wrote, "and every necessary direction given to the Ships in case the Rebels should attempt to force the lines." The smaller men-of-war were ordered to anchor as close in to shore as they could get to cover the approaches to Boston with their guns.

The sixty-eight-gun *Somerset* was positioned to prevent any boat from crossing the Charles River without General Gage's permission, and her captain, Edward LeCrass, was ordered to inform the selectmen of Charlestown that "if they suffered the rebels to take possession of their town or erect any works upon the Heights, the *Somerset* should fire upon them." After the evening guns were fired at sundown, "no Boat was to pass till day light, except those rowing Guard."

As the boats of the navy were pulling across the water from Charlestown to Boston and back, Admiral Graves was urging Gage to go on the offensive. The flèche, an insubstantial fortification, was already begun on Bunker Hill. Graves urged Gage to erect a serious redoubt there, and on the high ground at Roxbury as well, then burn both towns. Gage protested that his army was too weak for so ambitious a project. Graves offered what marines he could spare and suggested the 64th be removed from Castle William and the castle be garrisoned by sailors from the fleet, but Gage still declined to follow the admiral's suggestion.

Such an aggressive strategy was uncharacteristic for Graves, who had come in for criticism for his inactivity and would come in for more. In the wake of Concord and Lexington, at least, he was inclined "to act hostiley from this time forward by burning & laying to waste the whole country." In October of that year, under pressure from London to do something to bring the war to the rebels, Graves would finally act on that inclination, sending Lieutenant Henry Mowatt to sea with a squadron to burn virtually every major seaport town from Boston to the Canadian border. In the end Mowatt burned only one, Falmouth (now Portland), Maine, and it accomplished nothing beyond bringing many fence-sitting Americans over to the Patriots' side.

General William Heath, who, with Joseph Warren, had taken command of the American forces at Lexington and fought all the way to Cambridge, continued to exercise control over the militia as night came on. He posted guards near the foot of Prospect Hill, the height that most closely overlooked Bunker Hill, and deployed sentinels down the neck to Charlestown. He sent out patrols who were ordered to "be vigilant in moving during the night; and an immediate report [sent] to him, in case the enemy made any movements." The remainder of the militia were marched off to Cambridge. There, more guard units were formed and sent to Roxbury and other points south and west of Boston. Militia remaining in Cambridge were ordered to "lie on their arms," that is, sleep with their muskets at the ready.

The night passed, tense but relatively quiet. Around midnight the troops in Cambridge were alarmed to discover a ship moving through the dark up the Charles River. The men were turned out, ready for a fight, fearing the vessel was part of an attack on the town. But it was only an armed schooner, likely the *Diana* of six guns and thirty men, commanded by Admiral Graves's nephew, Lieutenant Thomas Graves. Far from attacking, she was part of the admiral's defensive line, and young Lieutenant Graves managed to run her aground on a falling tide. Luckily for him, the shoreline was too marshy for the American troops to get within musket range. Heath lamented, "If there had been a single field-piece with the militia, she might have been taken."

Soon after the first shots were fired on Lexington Green, express riders had raced off, raising the alarm and carrying word of the fighting to the nearby towns. The dissemination of the news did not stop there, however. Like a drop of ink that fell on Lexington and spread off in every direction, the frightening news moved farther and farther through the colonies. By the end of the day on April 19 the alarm had spread as far as Worcester and Newburyport in Massachusetts and Providence in Rhode Island. By the following afternoon Providence had "five hundred armed and ready to march, waiting only the Governor's Orders."

Word of the fighting moved as fast as the express riders' horses could run. On April 20 it reached New London and the neighboring coastal towns of Connecticut and spread west, reaching New York on the 23rd and New Jersey, Pennsylvania, and Delaware on the 24th. Along the way a rumor that Lord Percy had been killed, and in some cases Haldimand as well, attached itself to the news. Everywhere people were "animated with resentment," as one man in New York wrote.

Express riders reached Williamsburg, the capital of Virginia, on May 2 and continued south, reaching North Carolina the following day, though it was not until May 8 that word spread through that sparsely settled area. By May 9 the news of the fighting was carried around by sea to Charleston, South Carolina. No one who received word of the fighting failed to understand the significance. The waiting was over. The war had begun.

The morning of April 20 found the Americans still under arms and deployed in a great arc around Boston while the civilians struggled to get out of the potential line of fire. No one was sure what would happen next. "20th All confusion," wrote Deacon John Tudor. "Numbers of Carts &c carrying of Goods &c, as the rumor was that if the solders came out again they would burn Kill & destroy all as they march'd." How many American troops there were is not clear, but they certainly numbered in the several thousands, with more coming in all the time. Militia within a day or two's march did not hesitate to descend on Cambridge. Those farther away, or in other colonies, mustered and made ready to head off for Massachusetts, waiting on orders from their governors. The governors, in turn, were waiting to find out what the Provincial Congress of Massachusetts intended to do.

April 20 was a new day, new in many different and profound ways. As John Adams put it, "The Battle of Lexington on the 19th of April, changed the Instruments of Warfare from the Penn to the Sword." No one knew what would happen next.

A MILITIA BECOMES AN ARMY

The Americans had a significant armed force in the field, but they did not have an army.

Since the advent of the Provincial Congress and the smaller, more active branch of that body known as the Committee of Safety, the Patriot leaders of Massachusetts had done considerable work in organizing the military. They had selected general officers and encouraged constant training, initiated the organization of the minutemen, and established a system for quickly spreading the alarm. They instructed the various town governments to force the resignation of militia officers and, in those cases where the former officers were not reliable Patriots, see that they were replaced with men whose dedication to American liberty was above question.

They had also collected and secured a significant amount of war matériel. Chaplain William Emerson of Concord recorded in his diary in February of 1775 that "large quantities of military stores, sufficient for 15,000 men, were deposited in Concord." These included one hundred bell tents designed to shelter muskets stacked vertically, one thousand field tents, ten tons of lead balls, enough cartridges for 15,000 men to be issued thirty rounds apiece (which adds up to an astounding 450,000 cartridges), twenty hogsheads of rum and twenty of molasses, and one hundred hogsheads of salt, as well as candles, spoons, raisins, oatmeal, six casks of Malaga wine, fifteen hundred yards of Russian linen, and fifteen chests of medicine. Little wonder that Gage set his sights on that town.

All of this put the Massachusetts militia in good stead for turning out and opposing a British incursion, as the successful fight at Lexington and Concord showed, but it did not anticipate the militia forming into a permanent force. It did not provide for a quartermaster general to see about further supplies, or for terms of enlistment, the setting up of orderly camps, where the money would come from to pay for all this, or any of those things that differentiated a militia, who were only intended to be called up when needed, from a standing army.

Also, despite the impressive list complied by Emerson, Joseph Warren would soon write to his friend Joseph Reed that "we are in want of every thing, but nothing so much as arms and ammunition." A great deal of ammunition was certainly expended at the Battle of Lexington and Concord, but Warren also confided that "much time has been spent in procuring these articles, yet the people never seemed in earnest about the matter until after the engagement of the 19th."

Despite the fact that the men who turned out for the Lexington Alarm were militia, expected to stand down after the fighting, on the morning of April 20, they remained under arms. Indeed, there seemed to be no thought that the troops would disperse, or do anything other than become an army.

The situation of Phineas Ingalls, a sixteen-year-old minuteman from Andover, Massachusetts, was typical. At 7:00 A.M. on April 19 his company received the alarm. They mustered at the meetinghouse and marched off for Concord, about twenty miles away. The minutemen pushed hard all day and were within six miles of the town when they "heard that the Regulars had gone back."

Rather than return to Andover, however, Ingalls's company continued on to Menotomy (Arlington today), where they camped for the night. His diary entry for April 20 reads, "Early this morning we marched on the common on Cambridge and expected the enemy upon us every moment. They did not come." Ingalls's company remained in Cambridge, and they were not alone. Militia were arriving from every direction. "Folks came in very fast," Ingalls wrote. "Nothing happened today."

The morning after the battle, General William Heath was still the senior military officer in Cambridge, so he began to issue orders. He sent Captain John Brattle of Dedham with fifty men to "pass over the ground which had been the scene of action the preceding day, and to bury such slain as he should find unburied." He issued general orders that "Colonel Gardiner repair immediately to Roxbury, and bring all the bread that can be obtained," and "Colonel Bond bring all the cannon at Watertown, Newtown and Waltham, together with part of the ammunition, into camp at Cambridge." Heath, like everyone else, was trying to keep up with events as they raced ahead of him.

The other immediate problem centered on all those new mouths to feed. "All the eatables in the town of Cambridge, which could be spared, were collected for breakfast," Heath wrote, "and the college [Harvard] kitchen and utensils procured for cooking." The militia also collected up some beef and pork carcasses that had been prepared for the now defunct Boston market, and "a large quantity of ship-bread at Roxbury, said to belong to the British navy, was taken for the militia."

Heath sent word to the Committee of Safety and another committee of the Provincial Congress, the Committee of Supply, to send the provisions stored at Concord to Cambridge. By noon he received assurances that "every exertion in their power should be put in exercise, to forward supplies to the militia in arms." In the light of day, Heath reconnoitered the ground around Cambridge and established alarm posts in case the British sallied from the city. In the event the militia were driven back by any such attack, they were ordered to "rally and form on the high grounds towards Watertown."

Through fantastic effort Heath and the other officers saw that the men's needs were being met and the most immediate concerns addressed. Even so, before the rabble in arms could be called an army, there was a world of organization and infrastructure still needed.

Later that day General Artemas Ward arrived at camp in Cambridge. Ward was forty-seven years old, a graduate of Harvard College, and a veteran of the French and Indian War. Though he had taken part in the disastrous attack on Fort Ticonderoga under General James Abercrombie in 1758, his service had not been particularly active, certainly not on a par with Israel Putnam's. He ended the French and Indian War as a colonel of provincial troops, but the campaign had taken a toll on his health and he never fully recovered.

Ward had settled in Shrewsbury, about thirty miles from Boston, where he held a number of town offices and was active in colony-wide politics as well. He served as a member of the General Court until Gage dissolved it in disgust over the radical policies of members like Ward, who then went on to represent Shrewsbury in the First and Second Provincial Congresses. In October 1774, when Congress selected general officers as part of their expanded military efforts, Ward was chosen second in seniority after Jedediah Preble. Preble, however, declined the office, making Ward senior. Following Ward in seniority were Seth Pomeroy, John Thomas, a doctor from Kingston, near Plymouth, who had also served in the French and Indian War, and William Heath. Ward clearly had his supporters, given that he was chosen as a senior general, but he was also considered by many others to be largely incompetent in the military line.

When word of the fighting reached Ward on April 19 at his home in Shrewsbury, the senior general was sick in bed, but as soon as he was able he mounted up and rode east to Cambridge. He missed the battle, and he missed breakfast the following morning, but arrived in the afternoon to take command of the troops. He immediately called a council of war made up of the officers collected in Cambridge. The general officers who attended the meeting included himself, William Heath, and John Whitcomb, who had been added to the roster of generals by the Second Provincial Congress. Joining them were seven colonels, including William Prescott, who would play a significant role in the months to come, and five lieutenant colonels.

The council of war issued a series of general orders aimed at organizing and securing the American position. They issued orders for posting companies of guards at various approaches to Cambridge and instructed that "every officer and soldier keep close to his quarters, and be ready to turn out complete in arms at a moment's warning" and that each colonel appoint an adjunct, quartermaster, and sergeant major for his regiment.

Out of necessity, the council of war was creating new posts for the army and naming men to fill them. Still, they recognized the ad hoc nature of what they were doing and understood that such decisions were beyond their authority to make. Thus they made it clear that none of their decisions were permanent and issued an order that "all officers appointed before there is a regular establishment are appointed pro tempore."

There was one decision, however, apparently made that day, that would have profound implications for the immediate future and for the rest of the war. That was that the Provincial Congress would create an army on a "regular establishment," that is, a standing army that would remain in the field, rather than militia who would go home when the fighting was done. It is surprising, given the significance of that decision, that there is no record of when or where it was made, or by whom.

The Committee of Safety spent all of April 20 in session, as one might expect given the great upheaval that had just taken place, but no record exists of what was discussed. Nor is there any mention of forming a standing army in the scant records of the council of war. The only mention of any decision to create an army was written thirty years after the event by Timothy Pickering, a member of the Committee of Safety from Salem and future quartermaster general of the Continental Army. Looking back, Pickering recalled:

In the morning [of April 20] while at Medford I rec^d. notice that a number of militia officers assembled at Cambridge, desired to see me. I went thither. Genl. Warren was among them. They were consulting on the formation of an army. To me the idea was new & unexpected. I expressed the opinion which at the moment occurred to me—*that the hostilities of the proceeding day did not render a civil war inevitable: that a negociation with Gen*^l. Gage might probably effect a present compromise and therefore that the immediate formation of an army did not appear to me to be necessary.

Pickering was certainly in the minority, both in Massachusetts and in the other colonies, in his opinion that an army was not yet necessary, and it is not entirely clear what meeting he describes attending, whether the council of war or the Committee of Safety or some other gathering. Ward's orderly book does not mention Joseph Warren as attending the council of war, and Pickering's memory is failing him when he refers to Warren as a general. Warren would later hold that rank, but did not at the time.

The meeting Pickering attended was perhaps a joint conference between the military officers and the Committee of Safety, which was also meeting in Cambridge. Pickering refers to "militia officers," but the council of war would have understood that they did not have the authority to make so monumental a decision as forming an army (many of the military officers were also members of the Provincial Congress). Just as the Continental Congress would be scrupulous about maintaining civilian control of the military, a tradition that would carry on throughout the history of the United States, the Provincial Congress was also strict about maintaining control.

However the decision was reached, as of April 20 it was decided that the colony of Massachusetts would have a standing army, and it would be up to the civilian leaders, the Committee of Safety and the Provincial Congress, to create. They would soon find that, despite the thousands of armed men they had in the field, they would have to create it virtually from scratch.

THE BRITISH IN BOSTON

"The town is now surrounded by armed Rebels, who have intercepted all communications with the Country."

That was the succinct assessment of the situation in the diary of Lieutenant Frederick Mackenzie on April 21, as the new reality became clear. In his view, there were a number of factors to blame for the disaster he had just endured. There had been, he understood, a general muster of the American militia the day before, likely as a result of word leaking out about the raid. "This should have been known," Mackenzie wrote, though, in fact, he was wrong about the muster. "An Officer of more activity than Col° Smith," he felt, "should have been selected for the Command of the Troops."

General Gage, in Mackenzie's opinion, "had no conception the Rebels would have opposed The King's troops in the manner they did," though he should have, since "the temper of the people, the preparations they had been making all the winter to oppose the troops should they move out of Boston with hostile intentions, and above all their declared resolution to do so, made it evident to most persons, that opposition would be made."

Mackenzie was certainly wrong to suggest that Gage did not appreciate the danger. He did. What the young lieutenant of the Royal Welsh Fusiliers did not appreciate was the pressure that Gage was under from above to do something to stem the tide of rebellion.

Gage, of course, was particularly displeased with the events of April 19. There were any number of things that angered him, and one of them was the behavior of the British troops after leaving Lexington for the long retreat back to Charlestown. In a general order given out on April 22, Gage wrote that the men "behaved with much courage and spirit" but "shewed great inattention and neglect to the Commands of their Officers, which if they had observed, fewer of them would have been hurt." Gage went on to say that he expected in the future "they will behave with more discipline and in a more Soldierlike manner: and it is his most positive orders that no man quit his ranks to plunder and pillage." It was always Gage's goal to hold the moral high ground, and that was not possible with behavior such as that displayed by his redcoats.

Ensign Jeremy Lister, who volunteered to go with the light infantry and took a bullet in the right elbow, was all but spent when he collapsed on the slopes of Bunker Hill on the evening of April 19. A musician from the 23rd Regiment was sent to help him down to the waiting boats. Stumbling with exhaustion and supported by his helper, Lister managed to get to the waterfront, where the ships' boats were pulling back and forth from Boston with loads of grievously wounded men. As he waited for his turn, he came across a lieutenant he knew named Sunderland who had been shot in the chest at Concord Bridge. "I believe he was in Violent pain," Lister wrote, "and did not expect long to survive."

Finally it was Lister's turn, and he was helped into the boat by the blue-jacketed sailors and settled in place for the short trip to what was, at that moment, the only safe place in Massachusetts for a redcoat. Arriving at the landing in Boston he ran into his own regiment, the 10th Regiment of Foot, who had been ordered to Charlestown to relieve the exhausted troops and who were waiting to board the boats for the trip back.

It was 9:00 P.M. when Lister finally staggered back to the home in which he was lodged. He had endured "a March in the whole of about 60 Miles in the course of 24 Hours, about 24 Miles after I was Wounded and without a Morcel of Victuals," save for the small bit of biscuit and beef he had begged from the soldier in Lexington.

Exhausted as he was, Lister felt that he had to have a cup of tea.

Though others in the house, Lister wrote, "pronounc'd me light Headed in asking for Tea, I ought instantly to go to Bed," he prevailed, and tea was fetched. "Imagination may conceive," he added, "tho. it is beyond the power of Words to express the satisfaction I felt from that Tea, notwithstanding I was interrupted with a Thousand Questions."

It is hardly a surprise that Lister found himself the center of attention. Word of the fighting had swirled around Boston all day, and some of it had even been visible from the city. Merchant John Andrews wrote to a friend, "I stood upon the hills in town and saw the engagement very plain. It was very bloody for seven hours." He added, that it was "impossible to learn any particulars, as the communication between the town and country is at present broke off."

The people in Boston were desperate for information, and Lister, drinking tea with his left hand while his right arm hung useless in its torn and blood-soaked sleeve, had witnessed the whole thing. The questions flew like the musket balls of a few hours before, until Lister was asked if he had seen Lieutenant Sunderland, who had been lying wounded at the landing in Charlestown. Lister replied, "I had and supposed by that time he was dead," not realizing that Sunderland's wife was standing behind him.

Hearing the news, Mrs. Sunderland "immediately drop'd down in a swoon," Lister recalled, "which then diverted the Comp^ys attention a little from me, which I was not at all sorry for as I then got my Tea with a little more quietness." When he was told that he should not have given that answer, Lister replied that they should not have asked the question and that he did not know Sunderland's wife was there (in the end Sunderland did not die).

The glove on Lister's right hand had grown taut, "what with Blood and swelling of my Hand." When his tea was done, Lister had someone cut the glove off, and at long last he staggered upstairs for bed. A surgeon stopped by and put fresh lint on the wound and bandaged it, but he was likely too busy with more dire cases to do more than that. At last Jeremy Lister closed his eyes on the ordeal, eager for sleep, "but God knows," he wrote, "none fell to my share for a long time after."

For General Gage, the most pressing concern, once his men were out of harm's way, was to make sure that Boston was secured against attack. It was only a few days prior that the Americans were thought to be "frightened out of their wits" at the appearance of the regulars. Now that notion had been stood on its head, and Gage could not take anything for granted, including the unlikely but still real possibility of an assault on Boston itself.

It was three days after the battle before Gage sat down to write his report to Dartmouth. He concluded it by informing the American secretary, "The whole Country was assembled in Arms with Surprizing Expedition, and Several Thousand are now Assembled about this Town threatening an Attack, and getting up Artillery. And we are very busy in making Preparations to oppose them."

The obvious weak spot was Boston Neck. Gage, of course, had been beefing up the defenses there for some time, but now he no longer had to worry about offending Patriot sensibilities. A fatigue party of more than a hundred men was marched off with muskets and ammunition to the neck, "where a Battery is immediately to be constructed." Another hundred were sent off to augment the Royal Artillery.

There were other precautions taken. Every man was ordered to fill his cartridge box with sixty rounds and to sleep in his clothes, ready to turn out instantly. Prior to Lexington and Concord, most officers, such as Lister, were not housed with their men in the barracks but rather rented private accommodations. On April 20 orders were given "for the Officers to lay in their men's barracks 'till further notice." This may have been in reaction to a rumor going around the city that rebels would be laying in wait to murder the officers when they turned out for an alarm. Additionally, each regiment was ordered to assemble at their barracks, not their assigned alarm posts. Gage was beginning to worry about the possibility of a fifth column of rebels made up of the population still in the city.

Admiral Samuel Graves was also concerned about protecting his forces from attack. He issued a general order to his captains that "all scows, sloops, schooners & boats of every Kind (except the fishing boats) should be brought as they could be picked up & Kept to the Southward of the long Wharf." This would help prevent a waterborne attack on his vessels.

With all the boats and small ships rounded up, Roxbury Neck was the only avenue for attacking the city, and that was quickly becoming unassailable. Lieutenant John Barker of the King's Own wrote that the lines were "kept constantly in readiness for an attack which the Rebels threaten, but I dare say will not put in execution; they are now in such a good state of defense that it wou'd be no easy matter to force them."

Barker described abatis in front of the bastion on the left of the road that ran along Roxbury Neck. Abatis were felled trees piled parallel to and in front of an entrenchment with their limbs pointing in the direction from which an attacking army would approach. It was difficult and time-consuming to get through them, and troops struggling to do so were easy targets for the enemy hunkered down behind the earthworks. Abatis had been one of the elements of the French defense at Fort Ticonderoga in 1758 that contributed to the British army's staggering loss.

On the other side of the road were three lines of chevaux-de-frise, an obstruction comprised of a wooden pole with sharp shafts jutting out at right angles, much like a man-made and somewhat more sophisticated abatis that served the same function. Four guns covered the marshy areas beyond the road, and a week later four more guns and two mortars were added, along with two guns "which can play right up the Town of Roxbury."

Admiral Graves was particularly concerned about attacks on the great lumbering men-of-war, which were designed for line-of-battle combat on the open ocean, not as permanently moored floating batteries. Most vulnerable was the sixty-eight-gun *Somerset,* anchored close in to Charlestown Neck, which had protected the troops in the last leg of their retreat from Lexington. She was an easy target for field artillery on shore, or "any Battery which might be raised against her on a Hill on the Charles Town side where she cou'd not bring her guns to bear." Under perfect conditions it might take a ship like *Somerset* half an hour or more to get under way and out from under the guns. In the shallow water near

Charlestown in which she was moored, however, she could be stuck for much longer, until an exceptionally high tide could lift her out.

To protect against enemy fire from shore, Graves decided to erect a battery on Copp's Hill at the north end of Boston, the point of land closest to Charlestown and a block from the Old North Church. Under the direction of an artillery officer, Graves sent "an Officer & a Party of Marines from the *Asia*" to begin construction. Orders were sent to the *Somerset* to send a like-sized party to alternate workdays with the *Asia*'s men "until it is finished."

The idea of sailors constructing a shore battery under the admiral's orders was considered a pretty far-out notion. The whole affair "afforded much pleasantry to the Garrison," Graves wrote, "particularly among those who did not readily conceive of the intent, it was christened soon after by the name of the Admirals Battery and always spoken of with a smile."

As quickly as the new American army massed on the shoreline surrounding Boston, waiting for the British army to sally again, so the garrison in Boston fortified and braced for an assault from without and within. On the morning of April 19 Boston had been a place where fresh provisions would come in daily and regiments could march into the countryside and back for exercise. Twenty-four hours later it was as cut off from the shore as if it had been an island fifty miles out.

Chapter Nine

OFFICERS AND MEN

Once the decision was made to create a Massachusetts army, no time was wasted in gathering the armed forces. Joseph Warren penned a circular letter to the towns in Massachusetts, entreating them to "hasten and encourage by all possible means the enlistment of men to form the army, and send them forward to headquarters, at Cambridge, with the expedition which the vast importance and instant urgency of the affair demand."

On the same day another, somewhat less empathetic letter was written to the governors of the neighboring colonies, saying, "We pray your Honours would afford us all the assistance in your power, and shall be glad that our brethren who come to our aid may be supplied with Military Stores and Provisions, as we have none of either more than is absolutely necessary for ourselves."

The men of the nearby towns and more distant colonies complied, and no doubt would have even without the circular from the Committee of Safety. Men from New Hampshire, Rhode Island, and Connecticut grabbed up arms and provisions and headed off to war. A correspondent from Connecticut wrote to a friend in New York a few days after the battle with the news, "We are all in motion here, and equipt from the

Town, yesterday, one hundred young men, who cheerfully offered their service ... Men of the first character and property shoulder their arms and march off for the field of action. We shall, by night, have several thousands from this Colony on their march."

One of the companies preparing to leave from New Haven, Connecticut, was the Governor's 2nd Company of Guards under the command of Captain Benedict Arnold. In the case of New Haven, the town leaders opted to not send the local militia to Boston until the reasons for fighting at Lexington and Concord were better known. The young militiamen under Arnold's command were of a different opinion and opted to go despite what the town fathers said. When the old guard refused to open the town's magazine to allow the troops to gather their guns and powder, Arnold gave them five minutes to change their mind before he would have his men break the door down. In the face of such determination the city fathers complied, and soon Arnold and the "Footguards" marched off, part of the great influx of troops to Cambridge.

The logistical considerations were all but overwhelming, with little hope of getting things straightened out soon. More men were coming in every day, and already no one was sure of how many were already there or how many would ultimately arrive. A few days after the Battle of Lexington and Concord, John Adams rode from his home in Braintree to the army's headquarters in Cambridge. "I saw General Ward, General Heath, General Joseph Warren [Adams, like Pickering, refers to Warren by the title he will later hold] and the New England Army," the future president wrote in his autobiography. "There was great Confusion and much distress: Artillery, Arms, Cloathing were wanting and a sufficient Supply of Provisions not easily obtained. Neither the officers nor Men however wanted Spirits or Resolution."

From Cambridge Adams traveled along the road to Lexington and the scene of the action, talking to people along the way. This experience convinced him "that the Die was cast, the Rubicon passed, and as Lord Mansfield expressed it in Parliament, if We did not defend ourselves they would kill Us." John Adams, the short, stocky lawyer from Braintree, who had never until that point been at the forefront of radical activity, would, in the aftermath of the fighting outside Boston, become one of the most vocal and effective advocates for American independence.

In all about 20,000 men turned out for the Lexington Alarm. That said, not all of those were encamped outside Boston. Many who had headed off for the fighting turned back when they heard it was over. Many of the Massachusetts militia who turned out were not prepared to stay in the field, or did not intend to do so. As new troops were arriving from more distant communities or colonies, others were leaving camp and going home, adding to the confusion. Even weeks after the battle James Warren wrote to John Adams, then in Philadelphia for the Second Continental Congress, "As to the Army, it is such a shifting, fluctuating state as to not be capable of a perfect regulation. They are continually going and coming."

There is no way to know how many men were part of the ad hoc army around Boston in those first days of the war, though the number must certainly have been more than 10,000, or well over twice General Gage's force. By April 22, as the military and political leaders struggled to organize the troops they had, efforts were made to temporarily stem the influx of men. The committee of correspondence in Newburyport, Massachusetts, for example, received a circular letter from the Committee of Safety saying that "they have a sufficient number of men arrived, and therefore would not have any more come from the Northward for the present." The Committee of Safety would certainly want more men, but not before they had some level of organization in place.

Among those who did arrive in Cambridge was General Israel Putnam, who made his appearance on April 21, sans men or sheep but with plenty of enthusiasm for the fight. It was actually the second time he had headed off for battle in that neighboring colony. The year before, when Gage had ordered his troops to gather up provincial stores of gunpowder and secure them in Castle William, news of the affront quickly spread to the other colonies. By the time it reached Putnam the rumor had grown to include an attack on Boston by the regulars and the British fleet, leaving several Americans dead.

With perhaps more ardor than consideration, Putnam called for Connecticut's militia to turn out and march for Boston. Thousands grabbed up arms and prepared to head north as Putnam's call to action moved south to other colonies. Before any troops took to the road, however, additional news arrived indicating that the alarm was false. Putnam wrote to the leaders in Massachusetts, albeit likely exaggerating, "But for counterintelligence we should have had forty thousand men well equipped and ready to march this morning." Still, the significant number that did turn out was an indication of how ready the country was for war, even a year before the fight at Lexington Green. Word of this mobilization helped convince Gage to begin fortifying Roxbury Neck.

It was the morning of April 20 when the Lexington Alarm reached Putnam's hometown of Pomfret by way of a letter forwarded from Worcester to a local named Daniel Tyler, who happened to be Putnam's son-in-law. Putnam and his fourteen-year-old son, also named Daniel, were in the middle of plowing a field when Tyler hurried up with the news. Years later, Daniel Putnam would tell the story of how his father raced off at once, leaving Daniel with instructions to unhitch the horses and join him in Massachusetts as soon as he was able. Then the elder Putnam grabbed a horse from the stable and, still wearing his plowing clothes, rode off to spread the alarm, confident that this time it was the real thing.

The story of Israel Putnam leaving the plow to race off to war is one of the great, if now largely forgotten, legends of the Revolution. It is certainly plausible—Putnam was a farmer, and it was plowing season—but it also smacks enough of Cincinnatus to make one dubious. (Cincinnatus, the Roman leader who was called away from his plow at a time of crisis to take the office of dictator, and who resigned his absolute rule when the crisis had passed, was viewed by many as the ideal of military and civic honor. This was particularly true in the republican-minded United States following the Revolution.) Plow or no, Putnam did make the rounds of the nearby towns, raising the alarm and consulting with the local militia officers. By the time he returned home he found hundreds of men under arms and ready to follow him to Massachusetts.

Putnam was not ready to lead them, however, probably because he did not want to suffer the delay that would invariably come from having to move so many men a hundred miles to another colony. Instead, he assured them that other officers were on their way to bring them to camp at Cambridge. Then Israel Putnam, still wearing his plowing clothes, rode off for the field of battle.

By the following day he had arrived at Cambridge and thrown himself into the fight, or at least the preparations. He met with the Committee of Safety and wrote that same day to a militia colonel in Connecticut urging him to send 6,000 men to Cambridge "as speedily as possible." Ward's orderly book records for April 21, "This day, General Putnam, of Connecticut, attended the Council of War." In honor of the famous frontier fighter, the password, or "parole," of the day was "Putnam."

Another man who joined the fight around this time and who would play a pivotal role in the Battle of Bunker Hill was Colonel John Stark of New Hampshire, a seasoned combat veteran, as prickly as he was tough, of middling height but muscular and strong from a life of exertion. Stark had already gained a reputation as a hunter and woodsman before the outbreak of the French and Indian War. When the fighting started he was recruited into Rogers's Rangers, where he and Putnam served together.

John Stark had spent much of his youth hunting and trapping. During one of those trips he and a companion had been taken by Indians and held captive for some time, during which they endured beatings and other mistreatment. Throughout the ordeal Stark stood up to his captives, winning their respect and even the nickname "Young Chief." In the months he spent with the natives, first as a captive and then more as an adopted son, Stark learned a great deal about their techniques of hunting and warfare, lessons that would serve him well in the wilderness fighting to come.

Stark fought with Rogers's tough, hard-driving ranger corps in the wilderness around Lake George and Lake Champlain. There he came in contact with many of the men with whom he would fight in the American Revolution, such as Putnam and Artemas Ward, and those he would fight against, such as Thomas Gage. Like Putnam, Stark was a friend of George Augustus Howe, the two men fighting side by side on several occasions. Stark mourned the death of Howe for the rest of his life, though he admitted that the Americans in the Revolution were better off not having him as an enemy.

Stark took part in both Abercrombie's failed attack on Fort Ticonderoga in 1758 and Amherst's successful assault the following year. He spent the entire French and Indian War in the northern theater and took part in some of the war's toughest combat. When the peace was signed, Stark retired to his home in Dunbarton, New Hampshire. There he and his wife, Molly, and their eleven children ran their extensive farm and several mill operations.

Word of the fighting at Lexington and Concord reached John Stark while he was working at his sawmill. He immediately returned home, changed his clothes (unlike the impetuous Putnam), mounted up, and rode off south toward Massachusetts. Along the way he rallied his neighbors, and soon hundreds were following the famous Colonel Stark to the theater of action.

By April 22 Stark and his men had been incorporated into the army around Boston. On that day he was sent with 300 troops to the town of Chelsea, on the Mystic River about five miles northeast of Boston, "to defend the inhabitants of said town."

Artemas Ward remained in overall command with his headquarters in Cambridge and around 5,000 men in his camp. He sent General John Thomas to secure Roxbury with another 5,000 and stationed still more troops at posts circling Boston where they could keep their eyes on the city. The general expectation was that Gage would strike soon, while the American troops were weak and disorganized. Amos Farnsworth noted in his journal of April 22, "This night was Alarmed by the Regulars firing at our gard on the neck turned out And marched towards them but nothing more Ensued." The next few weeks would bring one alarm after another, with the newly minted soldiers grabbing their muskets and scrambling to their posts. Still the redcoats did not come.

A MOST DISTRESSED CONDITION

The Committee of Safety met on the morning of the fighting at Lexington and Concord and again the following day, April 20. There was no executive authority that the people of Massachusetts recognized, at least not those people numbered among the rebels, so the Committee of Safety took it upon itself to fill that role.

Dr. Joseph Warren was increasingly central to the work of the committee. Indeed, with Hancock and Sam and John Adams preparing to leave for the meeting of the Second Continental Congress in Philadelphia, the work of heading up the provincial government fell to Warren. For the next two months, from the fighting at Lexington and Concord to the Battle of Bunker Hill, two of the most epoch-making months in American history, Joseph Warren was the very epicenter of the military and political storm.

No one at that point was thinking in terms of grand strategy. It was not the plan of the Committee of Safety to lay siege to Boston. The strategy, such that it was, devised by the committee and the military leaders did not extend beyond organizing the army and preparing for a possible attack by the redcoats. Indeed, through the course of the yearlong siege of Boston there was little discussion of the fact that they were trying to lay siege to the city. Rather, the situation devolved into a stalemate in which there were few other military options.

Joseph Warren seemed to sense this early on. Even while others were still concerned about another British attack, Warren wrote to Arthur Lee, "I cannot precisely tell you what will become of General Gage; I imagine he will at least be very closely shut up in Boston." In fact, Gage beat the new American army to the punch and stopped all free communication with the countryside. No one passed over Roxbury Neck without his permission.

One of the first concerns of the men on the Committee of Safety was to get their friends out of Boston, before they were forced to suffer the deprivations that the Loyalists and the king's troops would soon feel.

Warren wrote to Gage on April 20, a very civil letter. Proud of the role he had played thus far in the Revolution, Warren reminded Gage that he had never tried to hide his activity. "Your Excellency knows very well," he wrote, "the part I have taken in publick affairs; I ever scorned disguise." He went on to ask "how many days you desire as may be allowed for such as desire to remove from *Boston,* with their effects, and what time you will allow the people in *Boston* for their removal." Gage was permitting only thirty wagons at a time to come into the city, and Warren suggested that this rule would slow things unnecessarily.

Gage did not reply to Warren's letter, as he did not consider Warren to be a legitimate government official. Gage was, however, willing to negotiate with the selectmen of Boston, who in turn informed Warren of their agreements and looked to the Committee of Safety for approval.

The selectmen met with Gage on April 21 to discuss the developing crisis in the town. Just as the Americans were expecting Gage at any minute to launch an attack against their lines, so Gage was at least aware of the possibility that the Americans might attack Boston, even if he was not overly frightened by the prospect. Gage's primary concern was that the Patriots still in the city would rise up and join in on such an attack. He knew most of them had guns secreted in their homes, and such an armed mob within his lines could be devastating. If that happened, Gage warned the selectmen, it might "issue in very unhappy consequences to the town," by which he meant Boston might be put to the torch, or worse.

Gage assured the selectmen that his men "should do no damage, nor commit any act of violence in the Town," if the selectmen in turn would make sure the people of Boston stayed out of any fight that might take place.

The next day the selectmen called a meeting of "the Freeholders and other Inhabitants of the Town of Boston," to inform them of the discussion they had had with Gage and to vote on an agreement with the governor. "After much debate and some Amendments," wrote John Rowe, "they Passed two Votes which were presented to the general."

In the first vote, the people of Boston agreed to keep the peace if Gage and his troops would do the same. In the second, the people reminded Gage that he had assured them, at the time he began fortifying Roxbury Neck, that "he had no intention of stopping up the avenue to the Town." Now they intended to ask the governor "to give orders for opening the communication, not only for bringing Provisions into the Town, but also that the inhabitants, such of them as incline, may retire from the Town with their effects without molestation."

The selectmen called on the governor the following day and read him the resolves voted on at the town meeting. A long conference ensued. Gage was happy to let the rebellious population leave. Boston was a fairly populous city with only one road in and out, and it depended on food and other supplies coming in to market every day. Just two days after the Battle of Lexington and Concord, John Rowe was writing in his diary, "All Business at an end & all Communication Stop'd between the Town & Country. No Fresh Provisions of any kind brought to this market, so that Boston is in a most Distressed Condition." It was only going to get worse, much worse, and Gage was eager to have fewer mouths to feed.

On the other hand, he did not want to augment the army at his gates by allowing all these armed rebels to leave Boston. Finally he agreed that if the people who wished to leave would deposit their firearms at Faneuil Hall, under the care of the selectmen and labeled with their names so that they might later retrieve them, then Gage would give those people permission to go. This was approved at yet another town meeting, and Gage even agreed to let them leave by land or water, saying "he would desire the Admiral to lend boats to facilitate the removal of the effects of the inhabitants."

Out of principle Gage would not communicate with Warren, but he also understood that Warren was the one who held the real authority beyond the town limits of Boston. He therefore asked the selectmen to write to Warren to request that "those persons in the country who may incline to move into *Boston* with their effects may have liberty to do so without molestation." The general feared that Loyalists beyond the protection of the army in Boston would be mistreated and would want to seek protection in the city. To this Warren and the Committee of Safety agreed, though it does not appear that many Tories took advantage of this arrangement That is hardly a surprise, given that the suffering in the city was already well known.

On April 27 the selectmen returned to Gage once more with word that all of the arms belonging to those wishing to leave, more than two thousand in all, were now stored in Faneuil Hall. After some more back-and-forth, Gage agreed that on the following day he would receive applications for passes to leave Boston "as soon as persons wanting them shall be ready to depart."

In the end it would not be so easy. Gage did not issue passes as freely as he suggested he would. John Rowe wrote, "April 28. This day I apply'd to get a Pass to go out with my Effects but could not prevail." The Loyalists who chose to remain in town howled in protest at Gage's allowing the rebellious faction to leave. As Gage explained to Dartmouth, the Loyalists felt that "none but the ill inclined will go out, and when they are Safe with their Effects, the Town will be set on Fire." In the Tories' way of thinking, the Patriots were serving as a human shield.

Another sticking point was "the Meaning of the Word Effects." When Gage said "effects" he meant personal effects only. This came as an ugly surprise to the many merchants in Boston who assumed it also meant their inventory of merchandise, in which they had considerable capital invested.

Merchant John Andrews, who planned to sail with his wife for Nova Scotia, felt that if "I can escape with the skin of my teeth, shall be glad, as I don't expect to be able to take more than a change of apparell with me." In truth, Andrews also hoped to escape with all the goods stored in his warehouse, as well. He and three friends had chartered a ship to carry them and their effects, including merchandise, to Halifax. On May 6 he wrote to a friend in Philadelphia, "You'll observe by this that I'm yet in Boston, and here like to remain."

Andrews's problem was not an inability to secure papers to leave but "the absolute refusal of the Governor to suffer any merchandise to be carried out of the town." Rather than endure the economic devastation that would come with his merchandise being commandeered or looted, Andrews chose to send his wife on ahead while he remained behind, minding the store and suffering the deprivations of living in Boston under siege.

As the complaints of the Loyalists grew louder, Gage felt pressured to halt the exodus. This he could not do overtly without breaking his word, so instead found means to slow it. Warren wrote to the governor of Connecticut, "The general is perpetually making new conditions, and forming the most unreasonable pretenses for retarding their removal from that *garrison*."

On May 10 the Provincial Congress wrote to Gage reminding him of his agreement and pointing out that they had received considerable intelligence that the people had met with "numerous delays and embarrassments," in trying to leave the town. "A delay of justice is a denial of it," they pointed out, "and extremely oppressive to the people now held in duress."

At the same time, and unknown to anyone, Joseph Warren sent a personal letter to Gage, appealing to the governor's reason and humanity. "As no living Person knows, or ever will know from me of my writing this," Warren wrote in the postscript, "I hope you will excuse a Freedom which I very well know would be improper in a Letter which was to be exposed to general View."

Warren addressed the issue of Gage's unwillingness to negotiate with the Provincial Congress. He asked Gage if he would be willing to sacrifice the interests of England and the peace in the colonies just for form's sake. He warned that the people of Massachusetts would not suffer Gage to break his agreement, and asked that Gage adhere to it "without hearkening to the mad Advice of Men I know have deceived you."

Despite the overblown condemnations of Gage he often churned out for public consumption, Warren seems to have harbored a real respect for Gage's decency and humanity. This comes through in the letter written to Gage directly after Lexington and Concord, on the same topic, and in this one. As in that earlier letter, Warren insinuated that Gage was being fed bad advice by men who "care not if they ruin you" and hoped that the governor's natural inclinations would lead him to a humane course of action.

Warren genuinely believed that most of what he saw as Gage's mistakes were the result of nefarious council he was receiving. Around the same time he was writing to Gage, Warren wrote a letter to Arthur Lee in London, touching in part on Gage's efforts to show that the Americans fired the first shot on Lexington Green. "My private opinion . . . ," Warren wrote, with no reason to be anything but candid, "is that he is really deceived in the matter, and is led (by his officers and some of the most abandoned villains on earth, who are natives of this Country, and who are now shut up with him in *Boston*) to believe that our people actually began the firing."

Gage was certainly a humane man, as Warren imagined, but he also had much more than just the comfort of the rebellious population of Boston to consider. Neither the official letter nor Warren's backdoor appeal did any good. Emigration slowed and finally stopped. Joseph Warren wrote to Adams, using a properly surgical metaphor, "General Gage, I fear, has trepanned the inhabitants of Boston."

CAPTAIN DERBY'S MISSION

If there was one thing that Joseph Warren had learned during his association with Sam Adams and the Boston radicals, it was the power of propaganda and the importance of being first to market with one's message. Days after the Battle of Lexington and Concord, the Provincial Congress assembled a committee to collect depositions concerning the fighting, "to be sent to *England* from the first ship from *Salem*." These depositions would support the suggestion that the regular troops had been the aggressors and had fired first.

For three days eyewitnesses to the fighting were sought out and their stories recorded. Warren penned a letter to "the Inhabitants of Great Britain," whom he called "Friends and Fellow-Subjects," containing a brief though largely accurate account of what had taken place on April 19, with a few notable additions and omissions. Despite the fact that no one knew, or knows now, who actually fired the first shot, Warren stated unambiguously that "the Regulars rushed on with great violence, and first began hostilities by firing on said Lexington Company." Warren recounted the atrocities committed by the troops on their way back to Boston but failed to mention the great violence done to them by the Massachusetts militia.

Warren's letter to the people of Great Britain, the depositions, and newspaper accounts of the action were packaged up and sent to Benjamin Franklin, who still served as Massachusetts's agent in London. Warren asked that Franklin print the enclosed papers and disperse them through every town in England. He warned Franklin that Gage had already sent off a "fallacious account of the tragedy," and Warren certainly hoped that the material from the Provincial Congress would be disseminated first.

The letters were carried to England by Captain John Derby of Salem in his fast schooner *Quero*. Derby was instructed to sail for Ireland and from there cross over to England to avoid any cruisers that might be on the lookout for him in the English Channel. Derby ignored that advice and made right for Southampton on the south coast of England, which he reached unmolested. On May 29 Derby personally arrived in London with the packet from the Provincial Congress. Despite leaving four days after Gage's ship, his speedy *Quero* arrived twelve days ahead of it, thus assuring that the American version of events was the first to be disseminated.

The news of Lexington and Concord rocked London, giving the already vocal opponents of Lord North's administration more reason for discontent and making their call for a change of administration louder. Lord George Germain, who would soon replace Dartmouth as the American secretary, wrote to a friend, "It is Strange to see the many joyful faces upon this Event, thinking, I conclude, that Rebellion will be the means of Changing the Ministry." Former governor Thomas Hutchinson, still rattling around London, wrote, "The Opposition here rejoice that the Americans fight, after it had been generally said they would not."

The king and his ministers were, of course, the most dismayed of all, and incredulous that the embattled farmers might have actually put the regular army on the run, but they could also detect the taint of propaganda in Warren's address, and so held their opinions until they could read the official dispatches from Gage. "I am impatient for the true and full account," Germain wrote. Dartmouth did not wait until Gage's reports to arrive before writing a letter to Gage saying, "It is very much to be lamented that We have not some Account from you of this Transaction." It was a pointless letter, particularly as Derby told Dartmouth that Gage sent his report four days before he, Derby, left. In fact, though, people were angry, and they were blaming Gage for the fact that Derby's documents arrived first.

Gage's report arrived on June 10. Most friends of the ministry had been waiting for the general's accounts, assuring themselves that they would prove the American versions were bogus. Thomas Hutchinson, who had firsthand knowledge of the armed citizens of Massachusetts, was not so certain. "I assured many gentlemen who would give no credit to Darby's account," he wrote in his diary, "that it would prove near the truth."

Hutchinson was right. When Gage's account was read, those hoping to disprove Warren's account "received but little comfort, from the accounts themselves being much the same with what Darby brought." In fact, the king's friends had been so sure that Gage's account would be more favorable, that they were, according to Hutchinson, "more struck than if they had not been so sanguine before. As one general exclaimed, 'How often have I heard you American Colonels boast that with four battalions you would march through America; and now you think Gage with 3000 men and 40 pieces of cannon, mayn't venture out of Boston!'"

Confirmation of the defeat of the British army shook the credibility of the administration and gave even more fuel to the opposition. One paper wrote, "The sword of civil war is drawn, and if there is truth in heaven, the King's Troops unsheathed it. Will the *English* Nation much longer suffer their fellow subjects to be slaughtered?" A group called the Constitution Society advertised for a collection of £100 "for the widows, orphans, &a, of the brave Americans inhumanly murdered by the K[ing]'s troops at Lexington, April 19th 1775, because they preferred death to slavery."

Dartmouth was understandably displeased and seems to have been the most annoyed that Derby's account was the first to arrive in England. This is perhaps understandable given that America was his responsibility and he had the most to lose in the propaganda wars regarding those colonies. In his next letter to Gage he began by pointing out, again, that the documents from the Provincial Congress had arrived ahead of the official reports. He mentioned that the initiative shown by the rebels had "its effect in leaving for some days a false impression upon the people's minds," though, of course, not as false as Dartmouth had hoped. He expressed his wish that in the future Gage would send such important correspondence "in one of the light vessels of the fleet."

The disaster at Concord and Lexington had happened largely because Dartmouth had urged Gage to be aggressive and make "a test of the people's resolution to resist." Now that the test had been made to the detriment of the ministry, Dartmouth stepped away from it in a most shameful manner. "I am to presume that the measure of sending out a detachment of your troops to destroy the magazine at Concord," he wrote, "was taken upon the fullest consideration of the advantage on one hand and hazard on the other of such an enterprise and all the probable consequences that were to result from it." The question fairly reeked of disapproval, and much of the rest of the letter continued in the same tone.

Gage probably guessed that he would take the fall if the situation in Massachusetts did not improve. He might have suspected that his position as governor and commander in chief would not survive Concord and Lexington. In late June, though, as Dartmouth's letter of tacit disapproval was sailing east to west, another letter from Gage, describing a second disaster, was sailing west to east. This letter described the bloodbath that was the Battle of Bunker Hill, and Gage must have known then that his tenure was at an end.

As Hutchinson wrote in his diary after hearing Gage's description of Concord and Lexington, "The prospect is dark and discouraging."

Chapter Ten

THE MASSACHUSETTS ARMY

The days following Lexington and Concord were a frenetic and confused time for the military, and just as much so for the civilian leadership in Massachusetts, primarily the Committee of Safety.

For a year the various militia units had been training, organizing, and collecting stores for the moment when the standoff would become an actual armed conflict, and when it did they found themselves overwhelmed by the magnitude of what confronted them and were only just able to keep up.

The same held for the Provincial Congress. As an ad hoc replacement for the General Court, the Congress had mostly involved itself with mundane aspects of administration and suggestions that the towns prepare their militias for war. It had not anticipated having to create and maintain an army, negotiate with Gage and with the other colonies, and set policy that would have continent-wide and indeed worldwide ramifications.

To make matters worse, the Provincial Congress and the Committee of Safety had no real legal standing. They were able to exercise authority only to the extent that the people would recognize that authority. James

Warren, a member of the Provincial Congress, wrote to John Adams that the work of the Congress was "attended with many difficulties, under the present Circumstances of our Government, in which recommendations are to supply the place of Laws, and destitute of coercive power, exposed to the Caprice of the People, and depending entirely on their virtue for Success."

The members of the Committee of Safety, forming as they did a sort of executive branch, met more frequently than the Provincial Congress. They were meeting the morning of the Lexington Alarm and assembled again the day after, when they found themselves tossed into the middle of the crisis (one observer said "The Committee of Safety, who are the *primum mobile* in the military movements, are crowded with business"). A bulk of the committee work fell to the committee's chairman, Joseph Warren.

After sending accounts of Lexington and Concord to England, the committee turned its attention to the monumental task that was the army. James Warren wrote to John Adams, "The principal Objects of our Attention have been the regulation and officering of the Army, and arming the men, and devising ways and means to support the enormous Expense incurred." The Committee of Safety found itself essentially micromanaging the nascent military effort. Records for the committee's workdays after Lexington and Concord show it voting that "orders be given to Captain Dexter to conceal the Cannon committed to his care," that "Major Bigelow be applied to furnish a Map and Horse to attend the Surgeons, and convey Medicines agreeable to their direction," and that "Mr. Pigeon, the Commissary-General, be directed to carry thirty-five barrels of Pork, and half a barrel of hog's fat, from the Town of Salem to the Town of Cambridge." Those were typical, and just a small sampling of the petty details with which the committee wrestled every day.

Some of the decisions made by the committee went beyond the distribution of hog's fat. On April 21 it approved the wording of an enlistment form to apply to all soldiers of the Massachusetts service. The form promised that the soldier would "solemnly engage and enlist" from the day the form was signed to "the last day of *December* next, unless the service should admit of a part of the whole sooner." It is unclear whether the members of the committee felt the war would not go on beyond December or did not think anyone would agree to serve more than eight months, but those short enlistments would come back to haunt them (though to be sure, it would then no longer be their problem, but that of George Washington and the Continental Congress).

The Committee of Safety voted to raise "eight thousand effective men" to be formed into companies of seventy rank and file. That number was soon changed to fifty rank and file to make it easier to complete a company from a given town without having to mix soldiers from various communities. Provincialism still ran strong, along with the militia spirit, and men wanted to stick with their neighbors and serve under the officers they knew.

Despite the thousands of men who had turned out for the Lexington Alarm, the number of troops still remaining in the field a week later was discouragingly small. Artemas Ward wrote to the Provincial Congress on April 24 begging it to take action in enlisting troops. "My situation is such," he wrote, "that if I do not have enlisting orders immediately I shall be left all alone. It is impossible to keep the men here, excepting something be done."

The enrollment forms that the minutemen and other militia had signed did not call for them to remain in the field for months, and while many of those who turned out on April 19 eagerly joined the new army, many others did not, and had no intention of doing so. Most of them were farmers, and it being planting season, they had to return to their farms and get their crops in the ground for the very survival of their families. Even as more troops were coming in from Massachusetts and other colonies, many were leaving camp, creating an uncertain and chaotic scene.

The civilian leadership was in mortal fear of another British attack and looked to the outlying communities to supply the army with troops, even on a short-term basis. "As many of the persons now in camp came from their respective Towns, without any expectation of tarrying any time," the Committee of Safety wrote to the nearby communities, "and are now under the necessity of returning, this is to desire that you would, with the utmost haste, send other persons to supply their places for a few days." The committee warned that the "most fatal consequences" must follow if the army were to become so weak as to allow Gage to break out of Boston. "We think none can be unwilling," the letter concluded, "to come for a few days to relieve their brethren who have been absent from their families."

It was a stopgap measure at best, one likely to add to the confusion. Nor is it possible to know, out of the swirl of activity, how many men responded to the committee's call for temporary stand-ins. A few certainly did. Amos Farnsworth wrote in his diary of June 5, "On Monday my Brother Came and took my Plase And on tusday about noon I Sot out on my jurney for home." However, as the Committee of Safety's enlistment forms began to circulate, and its efforts to bring order to the army began to have some effect, men began to enlist in the regular Massachusetts service, and the need for temporary relief faded.

Jedediah Huntington, a young officer from Connecticut, arrived in Cambridge on April 27. "I came into this place through Roxbury, last evening," he wrote to Jonathan Trumbull Jr.,

> and find great numbers of Troops, or rather armed men, in much more confusion than I expected, but perhaps with as little as possible, in their disordered state of the Massachusetts. Most of the soldiers here are inhabitants of this Province, who are now enlisting in a regular manner. General Ward is at Roxbury; General Putnam is Commander-in-chief at this place. Both have too much business on their hands.

Huntington referred to Putnam as the commander in chief. While this would appear to be a mistake, it was actually indicative of how badly organized and thought out the "army" was at that state. Putnam was commander in chief of Connecticut forces, and thus Huntington's superior. Rhode Island had its own separate command structure. Artemas Ward was only authorized to be commander in chief of the Massachusetts and New Hampshire forces, and while the officers from all the colonies with troops outside Boston looked to him for overall leadership, there was no clear chain of command. It was not until after the Battle of Bunker Hill that the Connecticut legislature would order Putnam to officially be under Ward's authority.

On April 22 the Provincial Congress met for the first time since the Battle of Lexington and Concord and began to look at some of the issues with which the Committee of Safety had been wrestling. They immediately upped the ante for the army surrounding Boston. Instead of the Committee of Safety's 8,000 they called for "an army of Thirty Thousand Men [to] be immediately raised and established." Of those, 13,600 were to come from Massachusetts.

The Congress also unanimously elected Joseph Warren as president pro tempore, Hancock and Sam Adams being then on their way to Philadelphia. The day after Warren was chosen president, the committee received a somewhat hysterical letter from John Hancock in Worcester. "Gentlemen," he wrote, "Mr. S Adams and myself, just arrived here, find no intelligence from you, and no guard . . . How are we to proceed? Where are our brethren? Surely we ought to be supported. I had rather be with you, and at present am fully determined to be with you before I proceed."

Hancock went on to request information on the outcome of the battle and to suggest that Boston and Castle William be captured by American forces. The close call at Lexington and the subsequent violence seemed to have unnerved the Boston merchant, which makes all the more amusing the fact that Hancock seriously considered himself a candidate for commander in chief of the army.

Along with increasing the number of men to be enlisted, the Congress set the establishment, or rate of pay, for the army. Colonels of a regiment of 598 men would have £15 per month, lieutenant colonels £12, and majors £10. Rates were set for adjuncts, quartermasters, chaplains, surgeons, and noncommissioned officers. Drummers received £2.04 and fifers the same. At the bottom of the list was the private soldier, who was paid £2 per month, about what an unskilled laborer might hope to earn. In addition it was stipulated that "a Coat for a uniform be given to each of the Non-commissioned Officers and Privates, as soon as the state of the Province will admit of it," which in the end was never.

The Congress ordered the establishment and the enlistment papers to be printed up and distributed. Prospective colonels fanned out in hopes of signing up their regiments. They met with a fair degree of success, and half of what would be the army laying siege to Boston was enlisted within a week of the Lexington Alarm. Regiments continued to arrive from other colonies, turning the Massachusetts service into a truly national army. Even so, it would be months, and only after the arrival of Washington, that real order would finally be made out of the chaos.

THE CONTINENTAL ARMY

Israel Putnam could not tolerate the idea of the army sitting inactive, and as an old soldier he knew how corrosive that was to discipline. He was constantly walking and riding the lines, urging the men as they strengthened the defenses. According to his son, "Old Put" felt it was "better to dig a ditch every morning and fill it up at evening than to have the men idle."

Thanks in part to Putnam's urging, the army began to dig in, building earthworks and other fortifications facing Boston. The general orders reflect this, with such directions as that of May 3: "Four captains, eight subalterns, sixteen sergeants, two hundred privates, be drafted, to go upon fatigue. Colonel Doolittle command the detachment."

Private Caleb Haskell from Newburyport recalled how Putnam came across a group of soldiers on that fatigue assignment slacking off.

"To what regiment do you belong?" Putnam demanded.

"To Colonel Doolittle's," the men answered.

"Doolittle?" Putnam replied in disgust. "Do nothing at all!"

Soon after, Putnam decided to give morale a boost by goading the British in Boston. On the afternoon of May 13 he turned out all of the troops stationed in Cambridge, save for those on guard duty, 2,200 men in total, and marched them off to Charlestown to "Shoe themselves to the Regulars," as Amos Farnsworth recorded. The line of march was a mile and a half long, stretched out along the road that a month before had been the scene of so much carnage, with Percy leading his men back to safety. They crossed the neck to Charlestown and marched over Bunker Hill and down the main street of the nearly deserted village, along the edge of the river that left them fully exposed to the eyes and guns of Boston. Then they crossed back over the neck and returned to Cambridge. James Warren wrote to his wife, "This movement produced a Terror in Boston hardly to be described."

From across the water the troops and civilians in Boston watched the parade, and the sailors on the men-of-war peered over the barrels of their long cannons. Putnam and his men were within easy range of both, but the British held their fire. "Between 2 and 3000 of the rebels came from Cambridge . . . ," Lieutenant John Barker wrote, "they kept parading a long time, they march'd into the Town, and after giving the War-hoop opposite the *Somerset* returned as they came." He added that the British troops expected that Putnam's column "wou'd have fired on the Somerset, at least it was wished for, as she had everything ready for Action, and must [that is, would] have destroyed great numbers of them, besides putting the Town to Ashes."

No doubt many of Putnam's men were eager to fire on the *Somerset,* but Putnam would never have allowed it. He may have been bold, and eager to provoke the British, but he was no fool. He would not invite the devastating fire of a ship of the line on his men when they were fully exposed. Fortifying Bunker Hill under the noses of the British was more in keeping with Putnam's idea of poking the enemy, not pointless small-arms fire on a man-of-war. Charleston was granted another month to live.

It's not clear if Ward ordered the parade or if the entire thing was Putnam's doing, but considering the caution of the former and the intemperance of the latter it is likely Putnam acted on his own. Indeed, the entire affair smacks of Putnam. He wanted to ratchet up the tension, to nudge the British troops toward action. That same tendency would be on display on the night of June 16 on the slopes of Bunker Hill, when the question became how far the American troops could push Gage before they got a violent response.

The Provincial Congress, meanwhile, continued to wrestle with issues of the army, including questions regarding the very nature of the force they were establishing. On May 8 they drafted a new enlistment form that more closely reflected the growing national character of the army. While those signing the new form still agreed to "truly and faithfully serve in the Massachusetts Army," they were now doing so "for the defense and security of the estates, lives and liberties of the good people of this and the sister Colonies in *America,* in opposition to Ministerial tyranny, by which they are or may be oppressed." The original enlistment form made no mention of any colony outside Massachusetts.

The returns of the army, that is, the official count of men, from the period between Lexington and Concord and Bunker Hill are so inaccurate and deficient that it is impossible to know just how many troops were present. It appears that there were about 16,000 in all, 11,500 from Massachusetts, 2,300 from Connecticut, 1,200 from New Hampshire, and 1,000 from Rhode Island. Though Massachusetts men still accounted for the lion's share and more, the army was quickly becoming a continental, not a Massachusetts, army.

This was very much what the Massachusetts leadership hoped for. Joseph Warren, writing to his friend Joseph Reed in Philadelphia, reminded Reed, "We are all embarked in one bottom; if one colony is enslaved, she will be immediately improved as an engine to subdue the others," a warning that hewed surprisingly close to the southern strategy the British would employ in the last years of the war.

What's more, as of May 10 the Provincial Congress of Massachusetts finally had a higher civil power to which it could appeal. On that day the Second Continental Congress convened in Philadelphia, and the Provincial Congress wasted little time in turning to them for help.

Two days after the Continental Congress convened, the Provincial Congress voted to select a committee to draft "an application to the Continental Congress, for obtaining the recommendation for this Colony to take up and exercise Civil Government as soon as may be." The fact was that the Provincial Congress did not actually view itself as a legitimate, lawful government body, and many of the members felt that Massachusetts had no real civil government at all. They turned to the Continental Congress to help them establish a genuine government.

In truth, the Continental Congress was no more or less a legitimate government body than was the Provincial Congress. Both were assemblies of elected officials selected by the citizens of the colonies (though hardly representational, since it is unlikely that any Tory took part in the voting). The one person most Americans still viewed as their sovereign, King George, considered both congresses to be completely illegitimate, and indeed illegal.

James Warren, for one, felt that the application to the Continental Congress was pointless; the Provincial Congress had all the authority they needed, and they should stop diddling and simply declare themselves the ruling government body. To his wife, Mercy Otis Warren, he wrote:

> But remember to revere our [Provincial] Congress [that last is written with a touch of irony], for if we have lost many good Members we have many left; and, if we have not all the Sense and property of the province among us, we have as good a Share as commonly is in such an Assembly, it will no longer therefore do to delay a question that should have been determined 6 months ago. Nevertheless we have gone no further than an application to the Grand Congress.

Warren, like his good friend John Adams, chaffed at the plodding, deliberative nature of congresses. "There is a degree of Timidity and slowness in our movements that my Soul abominates," he wrote. Warren had a bad cold at the time of that writing, which probably did not help his mood.

On May 15 the Provincial Congress realized that there was one other thing they wanted to ask of the Continental Congress. On that day they ordered "the Committee appointed to prepare an application to the Continental Congress, be directed to insert a clause therein, desiring that the said Congress would take some measures for directing and regulating the *American* Forces."

Joseph Warren had already taken a stab at getting the Continental Congress to take on the responsibility of the army. In his letter of May 3, in which he forwarded the depositions from Lexington and Concord, he also informed the Continental Congress of the Provincial Congress's decision to raise an army of 13,600 men from Massachusetts with a proportional number coming from New Hampshire, Rhode Island, and Connecticut. "We have the greatest confidence in the wisdom and ability of the Continent to support us, so far as it shall appear necessary for supporting the common cause of the *American* Colonies," he wrote.

By that Warren certainly meant that the Congress should consider supporting the army that was fighting for the common cause he mentioned, but the message was too subtle for Congress and they took no notice of it. Soon it would be time to make the suggestion again, in more emphatic tones.

As the days passed and the complexity and expense of the army grew, the Massachusetts leaders began to understand that they did not have the means or the authority to regulate a national army, particularly when they did not even think they had the authority to regulate their own colony. Earlier they had issued notes of credit for £100,000 to finance the operation, a huge financial burden. Even though each colony in theory supplied money and provisions to its own troops, it was clear that Massachusetts would be bearing most of the weight.

James Warren, who felt Massachusetts should just go ahead and form a government, was also ready for the Continental Congress to take over the army. This was as much to see better leadership as to avoid his colony's having to bear the expense. Warren wrote to John Adams on the subject. The troops, he wrote, "seem to me to want a more experienced direction. I could for myself wish to see your Friends Washington and L [Charles Lee] at the Head of it, and yet dare not propose it, tho' I have it in Contemplation."

Apparently Warren felt that the regional impulse of New Englanders was still such that they would not hear of a Virginian at the head of the army, and he did not dare suggest it. Charles Lee was British born, a former major in the British army and lieutenant colonel in the Portuguese army. He was a man with extensive military experience, far more than any other officer in America, including Washington. Apparently the idea of a former redcoat as head of the American army was so heretical that Warren did not even care to put his name on paper. It was certainly a purposeful thing that Warren wrote Washington *and* Lee, as opposed to Washington *or* Lee.

It is not surprising that Warren was already thinking of Washington as a potential commander in chief. Washington was arguably the most famous American military officer alive, and while others might see his being a Virginian as a problem, Warren did not. He might even have recognized at that early date that a commander in chief from the South would help in the effort to make the Continental Army truly continental. He also understood that his provincial assembly would never select a southerner. Only a continental congress would do that. "I hope that matter will be considered with more propriety in your Body than ours," he wrote. "If you establish a Continental Army, of which this will be only a part, you will place the direction as you please."

By May 16 the committee of the Provincial Congress had drafted its request to the Continental Congress. After a brief historical introduction, with an emphasis on the shared threat to all the colonies, the letter addressed the heart of the issue. Since the affairs taking place in Massachusetts "equally affected our sister Colonies and us," the Provincial Congress had thus far "declined, though urged thereto by the most pressing necessity, to assume the reins of civil Government without their advice and consent."

The lack of civil government complicated the issue of establishing an army. "But as the sword should, in all free States, be subservient to the civil powers," the Provincial Congress pointed out, "and as it is the duty of the Magistrates to support it for the people's necessary defense, we tremble at having an Army (although consisting of our own countrymen) established here without a civil power to provide for and control them."

The Provincial Congress asked the national body to "favour us with your most explicit advice respecting the taking up and exercising the powers of civil Government," which they would happily adopt, or, lacking advice from Congress, they would create their own form of government that would "not only promote our own advantages, but the union and interest of all *America*."

With regard to the army, the Massachusetts leaders were looking for more than just advice. "As the Army now collecting from different Colonies is for the general defense of the rights of *America,* we would beg leave to suggest to your consideration the propriety of your taking the regulation and general direction of it, that the operations of it may more effectively answer the purposes designed."

The application, as it was called, was personally carried to Philadelphia by the trusted Boston radical Dr. Benjamin Church. Joseph Warren sent with it a private letter to Sam Adams in which he expanded on some of the issues facing the Provincial Congress. "I would just observe," he wrote, "that the application made to you respecting the taking the regulation of this army into your hands . . . must be managed with much delicacy."

Though he is less explicit than James Warren was in writing to John Adams, Joseph Warren hints at some of the same difficulties. "I am a little suspicious, unless great care is taken, some dissensions may arise in the army, as our soldiers, I find, will not yet be brought to obey any person of whom they do not themselves entertain a high opinion." Warren and the Committee of Safety were finding it impossible to get Massachusetts men to serve even under officers who came from other towns in Massachusetts, and they despaired of getting them to serve under someone from another colony.

Sectional divides between the northern and southern colonies were already an issue, and there was fear that the southerners would consider the establishment of a new civil government in Massachusetts a step too far toward independence. Warren was no longer concerned about this, though. "If the southern colonies have any apprehensions from the northern colonies," he reasoned, "they surely must now be for an establishment of civil government here." With an army in the field and no civil government, "a military government must certainly take place; and I think I cannot see a question with them to determine which is most to be feared, a military or a civil government." The impulse toward civilian control of the military was deeply set in the American mind, even before there was an American army.

"THE MOST RIDICULOUS EXPEDITION THAT EVER WAS PLAN'D"

The idea of laying siege to Boston and depriving the British of supplies might have been a strategy arrived at by default, but it was one the Americans approached with great vigor. Nothing crossed Roxbury Neck, and the besieging army grew more bold about stopping anything from coming in from any other location as well.

As the weeks passed, the American troops and the Committee of Safety grew more aggressive about digging in. In the second week of May, a joint committee, made up of members of the Committee of Safety and the council of war, was assembled to reconnoiter the high ground in Cambridge and Charlestown and make suggestions with regard to defensive lines. The committee, under the leadership of Benjamin Church, recommended a series of breastworks, some with artillery, be constructed along the road from Cambridge to Charlestown, which would serve as a defense against exactly the type of amphibious move that began the march to Lexington.

The committee also recommended for the first time "a strong Redoubt raised on *Bunker's* Hill, with cannon planted there, to annoy the enemy coming out of *Charlestown,* also to annoy them going by water to *Medford.* When these are finished," the committee wrote, "we apprehend the country will be safe from all sallies of the enemy in that quarter."

With the British fairly well bottled up, the next step was to deprive them of supplies. Virtually no fresh meat made it into Boston. Instead, Gage and his men and the civilian population as well had to make do with meat packed in salt, the standard preservative of the day. The city was well stocked with both salt pork and salt beef, and more could be had thanks to the British command of the sea. Salt provisions, tough as leather and often very old, did not make a very satisfying alternative to fresh, but they were food, and their availability meant the people would not starve.

Some things were less easily imported. One was hay, necessary to feed the numerous horses attached to the army. There was no hay, or much of anything else, grown within the confines of Boston, and the fields on the mainland were beyond reach, but the numerous islands in Boston Harbor were largely unpopulated and used mostly for grazing animals and growing hay. It was there that the British army, with the waterborne superiority offered by the navy, looked for supplies of fodder and fresh meat.

Southeast of Boston, about nine miles away from the city by water, and close to the town of Weymouth, sits Grape Island. Like many other such islands, this small chunk of land was used chiefly to grow hay. On May 21 Gage dispatched a party of thirty men under the command of Lieutenant Thomas Innis of the 43rd Regiment to gather the hay, load it on board four sloops, and haul it back to Boston. One of the sloops mounted twelve guns, but those were removed to make room for the bulky cargo.

At 10:00 A.M. an express rider came charging into General Thomas's headquarters in Roxbury with the news that the regulars appeared intent on landing in Weymouth. Thomas immediately ordered three companies to march south and lend their support to the local militia. They grabbed up muskets and cartridge boxes and headed off for the ten-mile march from Roxbury to Weymouth. Also racing south in response to the alarm was Dr. Joseph Warren, who once again showed more willingness than any other political leader to not just legislate but to pick up a weapon and ride toward the sound of the guns.

The town of Weymouth, meanwhile, was gripped by panic at the approach of the British sloops. Hundreds of people, no doubt with tales of British atrocity on the Lexington Road still fresh in their minds, raced for the countryside. Abigail Adams in Braintree found herself in the path of the refugees. "People, women and children . . . ," she wrote to John, "came flocking down this way; every woman and child driven off from below my father's; my father's family flying."

This terrified flight demonstrates the fear that the redcoats had aroused in the civilian population. People raced from town without waiting to see if the regulars, all thirty of them, were actually landing at Weymouth, which they were not. When Warren and the companies from Roxbury arrived they could see Innis and his men on Grape Island, just offshore, carrying hay from a barn on the island down to the sloops and loading it aboard. They posed no obvious threat to anyone.

While the civilian population raced for safety, the local militia turned out in numbers. "The alarm flew like lightning," Abigail Adams wrote, "and men from all parts came flocking down, till two thousand were collected." It might have been a very bad day for the British troops, but happily for them the tide was out. A couple of lighters—smaller vessels used for loading and unloading larger ships—were lying grounded on the Weymouth mud flats, leaving the armed Americans stuck on shore.

"The distance from Weymouth shore to the said island was too great for small arms to do execution," Warren wrote in an account for the *Essex Gazette,* "nevertheless our people frequently fired. The fire was returned from one of the vessels, with swivel guns; but the shot passed over our heads, and did no mischief."

For several hours the two sides exchanged useless long-range fire while the troops lugged hay from the barn to the boats. The sound of the gunfire was clearly heard in the lines around Boston, where Amos Farnsworth wrote in his diary, "There was many guns herd to Day which we hear was by Regulars going to Weymouth After Some of our Cattle And hay But thay was Defeated By our Men."

Unfortunately for the regulars, the tide was flooding as the day wore on, and soon the lighters lifted clear of the mud and floated free. Hundreds of troops, "who were ardent for battle, got on board, hoisted sail, and bore directly down on upon the nearest point of the island." Both of John Adams's brothers were there. Abigail Adams told John that his younger brother and his militia company "gained honor for their good order that day. He was one of the first to venture on board a schooner to land upon the island."

With the lighters full of armed Americans bearing down on them, the thirty tired redcoats figured their luck had run its course. They raced back to their boats and got under way from one end of the island while the Americans landed on the other end. As the British passed a place called Horse Neck, they fired swivels and small arms at the people there but did not hit anyone. Amos Farnsworth, who knew the story second-hand, wrote of the British, "Thay was mad and fired Along the Shore."

The Americans let them go and focused on making sure the hay and cattle on the island would not fall into British hands. Lieutenant Innis and his men had managed to get away with some hay—Barker says seven or eight tons, Warren says one or two—but seventy or eighty tons were left behind, including several tons that had been carried down to the water and never loaded on board the sloops. The Americans put all that to the torch, and the barn as well. The cattle were loaded on the lighters and carried back to shore.

Lieutenant John Barker, for one, thought the whole affair was "the most ridiculous expedition that ever was plan'd." He criticized Gage for not sending nearly enough men or boats to do the job, but then Barker was not inclined to give Gage much credit for anything. The expedition did show that the spirit of Lexington and Concord was alive and well, and that the British could count on an armed mob, as well as organized troops, appearing whenever they ventured beyond their lines. It must have greatly increased the sense of isolation felt by the men in Boston. Nor were they finished engaging in gunfire over livestock and hay.

Chapter Eleven

THREE GENERALS

In Lord Dartmouth's secret dispatch, the one in which he strongly suggested Gage arrest the radical leaders in Boston, the letter that goaded Gage into sending troops to Concord, the American secretary also assured Gage that reinforcements were on the way. They would not be anything like the 20,000 men Gage had asked for but would include 700 marines, three regiments of infantry, and one regiment of light dragoons from Ireland. Gage would need a lot more food and hay.

The first of those reinforcements began to arrive in mid-May. Once again lines of white wedge-shaped tents sprouted on Boston Common as the new men were encamped as they arrived.

With those new troops, Gage would have around 6,000 effectives under his command. That was less than half the number of American troops currently encamped outside Boston. In the case of an actual fight, the American militia could be expected to turn out again to augment those troops, making the disparity at least three to one, or greater.

The secret dispatch from Dartmouth was delivered by Captain Oliver De Lancey of the 17th Regiment of Light Dragoons. He was the son of the De Lancey who advised Howe on Long Island and was sent from

London to assist with the purchase of mounts for the regiment. The dragoons, troops meant to fight on horseback or dismounted, would bring some horses with them, and Gage had been ordered to round up at least 200 more. Before he could act on that order, however, the opportunity was lost. Just days after De Lancey's arrival, and as a result of the letters he carried, the war had begun at Lexington and Concord. Boston was shut up tight and the rest of America in revolt. A month later Gage would write to Dartmouth, "Captain De Lancy went to New York two days after landing in order to purchase dragoon horses but the revolution that has happened in that town obliged him to return here again."

Along with the secret dispatch, De Lancey carried other letters from Dartmouth. One was written on February 22, assuring Gage that the reinforcements would leave soon (they were already at sea when the letter arrived) and that more might be sent as well. Dartmouth also wrote, "I have the farther satisfaction to acquaint you that the Major-Generals Howe, Clinton and Burgoyne are ordered upon service in North America and will take their passage to Boston on board one of His Majesty's frigates."

If sending the three major generals to Boston seemed to indicate a lack of confidence in Gage, that was because it did. The king and nearly all the members of Prime Minister Lord North's cabinet were disgusted by what they perceived as Gage's timidity and his conciliatory stance toward the rebels. Lord George Germain, who would supplant Dartmouth as American secretary, wrote to Lord Suffolk, head of the Northern Department, "I must then lament that General Gage, with all his good qualities, finds himself in a situation of too great importance for his talents."

In truth, the men in England, with no firsthand knowledge of the situation in America, did not appreciate the dilemma in which Gage found himself. Peter Oliver, staunch Loyalist and the Massachusetts chief justice, was stuck in Boston when he wrote to his brother-in-law (Peter's brother, Andrew, married Mary Sanford, sister-in-law to Thomas Hutchinson) in London, "You seem in England to be entirely ignorant of the temper of our people. They are as much determined from Florida to Halifax to oppose you at home, do what you will, as I hear the Ministry are determined to pursue their plan." It is no surprise that Thomas Hutchinson, who did understand the temper and nature of the people of Massachusetts, was one of the few Tories in London to suspect that Derby's first reports of Lexington and Concord were accurate.

Gage did not obfuscate or sugarcoat his reports, but the king and ministers refused to believe him and continued to insist that one good show of force would be enough to put the rebels in their place. On hearing about Lexington and Concord, George III wrote to the Earl of Sandwich, "Once these rebels have felt a smart blow, they will submit; and no situation can ever change my fixed resolution, either to bring the colonies to a due obedience to the legislature of the mother country or to cast them off!"

So, on April 20, as the men grievously wounded at Lexington and Concord were moaning in their barracks and the guards stood anxiously on the earthworks on Boston Neck, as militia from all over New England took up their guns and headed for Cambridge, and the Committee of Safety and the general officers contemplated the organization of a Massachusetts army, a frigate of twenty-eight guns set sail from Portsmouth, England. On board her were the three generals, William Howe, Henry Clinton, and John Burgoyne.

The frigate was named *Cerberus* after the three-headed hellhound of Greek mythology, a fact that was not lost on the humorists of the day.

Cerberus was not a large ship, and with her complement of 160 men she was a crowded one. The captain's great cabin, which was likely home to the three generals for the voyage, was a quarter the size of that enjoyed by Admiral Graves aboard *Preston*. Happily, though, *Cerberus* was a fast ship, as befitted a frigate, and on May 25 she stood into Boston Harbor, fired a salute to Admiral Graves, rounded up into the wind, and dropped her best bower anchor in seven fathoms of water. She had made the passage in just five weeks.

"About eight o'clock, heard the report of a great number of cannon," noted Ezekiel Price, a Boston exile, in his diary. The people he was with had various theories as to its origins. "Soon after, went down to Roxbury," he wrote, "found the firing of the cannon to be on account of the three new generals arrived from England." Then he added, apparently in reference to the things he had left behind in Boston, "None of my goods yet got out."

Of the three new generals, William Howe was senior, and also the only one who had served in America before, having fought in the French and Indian War. John Burgoyne was the junior of the three and, at fifty-three, the oldest. He had begun his military career at fifteen with a commission in the fashionable 13th Light Dragoons. His taste for clothes and high living earned him the nickname of "Gentleman Johnny" Burgoyne.

In 1743 Burgoyne eloped with Lady Charlotte Stanley, the daughter of one of England's leading politicians. Between that affair and the large debts he had accrued through his extravagant lifestyle, Burgoyne thought it might be healthier to live in Europe. In 1743 he "sold out," that is, sold his commission and left the service. He and Charlotte, to whom he was devoted, lived abroad for seven years. Eventually Charlotte's father forgave the elopement and helped Burgoyne secure a new commission in the army. It was that seven-year gap that led to Burgoyne's being older than, yet junior to, the other major generals.

Burgoyne had a solid reputation as a soldier. He distinguished himself in action during the Seven Years' War, and afterward was instrumental in developing the light cavalry for the British army. Though every inch the aristocrat with a firm appreciation for social hierarchy, Burgoyne insisted that his men be treated well, and his men in turn loved him for it.

Elected to Parliament, he took his duties seriously and held a dim view of the growing insurrection in America. In a speech in the House of Commons, given as he voted against the repeal of the tea duty, Burgoyne said, "I look upon America as our child, which we have already spoilt by too much indulgence. It is said that if you remove this duty, you will relieve all grievance in America; but I apprehend that it is the right of taxation which they dispute, and not the tax." The statement was a skillful blend of the obvious with an egregious amount of condescension, a style he would employ often in America.

The three major generals were intended to support Gage, but it would be wrong to think that any of them was any more skilled or experienced than their commander in chief. They weren't. Howe, Clinton, and Burgoyne would each get their chance to influence the outcome of the war. William Howe served as commander in chief after Gage's recall. He held that post until May 1778, during which time he managed to chase Washington's army around New York and New Jersey and to capture Philadelphia, all to little end.

Burgoyne is best known for his blundering attempt to hack his army's way through the woods from the southern end of Lake Champlain to Albany in the summer and fall of 1777. Though he had successfully taken Fort Ticonderoga and might have moved by water to the Hudson, Burgoyne's decision to cut a road through the wilderness wore his troops down and gave the Americans time enough to establish their defensive post. In October of 1777 they were able to force Burgoyne's entire army to surrender at Saratoga. It was that event that led to France's joining the war on the American side, and ultimately the American victory at Yorktown.

After William Howe resigned, Henry Clinton took over as commander in chief . He personally commanded at the Siege of Charleston, South Carolina, the biggest British victory of the war, but did little else. He found his headquarters at New York City so agreeable that he had little interest in stirring. His acrimonious relationship with Charles Cornwallis, commander of the British army in the South, helped bring about the Yorktown disaster.

That was all in the future. As the *Cerberus* came to anchor and the captain's gig rowed the three men ashore, the war was merely weeks old. In fact, the generals had only just learned that it had started. They were about to get a rude shock when they discovered what waited for them in America.

"THE BAULS SUNG LIKE BEES"

Across a narrow stretch of water northeast of Boston and west of the Charlestown peninsula there was, in 1775, an island known as Noddle's Island. Northeast of that, and separated from Noddle's by a strip of water that could be waded at low tide, was another island known as Hog Island. Noddle's was long and low and mostly flat. Behind it, Hog Island rose up in a high, gently sloped hill like Bunker and Prospect and the others that ringed Boston.

Today Hog Island has been subsumed into the stretch of land and landfill known collectively as Chelsea, and Noddle's, also no longer an island, is known as East Boston. Like so much of Boston today, it is hard to reconcile the densely packed urban landscape of Chelsea and East Boston with the all but unpopulated expanse of farmland that it was at the time of the American Revolution.

Noddle's and Hog islands, like Grape Island, were used mostly for growing hay and grazing animals. The Committee of Safety had its collective eye on them, even before the regulars made their surprise move on Grape. On May 14, the members resolved as their opinion that "all the live-stock be taken from *Noddle's* Island, *Hog* Island and *Snake* Island [a small island to the east of Noddle's], and from that part of *Chelsea* near the seacoast and be driven back." The committee recommended that the work be done by the local towns with "such a number of men, as they shall need, from the Regiment now at *Medford*."

Through his efficient network of informers, possibly by way of Benjamin Church, Gage got wind of the plan. On the day that the major generals arrived in Boston, Gage wrote to Admiral Graves, "I have this moment received Information that the Rebels intend this night to destroy, and carry off all the stock on Noddle's Island, for no reason but because the owners having sold them for the King's Use." Gage asked the admiral to see that the guard boats were particularly attentive and to take whatever other measures he thought best.

Graves assured the general that the guard boats would keep the "strictest look out" and that he would send an additional boat as far up-river as he could between Noddle's Island and the mainland. He also pointed out that stationing troops on the island was the "Most probable Means of preserving the Hay from being destroyed."

Admiral Graves had no need of hay, but he was still highly motivated to see Noddle's Island protected. There were a number of buildings on the island, including a home, a barn, stables, and outbuildings. Graves had rented one of the buildings to store "two large Cargoes of Lumber, Board and Spars." The material was for repairs needed by the frigate *Glasgow,* which had suffered damage in a grounding not long before. In addition Graves was storing "tar, pitch, junk, lumber and many other articles the store-schooner could not conveniently keep."

Graves wrote to Secretary of the Admiralty Philip Stephens, "The preservation of all these became of great Consequence, not altogether from their intrinsic Value, but from the almost impossibility of replacing them at this Juncture." Given that, it is surprising that Graves did not station a few companies of marines on the island. Perhaps he assumed Gage would follow his advice and station soldiers there, but Gage did not. As a result, the only protection for Noddle's Island was the guard boats patrolling the shore, the least likely direction for the enemy to attack.

It was late morning on May 27, a warm, lovely spring day, when 600 American troops splashed across the shallow water from Chelsea to Hog Island. Gunfire had echoed around Boston Harbor that morning as the fleet celebrated Graves's promotion to Vice Admiral of the White with a thirteen-gun salute from each of the ships, but now it was quiet.

The troops were a mix of men from Massachusetts, Connecticut, and New Hampshire, indicative of the growing national character of the army. Among them was the pious Amos Farnsworth from Groton, Connecticut, who wrote in his diary, "Went on hog island and Brought of [off] Six hoses [horses] twentyseven horn[d] Cattel And fore hundred And Eleven Sheep," a prodigious haul.

None of this activity was seen by the British. If the Americans were on the north side of Hog Island, the high slopes would have hid them from view. If the water was shallow enough to wade across, then it was likely too shallow for any guard boat to approach close enough to see what was going on. For several hours the troops remained unmolested as they made off with their bleating booty.

Around 2:00 P.M. a detachment of about thirty men was sent to Noddle's Island, Amos Farnsworth among them. "Went from hog island to Noddles island," he wrote, "and Sot [set] one Hous and Barn on Fiar."

The cattle rustling on Hog Island may have gone unnoticed, but it was hard for the British to miss the buildings and hay on Noddle's Island going up in flames. As columns of black smoke began rolling up from the fields on the low island, the ships in the harbor burst into activity. The journal of the flagship *Preston* reads, "At 2 P M. Saw a Number of Rebels on Noddles Island destroying some hay made the signal for Landing the Marines."

Aboard the ships scattered around Boston Harbor, marines turned up from below, their red coats on, white crossbelts in place, the short sea-service Brown Bess muskets in hand. They scrambled down the sides of the ships into the waiting boats, where the sailors in their blue jackets and round tarpaulin hats sat with sweeps held straight up. Aboard *Cerberus,* just one day in from England, they "disembarked our party of Marines P[er] Signal & sent our Boats on shore Man'd and arm'd to Assist the Troops." The *Glasgow* recorded, "The Adml made the Signal for all boats mann'd & arm'd to land the Marines on Noddles Island."

As the marines were heading for shore, Graves ordered the schooner *Diana* under the command of his nephew, Thomas Graves, to pass between Charlestown and Noddle's Island, stand in between the island and the mainland, and use her guns to prevent the rebels' escape. "There was no time to be lost," he wrote to Stephens, and with a dig at Gage added, "and assistance from the Army could not immediately be had."

It was low water between three and four in the afternoon when *Diana* stood into the river between Noddle's Island and the mainland, sailing slowly through the tricky shallows, her four six-pounder guns and twelve swivels blasting out to starboard and larboard. It was like running a gauntlet for Graves and his crew, with the men on Noddle's Island and American troops on the mainland peppering the little ship with small-arms fire.

Amos Farnsworth and the others were still wrestling with livestock when the *Diana* made her appearance. "Kil^d Some hoses [horses] and Cattel Brought off two or thre Cows one horse," he wrote. "I with five men got the horse and Before we got from Noddle's island to hog island we was fir^d upon by a Privatear Schooner But we Crost the river and about fiften of us Squated Down in a Ditch on the ma[r]sh and Stood our ground."

As Farnsworth and the others were falling back, the marines landed and pursued them past the burning buildings, toward the strip of water that separated the two islands. The Americans, squatting in their ditch just over the shallow river on Hog Island, now found themselves caught between the marines and the *Diana*. As the marines approached the river, the Americans opened up on them. "And thare Came A Company of Regulars on the marsh on the other side of the river And the Schoo-ner," Farnsworth wrote, "And we had A hot fiar untill the Regulars re-treeted. But notwithstanding the Bulets flue very thitch yet thare was not A Man of us kil^d Suerly God has A faver towards us."

Under fire from the marines and the schooner, Farnsworth and the others fell back to where the rest of the troops were waiting. It was around sunset when they crossed back over to Chelsea, their mission largely accomplished. They had deprived the British of a significant amount of fresh meat and fodder for their horses, but they seemed to be unaware of Graves's storehouse, which they had not burned. A few days later Graves would send men to empty the warehouse, with a gunboat nearby to hold off the rebels who threatened them.

Still, the navy would not get away unscathed from the fighting at Noddle's Island.

Admiral Graves had ordered his nephew, commanding *Diana,* "not to remain in the River upon the Turn of the Tide." Accordingly, as the sun was setting, young Graves put his helm up and began to head back toward

Boston Harbor, ghosting along with guns blazing in the fading light, and stabs of flame coming from the shore as the rebels gathering there returned fire.

Then, as she made her way past the island, the wind died completely, leaving the schooner drifting helplessly under the rebels' guns. The boats that had carried the marines to Noddle's Island were ordered to take her in tow. They pulled up the river through the blaze of musket fire, and tow lines were passed from the ship. The boat crews dug in with their long oars, pulling the schooner downriver, but "the Rebels kept a Continual fire upon them," the *Preston*'s journal recorded, "that they were at last ordered to cast off." Two men in the *Somerset*'s boats had been killed, two wounded.

The mainland was swarming with rebels, but Noddle's Island was deserted. Captain James Chads of the *Cerberus* ordered "two of our 3pdrs [three-pounder cannons] & a party of Seamen a Shore wh Ammunition &c." From a nearby ship, Graves sent two more guns. As the rebels fired on the drifting *Diana*, the navy guns fired on the rebels, as did the ship's boats, which pulled off a ways, then turned the swivel guns mounted on their bows toward the enemy.

The sound of the gunfire echoed all around Boston Harbor. Ezekiel Price wrote, "About sundown, the firing of cannon was very quick. Went down to St: Davenport's, but could hear nothing of the occasion of the firing." Admiral Graves could see the *Diana* was in serious trouble, so he ordered the armed sloop *Britannia,* a tender to the *Somerset,* to stand in to her assistance. *Britannia* drew as close as she could to the *Diana* and turned her guns on the rebels on shore.

It was around 9:00 P.M. when Israel Putnam arrived with two field guns and a reinforcement of men. With the sound of heavy gunfire filling the night, there was no way that Old Put could resist being in the middle of it. With him, serving as a volunteer, was his friend and admirer Dr. Joseph Warren, another one who could not stay away from the scene of action. The guns they brought with them were set up on shore and soon opened up on the drifting schooner, which returned fire for all she was worth. For two hours or more the warm night was torn apart by the blazing guns, firing at point-blank range.

Amos Farnsworth and his fellow soldiers had crossed from Hog Island to Chelsea and walked around to where the battle was now taking place. "About ten At night March^d, to Winnisimit ferry whare thare was A Schooner and Sloop Afiring with grate fury on us thare," he wrote.

Winnisimmet Ferry was a ferry landing on the mainland directly north of the gap between Charlestown Neck and Noddle's Island. The location today is in the town of Chelsea at the intersection of Winnisimmet Street and Ferry Street. At the time of the Revolution, heavy wooden beams, or ways, ran like tracks from the shore into the water for hauling boats out. As Graves reported, *Diana,* drifting under the rebel gunfire, "unfortunately got aground upon the Ferry Ways at Winnisimmet."

The tide was ebbing fast, and *Diana* settled on the ways. According to Admiral Graves "every means was tried to get her off," which probably meant pumping the fresh water over, tossing overboard anything that could be tossed, and perhaps "kedging," putting an anchor out and attempting to haul the vessel up to the anchor and free of the ways. Nothing worked, and with each passing moment the tide fell and she became more solidly aground.

Lieutenant Graves and his men put up a tenacious fight under impossible circumstances, with their vessel immobile and an enemy firing with field artillery and hundreds of muskets from the nearby shore. It was around 4:00 A.M. on the 28th when the tide finally ran out and *Diana* rolled over on her side, or "beam ends." The fight was over. Not only could Graves and his men not fire back, they could not even stand on the deck. Abandoning everything they had, save for the clothes on their backs (which were not much, given the warm night and the hot work), they were taken off by nearby boats and rowed to the *Britannia,* which was still standing by.

As the sun came up, the rebels waded out through the mud, Putnam leading the way, to strip *Diana* of everything worth taking. They liberated most of her rigging and sails, her carriage guns and her swivels, the contents of her great cabin, and even the clothes the sailors had abandoned. Then hay was stacked under her stern section and, according to Farnsworth, "we sot fiar to hur And Consumed hur thare."

None of the Americans were killed and only four wounded. One of the wounded, in Farnsworth's company, had a bullet go "throu his mouth from one Cheek to the other." Farnsworth summed up the night by writing, "Thanks be unto God that so little hurt was done when the Bauls Sung like Bees Round our heds."

News of the Battle of Chelsea, as it came to be known, electrified the Americans' camps. As Ezekiel Price heard the story, Putnam had led the entire expedition, from start to finish, and "it is said that this success has given the colonel [Putnam] and the country troops great spirits."

Once again the Americans had stood up to the vaunted regulars and come out the winners, fulfilling their mission on Hog and Noddle's islands and burning a Royal Navy vessel to the waterline. It was the first time since Lexington and Concord that the Americans and British had come to grips in any meaningful way. The next time would be at Bunker Hill.

ORDERS FROM LONDON

By the time they arrived in Boston, Howe, Clinton, and Burgoyne had had no fresh intelligence from that city for at least four months. Likely the last word they read from Gage was his optimistic January 18 dispatch to Dartmouth in which he told the American secretary that "the people's minds are greatly cooled and many begin to want courts of justice, and that the friends of government have showed themselves openly in many places."

Those opening days of 1775 had been a brief time of hope for Gage, when it looked as if he might be able to effect a change in the trajectory that America was on. He suggested to Dartmouth that "if a respectable force is seen in the field, the most obnoxious of the leaders seized and a pardon proclaimed for all the others, . . . government will come off victorious and with less opposition than was expected a few months ago."

In the five months since that was written, everything had changed, and the world that the three major generals stepped into when they came ashore in Boston bore no resemblance to the one described by Gage. "On our arrival," Clinton wrote, "we found, to our great astonishment and concern, that hostilities had already begun and that the King's troops were in consequence confined within a circle scarcely two miles diameter."

Burgoyne wrote, "It would be unnecessary were it possible, to describe our surprise or other feelings, upon the appearances which at once and on every side, were offered to our observation."

Letters from the generals sent back to England contained all the second-guessing of Gage one might expect. Clinton, who would "not presume to give an opinion" on the action at Lexington and Concord, did feel that "the first stroke in such a war ought to have been important and certain of success." Burgoyne, writing to Lord Rochford, secretary of state for the colonies, said the problem was not that Gage had tried to capture the stores at Concord; rather, the planning for the raid and "the want of preparation for the consequences" were responsible for "the per-plexity and disgrace which have followed."

The attack on Hog and Noddle's islands, coming just days after the generals' arrival, was a sharp illustration of the uncomfortable situation in which the British army found itself. In his letter to Rochford, Bur-goyne continued:

The cattle upon the neighboring islands in the harbour, (a poor stock, it must be confessed) were taken off in triumph; the houses of those who dared to supply provisions to the garrison, were burnt; an armed vessel of the fleet was burnt, and her guns taken away in the view of an admiral and lieutenant-general; and in the unfortu-nate situation to which things were then reduced, I do not know that they could have prevented these insults.

Howe also found reason to complain about Gage's performance and his overall strategy. He wrote to Adjutant General Edward Harvey that

the entire focus of the war should be shifted to the Hudson and Connecticut rivers. New York was more central to the colonies and considered more loyal to the king, and the Hudson provided access to the
interior. This was a strategy that would eventually become central to
British thinking.

If the ministers hoped that Howe would back up their claim that
Gage had men enough, they were disappointed. He called for a force of
19,000 men. With less, he felt, "this war may be spun out untill England
shall be heartily sick of it."

In the immediate aftermath of the Battle of Lexington and Concord,
Admiral Graves had recommended an aggressive move, taking the heights
at Roxbury and Charlestown and burning the towns. Gage had demurred,
arguing that he did not have men enough for such a move.

That situation was changing. In the first weeks of June, the reinforcements from Ireland that Dartmouth had promised began to arrive. With
them came the expectation that some move was imminent. Captain
Evelyn's thoughts were typical. He wrote to a friend on June 6 that since
Lexington and Concord things had been "tolerably quiet; but when the
forces from Ireland arrive, we shall no doubt commence an active campaign."

Gage likely would have made some move of his own accord, but now
he had considerable external pressure on him as well. Part of the pressure
was being applied by the three generals who had been sent out by Dartmouth to assist and had no desire to simply cool their heels in Boston.
Part of it was coming from Dartmouth himself, who sent another
lengthy letter to Gage by way of William Howe.

This latest letter, written on April 15, followed up on Gage's letter in
which he suggested that a sizable force in the field, the arrest of some of
the leaders, and a pardon for the others might mean a victory for government. This was an idea that Dartmouth embraced, and he informed
Gage that as governor and general he had everything necessary to put
the plan into action.

"The first two of these objects are already provided for," Dartmouth
wrote. With the reinforcements from Ireland, Gage had what Dart-

mouth at least considered a sizable force. He had permission to arrest the leaders of the radicals; in fact, Dartmouth had been pushing for him to do so for some time. As for the third, Dartmouth explained that "in virtue of the power already given to you by His Majesty's special commission under the Great Seal for pardoning treasons" he had the authority to pardon the rest.

Dartmouth felt that a proclamation announcing that policy would be "a proper test of that disposition towards submission which in your late dispatches you seem to think begins to show itself." The "late dispatches," of course, were written three months before Lexington and Concord. The entire situation was changed, the "disposition towards submission" tested and found seriously wanting. Events in America were moving way too fast for the trans-Atlantic communication of the eighteenth century.

Somewhat incredibly, and despite the fact that the start of the war had made Dartmouth's suggestion of a proclamation all but irrelevant, Gage issued one anyway. The situation was not unlike that prior to Lexington and Concord, where Gage obeyed orders from London though he probably knew better.

A worse decision on Gage's part, but not a surprising one, was turning to John Burgoyne for assistance in drafting the proclamation. Burgoyne had a reputation as a clever and sophisticated man of letters with some minor success as a playwright. He may well have offered his literary skills to Gage in a way that the commander in chief felt he could not decline. The proclamation came out in Gage's name, but it was written in Burgoyne's style, with all its overblown, pompous, and insufferable prolixity.

"Whereas, the infatuated multitude . . . ," it began,

who have long suffered themselves to be conducted by certain well known incendiaries and traitors, in a fatal progression of crimes against the constitutional authority of the State, have at length proceeded to avowed Rebellion; and the good effects which were expected to rise from the patience and lenity of the King's Government have been frustrated, and are now rendered hopeless . . .

For paragraph after paragraph it went on in that manner, at once patronizing and insulting. The proclamation touched on the recent history of the rebellion, how on April 19 thousands of armed persons "from behind walls and lurking holes, attacked a detachment of the King's Troops, who, not suspecting so consummate an act of frenzy, unprepared for vengeance, and willing to decline it, made use of their arms only in their own defense."

Since then, the text went on, the people had fired on the King's ships, stopped communication with the town of Boston, and "with a preposterous parade of military arrangement they affected to hold the army besieged." This last got a few laughs, even in London, where it was pointed out that the Americans did not *affect* anything, they did in fact hold the army besieged.

"In this exigency of complicated calamities, I avail myself of the last effort within the bounds of my duty to spare the effusion of blood," Burgoyne wrote for the governor, and offered "his most gracious pardon" to anyone who would lay down his arms, "excepting only from the benefit of such pardon Samuel Adams and John Hancock, whose offenses are of too flagitious a nature to admit of any other consideration than that of condign punishment" (one imagines Joseph Warren feeling pretty put out at not making that list).

The proclamation went on to declare martial law and to offer protection to "such persons as may have been intimidated to quit their homes in the course of this alarm," thus, in theory, allowing them to "return to their respective callings and professions," never minding the fact that there was not one thing the British army could do to protect anyone beyond the confines of Boston.

What Gage or Burgoyne thought they might achieve with that proclamation, beyond fulfilling Dartmouth's orders, is hard to imagine. It could not possibly have induced anyone to lay down his arms. In London it became the butt of the opposition's jokes.

To Americans, the insulting language was infuriating and reinforced the radicals' arguments. One soldier wrote in his journal, "Gages Proclamation read, a Blackguard thing," and expressed his indignation that

"Such a d-med Rascal" as Gage, "that has perjured himself so often," would deign to offer them a pardon. Abigail Adams understood that the proclamation, vile as it was, would only help the Patriot cause. In writing to her husband, she said, "Satan, when driven from the regions of bliss, exhibited not more malice. Surely the father of lies is superseded. Yet we think it is the best proclamation he could have issued."

Chapter Twelve

THE SIEGE OF BOSTON

By June 1775, after a siege of two months, with all communication shut off by land, the situation in Boston was growing decidedly grim. Peter Oliver, chief justice of Massachusetts, was at least able to maintain a sense of humor. Writing to his brother-in-law in London, he said:

> You who riot in pleasure in London, know nothing of the distress in Boston: you can regale upon delicacies, whilst we are in the rotations of salt beef and salt pork one day, and the next, chewing upon salt pork and salt beef. The very rats are grown so familiar that they ask you to eat them, for they say that they have ate up the sills already, and they must now go upon the clapboards. Indeed, now [and] then a hog swims across the water, and thinks it more honorable to be cut up in town, and ate at a shilling L[awful] M[oney] here per pound, than wasted out of town at 4 pence pr pound.

John Andrews, also trapped in Boston but not so sanguine about his situation, also railed against the price and scarcity of fresh food: "We have now and then a carcass offer'd for sale in the market, which formerly we would not have pick'd up in the street; but bad as it is it readily sells for eight pence Lawful money per lb . . . Was it not for the trifle of salt provissions that we have, 'twould be impossible for us to live."

Nearly half of the inhabitants of Boston had already left the city, fleeing like refugees and abandoning everything they had. About 6,500 civilians remained, mostly Loyalists of the working class. "You can have no conception . . . of the distresses the people in general are involv'd in," Andrews wrote to a friend in Philadelphia. "You'll see parents that are lucky enough to procure papers [permission from Gage to leave] with bundles in one hand and a string of children in the other, wandering out of town (with *only a sufferance of one* day's permission) not knowing whither they'll go."

Andrews was stuck. His entire net worth consisted of "between two and three thousand sterling" worth of furniture and goods that he was not allowed to remove from Boston. "I find an absolute necessity to be here myself, as the soldiery think they have license to plunder every one's house and store who leaves the town, of which they have given convincing proofs already," he wrote. Andrews suspected that the rule regarding merchandise was put in place specifically to detain people in Boston.

The people trapped in the city would not have been pleased to know that the siege would continue without respite for the next ten months. In those early days, however, there was nothing but uncertainty. One Loyalist trapped in the city wrote to a relative in England, "We are every hour expecting an attack by land or water. All marketing from the country stopt ever since the Battle. Fire and slaughter hourly threatened, and not out of danger from some of the inhabitants within, of setting the town of [on] fire." These fears were shared by much of the civilian population, who were at once afraid of the Patriots still in the city and afraid to let them leave.

On June 12 Gage wrote to Dartmouth reporting that he had "issued a proclamation for the exercising of martial law"; he included a brief description of the action on Noddle's Island and the burning of *Diana*. Dartmouth had in an earlier letter criticized Gage for not informing him of everything that was going on in America, and Gage sought to correct that defect. "As . . . it is your lordship's command that I should write fully upon the affairs of this country," he wrote, "I venture to give opinions I should not in any other situation take the liberty of doing."

Gage made good on that by telling Dartmouth something he did not want to hear, that the war was quickly becoming continent-wide, and rather than the 20,000 men he had once requested, he now felt that it would take 32,000 to suppress the uprising. He believed 15,000 should be employed in Massachusetts, 10,000 in New York, and 7,000 in the Lake Champlain region.

More to the American secretary's liking, Gage reported that the reinforcements from Ireland were beginning to arrive, including marines and part of the Royal Regiment of Artillery, with the rest expected shortly. "I do not, however, design to wait long for them before I make an attempt upon some of the rebel's posts, which becomes every day more necessary," he commented.

Though Gage recognized the continent-wide nature of the uprising, he intended to concentrate his force in Boston. New York was also in a state of rebellion, but he had far too few men there to do any good, and the reinforcements that Dartmouth was sending to New York would not be enough to help. Gage asked Graves to send a ship to sea to intercept those reinforcements and divert them to Boston.

This move put a crimp in Burgoyne's plans. Gentleman Johnny, ambitious and manipulative, had been angling for command of New York since before leaving England. He had planted the idea in the mind of Lord North, expressing his "surprise and concern that in the present crisis there was no person proper to manage the affairs of government in New York" and selflessly offering his service there at the head of three or four regiments.

Now, with New York all but abandoned, he had to come up with some other idea. The one thing he did not intend to do was while away the winter in Boston with no independent command and junior to three other general officers. Two weeks after arriving in America, Burgoyne was writing to Lord North suggesting he be sent as an envoy to some of the governors and the Continental Congress to negotiate with the friends of government and then return to England with the agreements he had collected as a first step toward reconciliation. His offer was not embraced by the ministry.

With the promise of reinforcements, the military was looking forward to some sort of breakout. The defeat at Lexington and Concord was humiliating enough, but to be trapped in Boston by "a rabble in arms," as Burgoyne put it, was too much. As the new troops arrived, the "effects on the spirit of the army was visible," Burgoyne reported. The question remained, what to do?

Burgoyne wrote to Rochford, "The sentiments of Howe, Clinton and myself have been unanimous from the beginning." The two primary strategic points around the city were the hills of Charlestown, in particular Bunker Hill, to the north, and Dorchester Heights, which was comprised of three hills arranged along Dorchester Neck, a truncated peninsula to the south of Boston. Both of those heights, as Burgoyne explained to his friend Lord Stanley, "command the Town, that is give an opportunity of erecting batteries above any you can make against them, and consequently are much more advantageous."

Every military officer on both sides recognized that the two points of high ground commanding Boston were the key to controlling the town. Of the two, Dorchester Heights was the more important, since cannons placed there could reach not only the town of Boston but the harbor as well, thus making the anchorage and waterfront untenable for shipping. With communications by land shut off, the sea lanes were the town's only supply line. Closing those would be the end for the British in Boston, as indeed it was the following March, when the Americans were at last able to mount artillery on Dorchester Heights.

In early June 1775, Dorchester Heights was unoccupied. The Americans were too focused on defending against a British attack to worry about taking an offensive position on the high ground, and they did not have the artillery to command the harbor. The four British generals, however, had little difficulty in reaching consensus on a plan. "First to possess Dorchester Neck by two redoubts," Howe wrote to his brother, Admiral Richard Howe, on June 12. The attack on Dorchester would be launched against two places simultaneously. "*Howe* was to land the transports at the point" at the north end of the Dorchester peninsula, Burgoyne wrote, and "*Clinton* in the centre." Burgoyne would "cannonade from the causeway or the neck," and each general would "take advantage of circumstances."

Once Dorchester Heights was taken, British troops would fall on Roxbury, sweeping down from Boston Neck to the northeast and Dorchester Neck to the southeast. A couple of hundred men would entrench in Roxbury, and Howe "would then go over with all we can muster to Charles Town Height, which is entirely commanded from Boston." Once Bunker Hill was taken, they would move on the American posts in Cambridge. "In either case, I suppose the Rebels will move from Cambridge, And that we shall take, and keep possession of it."

It was an intelligent and realistic plan, and according to Burgoyne, "the operations must have been very easy." He was probably right. For all the order and discipline that Ward, Thomas, Putnam, and the others had managed to bring to the American army in the two months of its existence, they were by no means ready to stand up against the British regulars in an open field of battle. There is every reason to suspect that the British troops would have rolled right over the American lines, just as they envisioned. They might have scattered the nascent army; indeed, they might even have delivered a serious check to the revolutionary movement.

It was decided that operations would begin on June 18—but the Americans never gave them the chance.

AN APPEAL TO CONGRESS

The Provincial Congress was worried. It was losing control of the army.

Joseph Warren had warned about this possibility when he first wrote to the Continental Congress urging them to take control of the armed forces and suggesting the possibility of a military government. In a private letter to Sam Adams he was more direct. He warned that "unless some authority sufficient to restrain the irregularities of this army is established, we shall very soon find ourselves in greater difficulties than you can well imagine."

Rumors and character assassinations were becoming common in the army and swept through the ranks like a communicable disease. Worse, the soldiers were beginning to take liberties with the private property of those who lived near the camps. Warren explained to Adams how the troops had first turned out with "nothing but the clothes on their backs, without a day's provisions, and many without a farthing in their pockets." The Patriots gave willing assistance to the soldiers, and where assistance was not given by those of a Loyalist bent, it was taken. "Prudence seemed to dictate," Warren wrote, that such liberties, born of necessity, "should be winked at."

Unfortunately, the attitude that the troops could simply take what they needed was becoming widespread and ingrained, and fewer distinctions were made between the property of Patriot and Loyalist. Warren, eager to find justification for the behavior of his countrymen, pointed out, somewhat weakly, "It is not easy for men, especially when interest and gratification of apatite are considered, to know how far they may continue to tread in the path where there are no land-marks to direct them."

The troops were also becoming more defiant of the orders of the Provincial Congress. Warren urged that the Continental Congress find a solution quickly, "as the infection is caught by every new corps that arrives." It was understood, at least by those in the Massachusetts government, what the solution required. A real civil government with the force of law had to be established in the colony, the army had to come under the direction of the Continental Congress, and the Congress needed to appoint a commander in chief who wielded more authority than Artemas Ward and who would bring the troops back into line before it was too late.

"You may possibly think I am a little angry with my countrymen," Warren wrote, and then assured Sam Adams that he was not. Warren tried hard to be circumspect and nonjudgmental. "It is with our countrymen as with all other men," he wrote, "when they are in arms, they think the military should be uppermost."

Joseph Warren may have been more inclined to see the problems as a temporary aberration, given that he, more than any other political leader in Massachusetts, was drawn to the military side of the rebellion. He was certainly not the only one to perceive the problem.

Elbridge Gerry, representative to the Provincial Congress from Marblehead and later signer of the Declaration of Independence, wrote to the Massachusetts delegates in early June. The people, he pointed out, had a very strong sense of their rights, since the rights of the colonies was the point that had been hammered home for so long in the growing dispute with England. Gerry wrote:

> They now feel rather too much their own importance, and it requires great skill to produce such subordination as is necessary. This takes place principally in the Army. They have affected to hold the military too high, but the civil must be first supported.

The problems between the civilian leadership and the military were apparently so widespread that word even reached the Loyalists holed up in Boston. Peter Oliver wrote to a friend, "The Army at Cambridge damn the Congress Orders, and the Congress are afraid of the Army, and Putnam will manage them all."

Gerry, like Warren, was looking to the Continental Congress to help establish a civil government in Massachusetts. Like Warren and others, too, he felt that "a regular General to assist us in disciplining the Army" was needed. Such a general, he felt, could train the Americans in a year or less "to stand against any troops, however formidable they may be with the sounding names of *Welsh Fusileers,* Grenadiers, &c."

Despite his being current commander in chief of the Massachusetts army, Artemas Ward was not mentioned for command of the Continental Army, not by Gerry or anyone else. There seems to have been a tacit understanding that Ward was not the man for the job.

There also seemed to be a growing consensus, at least among a certain faction of Massachusetts's leaders, as to who should be in the post of commander in chief. Gerry's letter closely echoes the earlier letter by James Warren on the subject. Gerry felt Charles Lee might "render great service by his presence and councils," though he knew "the pride of our people would prevent their submitting to be led by any General not an *American.*"

"I should heartily rejoice to see this way the beloved Colonel *Washington,*" Gerry continued, "and do not doubt the *New-England* Generals would acquiesce in showing to our sister colony, *Virginia,* the respect which she has experienced from the Continent, in making him Generalissimo." Gerry stated that Joseph Warren agreed with him on that point. John Adams, also a supporter of Washington, later claimed to have been the one to nominate him for the post of commander in chief. With the exception of John Hancock, who wanted the job for himself, the New England leadership seemed pretty well aligned behind Washington for head of the army.

Though the Massachusetts Provincial Congress was growing frustrated and impatient, the Continental Congress was in fact considering its various requests. On June 9 the delegates passed a resolution concerning the civil government of the colony. In it, they declared that no obedience was due the act of Parliament that altered the charter of Massachusetts or to any governor or lieutenant governor who would act to subvert the charter. Therefore, those offices were to be considered vacant. There was no legislature, either, since Gage had suspended it. Taken altogether, the Congress was of the opinion that no government currently existed in Massachusetts. The situation could not continue that way; "the inconveniences, arising from the suspension of the powers of Government, are intolerable," particularly given that General Gage had begun waging war.

The Congress was trying to tread a fine line between allowing Massachusetts to form a government and giving permission for anything that looked like a declaration of independence, which many in the Congress were wary of. It recommended, therefore, that each town in Massachusetts choose a member for an assembly, which would function as a lower house, and that assembly should then elect a council, which would form an upper house. Then the "assembly and council should exercise the powers of Government, until a Governor, of his Majesty's appointment, will consent to govern the colony according to its charter."

It was a decent compromise, and pretty much what Massachusetts already had with the Provincial Congress and the Committee of Safety. It gave the leaders in Massachusetts the permission they sought to form a new government, while assuring the more conservative members of Congress that they were not doing anything so radical as throwing off the authority of the king by forming a new government. The resolution ignored the fact, of which they were all perfectly aware, that Governor Thomas Gage *was* a governor of His Majesty's appointment. What they wanted was a governor appointed by the king who would take their view that the king had no right to alter the charter. That was something they were not likely to get.

Congress's adopting the army was a more ambiguous process. On June 10, Hancock, as president of the Continental Congress, wrote to the Massachusetts Provincial Congress that "the Congress have been so pressd with Business that they have been prevented Determining upon the other matters mentioned in your Letters," by which he meant taking over the army.

Though Hancock claimed that the Congress had had no time to consider the administration of the army, it had been considering army affairs. On the day after Benjamin Church arrived in Philadelphia with letters from the Provincial Congress, a committee was appointed to "borrow the sum of six thousand pounds for the use of America . . . and that the s^d [said] com[mittee] apply the s^d sum of money to the purchase of gunpowder." The most interesting aspect of this was that the gunpowder was, according to Congress, "for the use of the Continental Army."

It is the first official use of the term "Continental Army." Though there was no formal vote to adopt the army, at least none that was recorded, the Congress began increasingly to think of the troops around Boston as a national army under its direction. On June 9 it requested that New York forward to Massachusetts five thousand barrels of flour for the Continental Army. Colonies as far south as Maryland were asked to collect saltpeter and sulfur for the manufacture of gunpowder "for the use of the continent."

On June 14 the Congress voted to raise "six companies of expert rifle-men" from Pennsylvania, Maryland, and Virginia to "join the army near Boston"—the first time Congress had actually authorized men for the military—and drafted an enlistment form that signified that those who signed were enlisting as "a soldier, in the American continental army." That same day a committee consisting of George Washington, Philip Schuyler, who would serve as a major general, Silas Deane, Thomas Cushing, and Joseph Hewes was convened to "bring in a dra't of rules and regulations for the government of the army."

Bit by bit the Continental Congress was taking over the organizing, running, and financing of the army around Boston. Before that transition was complete, the ad hoc force that had developed out of the Lexington Alarm would be put to one last, bloody test.

COUNTERSTROKE

British plans for an attack on Dorchester Heights were not a particularly well kept secret. On June 13 the New Hampshire Committee of Safety wrote to the Massachusetts Provincial Congress, reporting:

> By a gentleman of undoubted veracity (who left *Boston* last *Friday* and who had frequent opportunity of conversing with the principal officers in General *Gage*'s Army,) we are informed there is a great probability . . . that General *Gage* will secure some advantageous posts near *Boston,* vis: *Dorchester* and *Charlestown.* We are unac-quainted with the importance of those posts, but if this hint should be in any degree useful, it will give us pleasure.

By the date, the "gentleman of undoubted veracity" must have heard of the plan almost as soon as it was agreed upon by the generals. On the same day that the New Hampshire committee was writing to the Provincial Congress, the Massachusetts committee of safety was reporting that "it is daily expected that General Gage will attack our Army now in the vicinity of Boston."

This could hardly be considered proof that they were alerted to the generals' plans, since that sort of warning had occurred frequently over the past two months. Diaries of soldiers mentioned frequent alarms. Four weeks earlier, by way of example, General John Thomas received information of a pending attack in Roxbury. "The information is Simular to what I have Recvd almost Every Day this 10 Days Past," he wrote back to headquarters. The letter from New Hampshire was specific about the places that would be attacked, though, and they were certainly the places the Committee of Safety and the council of war would expect Gage to hit. They likely paid closer attention to this new intelligence than they would have to something more general.

Nor was that the only warning they received. In a report after the battle, the Provincial Congress wrote that days before, they had "good intelligence that General *Gage* was about to take possession of the advantageous posts in *Charlestown* and on *Dorchester Point*." It is interesting to note that the Provincial Congress report specifically mentions the point, a detail that the warning from New Hampshire did not include, but one that was in Burgoyne's description of the planned action. This would certainly suggest that there were a few loose lips in Boston. Later, Thomas Hutchinson in London would write that a gentleman who had arrived there from Boston "heard General Burgoyne, as well as inferior officers," talking about the plan.

The Committee of Safety certainly had all the information it needed. The only realistic way to stop Gage and the regulars from taking the high ground was to take it first. The committee on June 15 wrote:

> Whereas it appears of importance to the safety of this Colony, that possession of the hill called *Bunker's Hill,* in *Charlestown,* be securely kept and defended, and also some one hill or hills on *Dorchester Neck* be likewise secured; therefore *Resolved unanimously,* that it

be recommended to the Council of War that the above mentioned *Bunker's Hill* be maintained by sufficient force being posted there.

The committee did not know what the situation was on Dorchester Heights and instructed the council of war to investigate, but there did not seem to be much interest on the American side for taking Dorchester. Charlestown to the north was a natural extension of the lines that ran from Roxbury all along the Back Bay, but the Dorchester peninsula was pretty well detached from the rest. In terms of creating an immediate threat to Gage, Dorchester Heights was two miles or more from Boston, whereas Charlestown was less than a mile from the city's North End.

The Americans' focus, therefore, was Charlestown. The idea of taking the high ground in that town was not a new one. An earlier resolve of May 12 had suggested fortifying Bunker Hill as part of the recommended fortifications between Cambridge and Charlestown, but nothing had ever been done about it. Certainly it was a provocative move. The rebels could fortify all they wanted around Cambridge, and Gage could have just as easily ignored them. A works on Bunker Hill, within long cannon range of Boston, was something else.

If there was a chief provocateur in the American ranks it was Israel Putnam, and it is no surprise that he is credited with being the foremost advocate for fortifying on Bunker Hill. According to the account written by his son Daniel some years later, Putnam had been distracted and lost in his thoughts quite often following the march he made through Charlestown to taunt the British. All of his life Putnam had been in the habit of muttering to himself, of thinking out loud, and according to Daniel that became chronic after the march. Putnam spent days wandering around saying such things as "Yes, yes, they must" or "I'll go with my regiment anyhow" or "I know 'em of old, they fire without aim."

The other officers, apparently, were somewhat divided on the advisability of taking Bunker Hill. While some sided with Putnam, others, such as Artemas Ward and Joseph Warren, were opposed on the grounds that they did not have any big guns to fire on Boston, and even if they did, they did not have enough gunpowder.

Putnam told them that they were mistaking his purpose. He did not want to fire on the British in Boston, he wanted to make the British come out and fight. This was exactly what the others were afraid of, and they pointed out that there was a good chance the troops on Bunker Hill could be surrounded and cut off. To this argument Putnam supposedly replied that, in that case, "we shall set our country an example of which it shall not be ashamed, and show those who seek to oppress us what men can do who are determined to live *free* or not live at all!"

Even if Putnam did not actually say that, it certainly was in keeping with his philosophy. Warren was supposed to have said in response, "I must still think the project a rash one. Nevertheless, if it should ever be adopted, and the strife becomes hard, you must not be surprised to find me with you in the midst of it."

Old Put surely would not have been surprised. Since the first gunfire of the Revolution Dr. Warren had raced off to be where the action was, at Lexington and Grape Island and Noddle's Island. Being a civilian, and not a soldier who was part of a regiment with an assigned post, Warren had the freedom to go where he pleased, and he took advantage of it.

Warren's passion for military affairs did not go unnoticed, and it's likely he made his ambitions in that line known. On June 14 the Provincial Congress sent a committee to "wait on the Hon. Joseph Warren, Esq., and inform him that this congress have made choice of him for second major-general of the Massachusetts army, and desire his answer to this congress of his acceptance of this trust."

It was an extraordinary move. Warren was thirty-four years old with no prior military experience. Every other man who held a general's rank was a veteran of the French and Indian War, a combat veteran, and old enough to be Warren's father. Warren of course accepted, which made him senior to everyone in the Massachusetts establishment save for Artemas Ward and John Thomas.

The Provincial Congress had apparently intended to give him the rank of "physician-general," but Warren had preferred "a more active and hazardous employment," which would suggest there was some negotiation going on behind the scenes. Wrangling aside, the Provincial Congress was sufficiently convinced of Warren's abilities that they offered him the number three position in their army.

The Congress's timing was perfect. In just days Warren would get all the active and hazardous employment anyone could want, in the first real battle of the American Revolution.

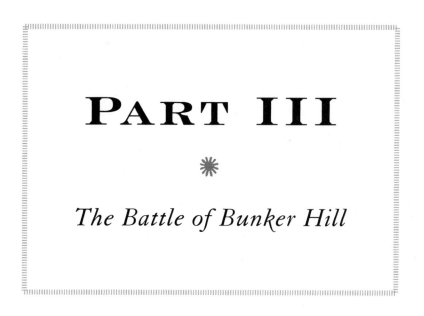

PART III

*

The Battle of Bunker Hill

Chapter Thirteen

CHARLESTOWN HEIGHTS

The Charles River, which separated the towns of Boston and Charlestown, snaked its way up from the southern part of Massachusetts. At the time of the Revolution there was a wide bay of channels and mud flats, known as Back Bay, to the west of Boston into which the Charles drained. Around Boston's North End the river narrowed again as it ran between that town and the peninsula of Charlestown, before channeling past Noddle's Island and emptying into Boston Harbor.

Charlestown sat directly north of Boston. At the point where Copp's Hill at the North End of Boston reached out toward Charlestown, the river was at its narrowest, only a bit more than a thousand feet across.

The peninsula on which Charlestown was located was about half the size of that on which Boston sat. It was roughly triangular in shape. The base of the triangle formed the north side of the peninsula, which was bordered by the Mystic River. At the western end of the base was Charlestown Neck, which, like Boston Neck, was a skinny pass that formed the only land route onto the peninsula.

Charlestown Neck was more narrow and low than Boston Neck and at high tide could actually flood, turning the peninsula temporarily into an island. On the south side of the neck was a mill pond, formed by a causeway that ran like a seawall from the mainland to the edge of the town. This causeway prevented any ship or boat from coming within 1,500 feet of the neck, the reason that the ships of the British navy could make it uncomfortable, but not impossible, for traffic to cross back and forth.

At the other end of the peninsula, the eastern corner of the base of the Charlestown triangle, was an area called Moulton's Point, or sometimes Morton's Point, at the confluence of the Mystic and Charles rivers. The town of Charlestown itself was located at the southern point of the tri-angle, the apex, and the point closest to Boston. Lengthwise, from Charlestown Neck to Moulton's Point, the peninsula was about a mile long. At its widest, running from the town of Charlestown to the banks of the Mystic River on the north side, it was about half a mile.

The town itself lay pressed between the heights and the Charles River, huddled at the base of the rolling hills that dominated the Charlestown countryside. There were around four or five hundred buildings arranged along a dozen or so irregular streets. The town was clustered tightly near the southern point of land and from there spread east, where the build-ings grew more sparse. A few wharves pointed like fingers at Boston across the water. Before the outbreak of fighting on April 19, the popula-tion had been around two or three thousand, but by June the town was all but abandoned.

The topography of the peninsula consisted of three hills that grew progressively higher from east to west. At the eastern end, at Moulton's Point, was Moulton Hill, a round hump thirty-five feet high and the smallest of the three. That area was named for one of Boston's earliest citizens, a shipbuilder named Robert Moulton who had settled there in 1631.

At the western end of the peninsula was Bunker Hill, named for George Bunker, a contemporary of Moulton's. Bunker Hill rose up from the eastern end of Charlestown Neck and at the time of the Revolution reached a height of about 110 feet. It was a rounded, smooth, gently slop-ing hill, more an elongated oval shape when viewed from above, running northwest to southeast, parallel to the Mystic River. The north and south sides of the hill sloped gently down to the water, while the eastern end merged with the high ground between Bunker and Moulton's hills.

It is a well-known bit of American trivia that the Battle of Bunker Hill took place on Breed's Hill, but that is a fact that would have surprised the Americans who fought there on June 17. There was actually no place called Breed's Hill at that time. The high ground that forms the center part of the peninsula, rising up sixty-two feet from the town of Charlestown along the waterfront, while certainly a hill, had no particular name. Part of it was known as Russell's Pasture, part Green's Pasture, and part Breed's Pasture. Some sources suggest that this area was considered part of Bunker Hill, that no distinction was made between the two. Others referred to it as Charlestown Hill, though notably none of those who did were from the Boston area.

Richard Frothingham, the nineteenth-century historian who is the foremost authority on Charlestown's history, was never able to locate a reference to "Breed's Hill" prior to the Battle of Bunker Hill. The name Breed's Hill came into use almost immediately after the battle and is used today, but it was unknown up until the day of the fighting. Thus the Battle of Bunker Hill, we find, was fought on Breed's Hill, which was not in fact Breed's Hill at all.

The hills were chiefly pasture land, open fields covered with grass that was probably knee high. One contemporary writer noted that "almost every housekeeper in Charlestown having a separate pasture for a cow, it was intersected by a vast number of fences" except for the area around the summit of Bunker Hill. The British troops would suffer greatly because of those fences. A few trees and orchards dotted the slopes, but for the most part it was open country, with no cover for troops on the march.

With the hills rising above the town and clear of cover, a battery on the Charlestown high ground would have an unobstructed field of fire on the city to the south. Whoever controlled the Charlestown Heights controlled Boston. By decree of the Committee of Safety, June 17 was set as the date when American and British troops would determine who that would be.

MARCHING ORDERS

The Battle of Lexington and Concord was a spontaneous event, a fight that grew organically from the Lexington Alarm and was carried out with no leadership beyond what little was provided by Heath, Warren, and the lower-ranking militia officers present. In that respect, the Battle of Bunker Hill might be considered the first real battle of the American Revolution, insofar as it was the first that was entered into deliberately and under the authority of some sort of military chain of command.

For all that, the action at Bunker Hill was not particularly well planned or thought out. Though it had been officially recommended more than a month before that a redoubt be established on Bunker Hill, nothing had been done to make it happen. When the sudden rush of intelligence regarding British plans to fortify Bunker Hill appeared in the second week of June, the Americans found themselves scrambling to react. The results were predictable. Captain John Chester, who fought toward the end of the battle, wrote, "Possibly the whole attempt was rather premature, and not thoroughly well planned. If we might again attempt it, we should, undoubtedly, have contrived and executed much better."

The official report of the Committee of Safety to the Continental Congress regarding the Battle of Bunker Hill states that "the New England army had, about the 14th ult., received advice that General Gage had issued orders for a party of the troops under his command to post themselves on Bunker's Hill." Since the Committee of Safety ordered the hill entrenched on June 16, they left themselves no more than two days to plan and organize their move.

In truth, considering how little preparation was done, they probably did not need even that much time. No written orders to the officers commanding the men on Breed's Hill survive, if indeed they ever existed. The Committee of Safety's report says simply, "on the 16 ult. orders were issued that a detachment of one thousand men should that evening march to Charlestown, and intrench upon that hill." The planning does not seem to have been any more extensive than that, and the men on Breed's Hill would pay the price for that lack of forethought.

The orderly book kept for Artemas Ward records, "Frye's, Bridge's, and Wm. Prescott's regiments to parade this evening, at six o'clock, with all the entrenching tools in this encampment." The regiments, only partially complete, were made up of Massachusetts men under Artemas Ward's command. Colonel James Frye's regiment had 493 privates; that under Colonel Ebenezer Bridge had 315. The third was under the command of William Prescott and numbered 456 men. It is likely that not all of those men were in camp. Certainly they did not all go to Bunker Hill.

Additionally, around 120 Connecticut men from Israel Putnam's regiment were detailed to join the Massachusetts troops as a fatigue party. Lieutenant Colonel Experience Storrs, a Connecticut officer, wrote in his diary on June 16, "Expecting an engagement soon, P.M. Orders came for drafting 31 men from my company, and the same from all the companies belonging to Connecticut."

The Connecticut troops were under the command of Captain Thomas Knowlton, a thirty-four-year-old officer from Ashford, Connecticut. Knowlton had served in Canada and Havana during the French and Indian War and had turned out with the Connecticut militia for the Lexington Alarm. A skilled and courageous officer, Knowlton would prove his worth at the Battle of Bunker Hill, though, like a number of other officers, he was not actually in favor of the operation. His career ended little more than a year later when he was killed in the thick of the fighting at Harlem Heights in New York.

Along with the infantry troops, an artillery company under the command of Major Scarborough Gridley with two field pieces was ordered to accompany the men. Some accounts suggest that the two guns were ones taken from the *Diana* at Noddle's Island. Also with the detachment bound for Bunker Hill was the army's chief engineering officer, Colonel Richard Gridley. Gridley was sixty-five years old, father of Scarborough Gridley and responsible for the younger man's promotion to officer of artillery, which caused some grumbling in the ranks. The elder Gridley, though an American, had held a regular British army commission and served with distinction in the French and Indian War. He was chief engineer at the reduction of Louisburg and was with Wolfe at the capture of Quebec. For his service he had been given half pay for life from the British army, which he gave up to side with his native country.

In overall command of the troops marching for Charlestown was Colonel William Prescott. Prescott was forty-nine years old. He stood over six feet in height, his head bald on top, his hair brown where it still existed, with blue eyes and a large and muscular frame. More than anyone else's, the Battle of Bunker Hill would be Prescott's show.

Like so many of his fellow officers, William Prescott was a veteran of the fighting in Canada during the previous conflict. So impressed were his commanding officers by his martial skills that they offered Prescott a commission in the regular army, an offer even George Washington never received, try though he might for one. Prescott declined, though, and returned to the large estate he had inherited in Pepperell, Massachusetts.

He held various civil posts there and with the militarization of 1774 was given command of a regiment of minutemen. On April 19 he and his soldiers turned out for the Lexington Alarm, though they did not make it to Lexington in time for the fighting. Prescott continued on to Cambridge, and once the regular army was established he joined with the rank of colonel. On June 16 he received orders to go to Bunker Hill.

The men mustered at 6:00 P.M. on the commons in Cambridge. They did not know why. The Committee of Safety ordered that the plan to fortify Bunker Hill be kept a profound secret, and somewhat surprisingly it was. Peter Brown, a private in Prescott's regiment, wrote to his mother, "Friday the 16 of June we were ordered on parade at six 'o Clock, with one days provision and Blankets ready for a March somewhere, but we knew not where but we readily and cheerfully obey'd."

Peter Brown was from Westford, Massachusetts, where he had taken his part as a private in the local militia. At the Lexington Alarm he turned out with his company and joined in the fighting as the British retreated, "pursu'd with the rest and fought that day." When the fighting was done he "tarried at Cambridge that Night, being forbid to go home."

Brown remained in camp after Lexington and Concord and seems to have joined the newly organized army for lack of anything better to do. "Soon after this," he wrote, "there was an Army establish'd all business then being stagnated, and a great deal wholly broke up, I did not know what I could do better than to enlist." He did assure his mother, however, that he was "hearty in the cause."

Also ordered to march that evening was Amos Farnsworth, who had recently been in the thick of the action on Noddle's Island. Farnsworth was also a part of Prescott's regiment, and for most of the 16th he was unaware that anything was in the offing. In the afternoon, however, he wrote in his diary, "we had orders to be redy to march at Six[.] Agreeable to Ordes our Regiment Preadid [paraded] and about Sun-set we was drawn up and herd Prayers."

The prayers, "fervent and impressive," were offered up by Dr. Samuel Langdon, president of Harvard College. That done, the troops, with their muskets, one day's provisions, and blankets, milled about the Cambridge Common as the sun sank in the west and the evening grew dark enough to mask their march.

Around 9:00 P.M. they moved out, falling into columns along the dusty road, William Prescott leading the way. "And about Dusk Marched for Bunkers Hill," Amos Farnsworth wrote, "under Command of our own Col Prescott." Farnsworth, of course, wrote that diary entry a day or two later. On the night of June 16 neither he nor any of his fellow privates knew where they were going.

The column moved east. Alongside the tramping men rattled carts filled with entrenching tools, and the two cannons on their creaking field carriages took their place in the procession. The road rose up as it crossed the southern part of Winter Hill, north of Phipp's Farm, where the British flank companies had splashed ashore on the night of April 18. The Connecticut troops under Putnam were camped at Inman's Farm, on the road between Cambridge and Charlestown Neck. It is likely there that Knowlton and his 120 men fell in with the column.

It is also likely that there General Israel Putnam joined the troops. Putnam had no official part in the action; there are no extant orders directing him to the field of battle. In fact, though Putnam deferred to them, neither Artemas Ward nor the Committee of Safety had any official authority over him and his Connecticut men. The committee had apparently felt authorized to order Connecticut troops to join those from Massachusetts at Bunker Hill, but Putnam had not been part of those orders.

On the other hand, there was no possibility of Putnam not taking some role in the fighting. He had marched his troops through Charlestown to taunt the British and had long been an advocate of entrenching on Charlestown Heights. Putnam knew from experience that Americans, once they were dug in, would fight like the devil. It was purported to be his favorite maxim that "the Americans are not at all afraid of their heads though very much afraid of their legs; if you cover these, they will fight forever."

Putnam's son Daniel, who was with his father in camp, suggests that there was an understanding between Prescott and Putnam, with Artemas Ward's knowledge, that the Connecticut general would take some part in the move to fortify Bunker Hill. It is difficult to gauge the accuracy of that; there is no other source beyond Daniel's statement, written secondhand and many years after the event.

In any event, Putnam was certainly there. His presence on the battlefield, which was undeniable and ubiquitous, would lead to years of acrimonious debate as to who was actually in command at the Battle of Bunker Hill. In the long view of history, a few things become clear.

William Prescott was the man officially tasked by Artemas Ward with command of the entrenchment at Bunker Hill, and it was Prescott who commanded the troops in the redoubt during the fighting. Putnam did not try to interfere with anything that Prescott was doing. Putnam, rather, took it upon himself to be everywhere Prescott was not; riding back to headquarters, going between Bunker Hill and Breed's Hill, organizing those troops who were not with Prescott in the redoubt. Thomas Grovesnor of Putnam's regiment, who was wounded at the Battle of Bunker Hill, would years later state, "Colonel Prescott was constantly with the troops; but General Putnam was backwards and forwards from Cambridge during the day, to bring on reinforcements."

To say the command situation at Bunker Hill was confused is to understate the situation. Because of Putnam's superior rank and reputation, and the fact that he was exerting some degree of command and control, many of the men who were not directly under Prescott's command looked to him for leadership and assumed he was the commanding officer. Others, such as Colonel John Stark of New Hampshire, appear to have operated completely on their own, never conferring with either Putnam or Prescott.

It takes a genuinely disorganized and ill-planned action, carried out by an army lacking a clear command structure, for there to be a question after the fact as to who was in charge. That was the situation as the 1,200 or so Continental troops marched through the late evening for Charlestown Neck and Bunker Hill beyond.

"A SMALL REDOUBT, ABOUT EIGHT RODS SQUARE"

The column passed Winter Hill, turned south for Charlestown Neck, and crossed that narrow strip of land between the Mystic and Charles rivers. "Jest before we turned out of ye rode to go up Bunkers-hill; Charlestown," Farnsworth wrote, "we was halted." At last the rank and file were told the object of their march, though most had probably guessed by that point. Sixty men were selected from the column to head off to Charlestown under the command of Captain John Nutting, who had been the commander of the minutemen in Prescott's hometown of Pepperell. This small division was intended to secrete themselves in the town and keep an eye on Boston for any sign of British movement.

Farnsworth was one of the men selected to go to Charlestown. "Capt Nutten heded us Down to ye town house," he wrote, "we Sot [set] our Centres [sentries] by yᵉ waterside; the most of us got in the town house But had orders not to Shut our eyes." Farnsworth was lucky in his assignment. While most of the men who had marched for Bunker Hill spent the night in backbreaking labor, he and his compatriots in the town house were faced with nothing more difficult than having to stay awake.

One soldier who did not go to Charlestown was Josiah Cleveland, a

Connecticut private. "We were halted at the Neck by General Putman," he wrote, "and ordered to load with two balls." Once the men were told of their mission and the division for Charlestown marched off, the rest continued on toward the high ground. "We marched in profound silence," Cleveland wrote, "General Putnam at our head." Cleveland, a Connecticut soldier, seemed to regard Putnam as the commanding officer.

From the end of Charlestown Neck the troops began to ascend the gentle slope of Bunker Hill. They moved quietly through the knee-high grass toward the summit, passing by what remained of the flèche that had been erected by the British as a defense against any further attacks on April 19.

The men came up over the edge of the rise and onto the broad, flat top of the hill, the wagons with the entrenching tools and the field guns bouncing after them, and there they stopped. Before the first pick bit into the first patch of sod, the most important question of all had to be answered—where would the redoubt be located?

The answer to that question would make all the difference. A redoubt on Bunker Hill would have anchored the left flank of the American lines. Properly outfitted with artillery it would have commanded Charlestown Neck and effectively cut off any chance of an overland attack from that direction, as well as controlling waterborne traffic on the Charles and Mystic rivers west of Charlestown.

However, a redoubt there would have been more than a mile from the closest point in Boston, extreme range for a twelve-pounder gun, and smoothbore cannon firing round shot were not much use at extreme range. It is entirely possible that General Gage, waking to see a new-built redoubt on Bunker Hill, would not have felt the need to launch an immediate attack. He might not have seen it as an intolerable threat to his position in Boston.

Breed's Hill was something different. It was a little over half a mile from the Admiral's Battery on Copp's Hill. Heavy guns there could sweep the entire North End of Boston as well as the Charles River from Noddle's Island to the Back Bay. Though lower than Bunker Hill, its proximity to Boston made it more of a threat.

If indeed the thinking was to create something the British would view as a clear and present danger, then fortifying Breed's Hill would do it. Lord Percy, for one, saw the threat it posed. Writing to his father he said, "The Rebels . . . flung up a very strong intrenchment in order to annoy both this Town & the shipping."

The Committee of Safety had been unequivocal in their instructions that the fortification was to be located on Bunker Hill, but even so definitive an order left room for discussion. Lengthwise, the top of Bunker Hill was 1,500 feet long. Did the pasture now called Breed's Hill constitute part of Bunker Hill? A decision was needed as to where on the hill the redoubt should be placed.

That decision was made by the officers standing in the grassy field on the night of June 16, though it is not entirely clear which officers they were. The only account of the meeting is secondhand, as are so many of the sources for the Battle of Bunker Hill. Samuel Gray, an American soldier, writing to a friend from Roxbury a few weeks after the battle, promised to give what facts he could concerning the events surrounding the decision, which he called, "a very confused transaction." According to Gray:

> the engineer and two generals went on to the hill at night and reconnoitered the ground; that one general and the engineer were of the opinion we ought not to entrench on Charlestown Hill till we had thrown up some works on the north and south ends of Bunker Hill, to cover our men in their retreat, if that should happen, but on the pressing importunity of the other general officer, it was consented to begin as was done.

The engineer, of course, was Richard Gridley. One of the "generals" had to have been Colonel Prescott, his rank misstated. He was the officer ordered by the Committee of Safety to take Bunker Hill, and it is impossible that he would not have been involved in that decision.

It is only reasonable to assume that the second general was Israel Putnam. Several accounts place him on the hill that night, including

Lieutenant Grosvenor's, which states, "General Putnam was with us and attended to laying out the ground for erecting the redoubt." Given Old Put's character it is hard to imagine him staying away. For that same reason, it is most likely that Putnam was the general advocating for the redoubt to be located on Breed's Hill. Putnam had already displayed a strong inclination to twist the lion's tail, and his seniority, reputation, and force of personality might have been enough to move Prescott and Gridley to disobey direct orders from the Committee of Safety.

It is also possible that Putnam was not involved in the decision at all. Prescott's son, Judge William Prescott, penned a long account of the battle based on the stories he had heard, likely many times, from his father. He wrote that after the troops passed the neck his father "called Colonel Gridley and the field officers around him, communicated his orders, and consulted them as to the plan intended for the fortification. Bunker Hill was named in the orders, but the whole height, it is said, was at that time often called by that general name." Judge Prescott, however, had a vested interest in showing that Putnam played little part in the battle and does not mention him at all in the course of his account, save for at the end when discussing how Putnam was not in command.

On the other hand, Putnam may have been advocating for Bunker Hill. It is certainly the case that he spent most of the battle on that height, and during the fighting tried to get men to throw up some sort of defense there. Prescott was without doubt in command on Breed's Hill, and he may have been the one to first push for that location. The fact is, we have only secondhand accounts and guesswork with which to reconstruct this monumental choice.

However it happened, the decision was made to fortify Breed's Hill, which even afterward the Committee of Safety would consider contrary to their instructions. In their official report, the committee chose to take a generous view of that disobedience, writing to the Continental Congress that rather than entrenching on Bunker Hill, the men "proceeded to Breed's Hill, situated on the farthest part of the peninsula next to Boston, for by some mistake this hill was marked out for the intrenchment instead of the other."

It is clear in hindsight that the Committee of Safety had no real vision of what they were trying to accomplish. One small redoubt would never be enough to hold off a determined assault by the British regulars, and 1,200 men were far too few to create more than that in one night, particularly as that night of June 17 was all but the shortest night of the year.

For about half an hour the debate went on, the men with their muskets and entrenching tools standing around on the dark slope of the hill while the commanding officers discussed where to place the redoubt. When it was at last decided, Colonel Prescott marched the detachment of men along the pastures that made up the wide top of Breed's Hill to the edge of its southern slope, as close to Boston as one could get on the crest of the hill, and there Colonel Gridley marked out the dimensions of the fortification.

The troops had been waiting for hours to begin. Now they piled their blankets and their packs with their day's rations to the side and exchanged their guns for entrenching tools. It was just before midnight when the picks and shovels finally tore into the earth, and "the clocks of Boston were heard to strike about 10 minutes after the men first took their tools in their hands." With a skill and strength born of a lifetime of farm work, which was the lot of most of the men there, they began digging down and piling up dirt along the lines marked out as the walls of the fortification.

The redoubt was not large. The Committee of Safety's report called it "a small redoubt, about eight rods square." A rod was five and one half yards (the same length as a perch), making eight rods around 132 feet. Peter Brown described the works as "ten Rod long and eight wide." British accounts would describe the men as entrenched up to their chins, making the walls of the redoubt around five feet in height.

The men worked like demons. Dawn would come around four in the morning, and they knew that once the British discovered them, the pounding would begin. If their cannon could, in theory, hit Boston from Breed's Hill, then the dozens of guns in Boston pointing their way could certainly hit them. Amos Farnsworth, struggling to stay awake in Charlestown, may have heard the soft scrape of shovels coming from the hill behind him. Those men, he noted, "begun thair intrenchment And Careed it on with the utmost Viger all Night."

Prescott was worried that the British would get wind of their work and begin a cannonade before the walls were high enough to afford any protection. Several times, in the company of a few of his officers, he trekked down to the edge of the Charles River to look out over the dark water, toward the town of Boston five hundred yards away. He listened for any sound of alarm from the admiral's battery on Copp's Hill or the men-of-war that swung lazily on their anchors. Reassuringly, he could hear the distant call of "All's well!" coming from the deck watch of the various ships. The British seemed to have no idea of what was happening less than half a mile away.

As the hours crept by, the redoubt quickly took shape. It was roughly square, 130 feet on each side. The front faced toward Charlestown and was augmented by three redans, or wedge-shaped projections, one from the center and one from each of the front corners, that allowed troops to enfilade, that is, shoot down the line of an enemy attacking the wall. A sally port, the only way in or out of the redoubt, except for going over the top of the walls, was built into the north side.

The working conditions were miserable. The weather had been dry, and the digging raised great clouds of dust. The men "were almost Suffocating with Dust & Choakin for want of liquor," one man wrote. "They expected to have been releaved early in the Morning but no releaf came."

Colonel William Prescott was the prime mover behind the men's efforts; it was his presence and determination that made them press on and drove them through the night. Israel Putnam's movements are often difficult to follow. It appears that he returned to camp during the night to make arrangements for the following day. Prescott, though, was a constant. As Private David How would recall years later, "If it had not been for Colonel Prescott, there would have been no fight. He was all night and all the morning talking to the soldiers, and moving about with his sword among them in such a way that they all felt like fight."

It was only three and a half hours from the time the digging began to when the sky began to lighten in the east, the first gray streaks of dawn intruding on the night's blackness. Slowly the thin light spread over Boston Harbor, just enough to distinguish the dark humps of the islands from the sea around them. The men in the redoubt did not pause to watch the sun rise on that flawless summer morning. Sweating, exhausted, filthy, and choked with thirst, they did not stop in their digging and their piling dirt on dirt as they built their ramparts higher. The walls of the redoubt and the darkness were their only protection, and soon one of them would be gone.

Around this time the detachment under Captain Nutting that had been sent to Charlestown to watch for any surprise gave up their posts and trudged uphill to the site of the digging. Another patrol under Captain Hugh Maxwell, which had likewise been sent to Charlestown to watch for an alarm in the British camp, returned and joined the men laboring at the earthworks.

At last the edge of the sun broke the clean horizon of the sea, and still the men dug. Privates, subalterns, officers, they all dug. Colonel Prescott moved among them, sword in hand, his words pushing them on. Down below, in the Charles River, halfway between Charlestown and Boston, the British ship *Lively,* of twenty guns and 130 men, floated motionless at anchor, looking more like a delicate model than an engine of war. Suddenly a plume of gray smoke jetted from her side. An instant later, and at almost the same time, the men in the redoubt heard the scream of the round shot go by and the dull thud of the gun firing a quarter mile away.

The redoubt had been seen. The battle had begun.

Chapter Fourteen

FIRST LIGHT

I t was eight bells in the middle watch, 4:00 A.M., when someone aboard His Majesty's ship *Lively* first noticed the fresh-turned earth walls of the American redoubt a thousand yards to the north.

The ship was moored in the middle of the Charles River, midway between Charlestown and the North End of Boston. It was a calm morning, "Modt [Moderate] and fair weather," her journal read. "Discover'd the Rebels throwing up a Redoubt on a Hill at the Back of Charles Town. Began to fire upon them."

Lively began her bombardment with amazing alacrity. She and the other ships may have already been cleared for action, that is, their extraneous gear stowed, guns ready for loading and firing. The journals say nothing about clearing for action, so it is possible, given the tense situation that had existed for two months, and the presence of a hostile army on the nearby shore, that the ships were kept in a constant state of readiness.

The gunners were shooting uphill, and the guns must have been at extreme elevation; even then it is possible they would not reach the redoubt. Not so for the Admiral's Battery, now known as the Copp's Hill

Battery, since Gage, seeing how useful it might be, took it over. "Insensibly," Admiral Graves wrote, "it lost its original nickname, and instead thereof was called by the army from hence forward Copeshill Battery." Graves had taken considerable pride in the "Admiral's Battery" and was likely quite annoyed to have it commandeered and rechristened by the army.

It is certainly understandable, however, why Gage would want control of it. The Copp's Hill Battery commanded nearly all of the Charlestown peninsula and the water around the North End. It was about twelve hundred yards from the redoubt, the closest point in Boston, and only a bit lower in elevation. It was not a difficult shot.

One by one the guns of the battery and the ships at anchor opened up on the offending redoubt. The frigate *Glasgow* had replaced the ponderous *Somerset* close in to the mill pond at Charlestown. At 4:30 A.M. she adjusted the cables on the two anchors mooring her and "Carried out the Stream Anchor to bring the Ship to bear on Charles Town Neck."

Throughout the night, William Prescott had worried that the activity on Breed's Hill would be discovered, and he was pleased to find no alarm raised until sunrise revealed the works. In fact, the entrenching was not as profound a secret as he believed. General Howe would write a few days after the battle, in apparent disgust at the lax attitude of the soldiers, "As a specimen of our knowledge of service, the centrys on the Boston side had heard the Rebels at work all night without making any other report of it, except mentioning it in conversation in the morning."

The sentries were not the only ones who heard the sound of shovels in the night. Just as he would later personally reconnoiter the Heights of Guana before formulating his plan for the Battle of Brooklyn, Henry Clinton had been patrolling the Boston waterfront, peering through the starlit night, trying to divine what was going on out there. On June 16 he scribbled a postscript on a paper: "Friday night just returned from reconnoitering and have strong suspicions that our C. [Charlestown] operations must proceed the other [Dorchester] . . . I have given in a proposal in writing, if we were of active dispositions we should be landed by tomorrow morning at daybrake as it is I fear it must be deferred."

It is significant that this was written the night before the battle, and thus is not the product of perfect hindsight, as so many such observations are. The whole affair is classic Henry Clinton. He took the initiative that none of the others did, used it to devise a unique strategy, and urged its immediate implementation, only to be ignored. It was the same way in which circumstances had played out at the Battle of Brooklyn. There, Clinton took it on himself to find the open pass on the Old Jamaica Road and advocated a bold move based on that intelligence. On Long Island, his advice was eventually taken, and the result was an overwhelming British victory. At Charlestown, his advice was dismissed.

In another note, Clinton wrote, "In the evening of ye 16th I saw them at work, reported it to Genls Gage and Howe and advised a landing in two divisions at day brake." Howe apparently liked the idea "but G Gage seemed to doubt their intention."

Despite the long-held belief that the British command was surprised at first light on June 17 to find the Americans entrenched on Breed's Hill, they were in fact aware that something was going on the night before. Still, no one besides Clinton was moved to take immediate action, and Gage was probably in bed when the first flat report of the *Lively*'s guns jolted him awake. He made his way to the observatory on top of Province House, the governor's residence, or to Copp's Battery and there first saw that the Americans had, in Burgoyne's words, "pushed intrenchments with great diligence during the night on the heights of Charlestown."

Gage likely brought a telescope with him and through the glass could see the men still furiously wielding their shovels, even as the round shot made dark streaks in the sky around them. Burgoyne added, "We evidently saw that every hour gave them fresh strength; it therefore became necessary to alter our plan, and attack on that side," and not Dorchester, as first intended.

Gage immediately ordered a council of war. No formal record of this council survives, nor is it known who was in attendance. Howe, Clinton, and Burgoyne were certainly there. Most likely Brigadier General Robert Pigot, who would serve as second in command at Bunker Hill, was also there, along with Lieutenant Colonel James Abercrombie, who had command of the grenadier companies, and Major John Pitcairn, who commanded the marines.

Lord Percy was probably not in attendance, having duty on the lines at Boston Neck. There is no evidence to suggest that Admiral Graves was there, either. Gage may have had enough of the cantankerous and uncooperative old man, but given that they would be attacking a place that was all but an island, the navy could be expected to play a big part.

It was universally agreed from the onset that the redoubt could not be suffered to remain. William Howe wrote to his brother, "This work was no sooner observed, than it was determined they must be removed from thence as soon as the troops and boats could be got in readiness for that purpose." The only question was how to root it out.

Henry Clinton, of course, had a plan. He felt it was crucial to strike immediately, within an hour or so of the decision being made. The attack would come from two directions. Howe would land with his force at a spot Clinton designated as "S.D. 2." It is not clear where that was, though it may have been Moulton's Point, where Howe did eventually land. Meanwhile, Clinton would take 500 men and take possession of the "Jews burying ground." Again, it is not clear where that is, as no such cemetery now exists, nor was it marked on any contemporary maps. Clinton described it as "within half gunshot of the narrow neck of communication of the Rebels."

Whatever landing places Clinton was advocating, it is certain he wished to get his men between the redoubt and Charlestown Neck to cut off any retreat and allow him to hit the rebel works from behind, while Howe made an assault from the other direction. It was a good plan, perhaps the best possible when all the strategic elements were considered. By moving fast, the attack could be launched before the rebels could substantially improve their redoubt. Clinton's plan took advantage of the British navy's control of the water to get troops in behind the American lines. It cut off any retreat from the peninsula and enveloped the American position with attacks from two sides. However, as Clinton noted, "My advice was not attended to."

It is not clear why Clinton's plan was dismissed. Gage may have been concerned that putting a force between the redoubt and the neck risked having those troops get caught between rebels sallying from the redoubt and reinforcements coming from Cambridge, thus trapping the British the way Clinton hoped to trap the Americans. Then again, Clinton's abrasive personality could often dissuade others from taking his advice.

Most likely, however, Clinton's plans were just considered unnecessarily complicated. From their vantage point in Boston, the officers could see only the south wall of the redoubt, and they did not know what they were looking at. "The general Idea was that the ridoubt was only a redan," Clinton wrote, that is, it was little more than a glorified flèche, opened in the back, and not a four-sided earthwork. From where they stood the British officers could not see the north side of the Charlestown Peninsula. They had no idea what was there.

In the council of war's opinion, "the hill was open and of easy assent and in short it would easily be carried," Clinton wrote. He disagreed. He felt that the redoubt was complete and reported that behind it there was "a double stone wall with a lane between by Which they [the rebels] could retire safely." Clinton may have earlier scouted the ground, or he may have been writing with the advantage of hindsight, but either way, he was certainly closer to being correct.

The story of the fight on Breed's Hill is one of terrific blundering on all sides. For the Americans, the blundering took the form of a frightful lack of organization, a failure to think through the objectives of the mission, and an unwillingness to commit the resources needed for anything beyond colossal failure. The end result would have been much worse for the Americans if the British had not blundered just as badly.

British blundering centered around an arrogant view of the ease with which the Americans would be driven off the hill. They did not employ anything more nuanced than a frontal assault because they felt they did not need to. They failed to take advantage of the most obvious benefits of their naval superiority. They did not even bother to reconnoiter the American redoubt before deciding how to assault it.

Howe's plan called for all the troops to be landed at Moulton's Point, but the water off that point was very shallow. The landing could only be effected at high tide, which was around two o'clock that afternoon, thus handing the Americans at least seven more hours to entrench and reinforce.

Once the troops were ashore, Howe envisioned sending a column up Breed's Hill while another marched along the shore of the Mystic River to flank the redoubt. It was a good plan, based on what Howe could observe from Boston, but Howe did not know the extent of the American defences, and in all the hours he was waiting for the tide he never once sent a boat around to reconnoiter. Indeed, it was not until he personally came ashore at Moulton's Point that he understood what he was up against.

The hills of Charlestown were certainly open country, but they were also crisscrossed with rail fences. Those fences would not have seemed much of an obstacle viewed from Boston, but one would think professional soldiers such as Gage, Howe, or Burgoyne would have seen the danger of troops bunching up under the enemy's fire as they slowed to climb over them or take them down.

Was Major Pitcairn there, or Lieutenant Colonel Francis Smith, or any of the men who had endured the slaughter of Lexington and Concord? Howe, Clinton, and Burgoyne had been in America for about three weeks and still harbored considerable disdain for the farmers in homespun who dared take up arms against the vaunted redcoats. It was the same attitude held by Gage, Percy, Smith, and the others before they had seen, at Lexington and Concord, what America soldiers could do when properly motivated and fighting in a manner in which they were comfortable. "Whoever looks upon them as an irregular mob, will find himself much mistaken," Percy had written after learning his lesson. Now it was the major generals' turn.

"THE ENENMY APPEARED TO BE MUCH ALARMED"

*"Saturday June y*ᵉ 17. The Enenmy appeared to be much Alarmed on Saturday Morning when they discvered Our operations and immediately

began a heavy Cannonading from a batery on Corps-Hill Boston and from the Ships in yᵉ Harbour." So wrote Amos Farnsworth, rejoining the others in the redoubt as the heavy fire from the ships and the Copp's Hill Battery tore up the air around them and thudded into the side of the hill.

The men did not pause in their work. The more substantial the breastwork, the safer they would be, so they pushed on, digging and piling dirt on the mounting walls. The art of building earthworks was fairly advanced by the late eighteenth century, and there were a number of structural elements that could be added to the walls to make them more substantial and more difficult to assault. These included fascines and gabions, which were bundles of wood used to give structure and reinforcement to walls, as well as chevaux-de-frise and abatis, such as Gage had used on Boston Neck. The redoubt on Breed's Hill had none of those things. As Clinton observed, it was "neither picketted pallasaded or ditched." There had been no time to prepare any of that. Instead, the works built in the early morning hours of June 17 were nothing more than sloping piles of dirt, around five feet high and more than a hundred feet long.

Peter Brown well recalled the heavy gunfire at sunup. "We not having more than half our fort done," he wrote, "they began to fire (I suppose as soon as they had orders) pretty briskly for a few minutes, then ceas'd but soon begun again." One observer in Boston claimed that Graves had initially ordered *Lively* to stop firing, and that may be the interval to which Brown refers. Brown also noted that with the coming of the light "we saw our danger, being against Ships of the Line, and all Boston fortified against us."

As daylight spread over the Charlestown peninsula, William Prescott took his first real look at the strategic situation he had placed himself in, and he was not altogether pleased. Given that the wall with the redans, which would be considered the front of the redoubt, was facing Charlestown, and the wall with the sally port was on the opposite side, Gridley and the others must have expected the British, if they came, to land at Charlestown and make an assault from the south.

Now, looking at the lay of the land around him, it occurred to Prescott that the enemy might instead land at Moulton's Point on the eastern end of the peninsula and attack from that direction. There was about one hundred yards of open ground along the top of Breed's Hill to the east of the redoubt, giving the disciplined redcoats ample room to mount an assault. With the walls of the redoubt only 130 feet long, it would not be possible to crowd more than 150 or so men in place to fire at the enemy. Prescott could see that he needed a longer firing line facing east.

"Having thrown up a small redoubt," he wrote to John Adams, he "found it necessary to draw a line about twenty rods in length from the fort northerly, under a very warm fire from the enemy's artillery." What Prescott calls a line was generally referred to as the breastwork, essentially a freestanding extension of the eastern wall. The northeast corner of the redoubt was near the edge of Breed's Hill, and the breastwork, continuing the line of the eastern wall, ran down the northern slope of the hill, an earthen wall running north about one hundred feet. Men who had been digging for hours in the redoubt were ordered out of those protective walls to throw up this new work.

Colonel Gridley had gone off somewhere, perhaps to rest or bring up artillery (Prescott wrote that "the engineer forsook me," but Gridley returned during the fighting), and Prescott was left to oversee the work. The fire from the British ships and batteries was terrific; the distant report of the guns, the scream of the round shot overhead, and the concussion of the balls hitting the earth all added a terrifying element to the exhausting work.

Abel Parker was with John Nutting's company keeping watch in Charlestown. When they arrived at the redoubt around dawn they found "the fort was in considerable forwardness, and the troops commenced throwing up the breast-work . . . We had not been long employed in that work, before the cannon shot from the hill in Boston, and the vessels lying in the river were pouring in upon us in great profusion." Despite the storm of iron, the men kept at it until the breastwork "would answer the purpose for which it was designed."

The report of the Committee of Safety suggested that the breastwork was meant to extend to the bottom of the hill, nearly to the Mystic River. That certainly would have made it more effective as far as preventing the British from flanking the redoubt by marching out of gunshot along the edge of the river, but the men "were prevented completing it by the intolerable fire of the enemy."

Though the breastwork made it only partway to the river, its northern end was anchored in a swampy area through which the regulars would have had a hard time marching. About two hundred yards west of the point where the breastwork ended stood one of the many rail fences that divided the Charlestown peninsula into a patchwork of pastures. Like the breastwork, the fence ran in a north-south line for about three hundred yards down the slope and nearly to the bank of the Mystic River.

The rail fence was not a particularly formidable barrier, made "half of stone and two rayles of wood." It was augmented, however, by a shallow trench in the ground running along the western side of the short stone base. "Here nature had formed something of a breastwork," one soldier wrote, "or else there had been a ditch many years agone." Insubstantial as the rail fence was, it would become a crucial link in the Americans' defense.

Together, the breastwork and the rail fence amounted to a defensive line that ran from the redoubt on Breed's Hill nearly to the Mystic River. Unfortunately, those two works were not connected. A gap of about two hundred yards remained open between where the northern end of the breastwork terminated and where the rail fence began, two hundred yards west of there. Part of that gap was rendered impassable, or at least difficult to pass, by the swampy area.

One map of the battlefield, drawn by British ensign Henry De Berniere, shows three small flèches, the V-shaped defenses, positioned in the gap between the breastwork and the rail fence. It is unclear when those were erected, but whenever it was done, it must have been done hastily, and they were likely crude affairs, probably built up out of rails pulled down off other fences. De Berniere's map, which was quite accurate in other ways, is the only such contemporary drawing to show these three flèches. They are not mentioned in any known reports, letters, or journals. Nonetheless, they probably stood as De Berniere showed them. Prescott would surely have recognized the danger that this two-hundred-yard gap represented in his defensive line and taken some measures to block it up.

It was around this time, with the British pouring fire at the redoubt, that the Americans suffered their first casualty. Private Asa Pollard and a few other men had, for some reason, ventured out of the redoubt when a round shot struck Pollard and killed him instantly. The wound delivered by a cannonball, as opposed to a musket ball, would have been gruesome indeed and frightening to the raw troops in the redoubt.

Word was sent to Prescott with a request for orders as to what to do. Prescott, likely sensing that it would not help morale to make a fuss over the man's death, and not wanting to slow down the digging for a funeral service, ordered that Pollard be buried immediately.

"What?" asked the subaltern who had gone for instructions. "Without prayers?"

That was exactly what Prescott meant, but one of the soldiers in the redoubt was a chaplain, and he insisted on performing a ceremony. Seeing this, Prescott ordered the men to disperse, but the chaplain managed to gather a small crowd again as Pollard was buried in one of the ditches left in the wake of digging the redoubt. It was around this time that some of the men began to slip away, unnerved by Pollard's death and the incessant cannonade.

Morale was indeed reaching a low point. "We began to be almost beat out," Peter Brown wrote, "being fatigued by our Labour, having no sleep the night before, very little to eat, no drink but rum, but what we hazzarded our lives to get, we grew faint, Thirsty, hungry and weary." As the sun climbed overhead the morning grew hotter, making the tiring, dusty work more torturous for the men in the redoubt. They had expected relief to come at daybreak—more men to wield shovels, and wagons bearing food and water—but none did.

The troops laboring away at the dirt walls began to grow suspicious. "The danger we were in made us think there was treachery and that we were brought there to be all slain," Brown wrote. Eventually he came to understand that it was incompetence, and not treachery, that had led to their suffering. "I must and will say," he added, "that there was treachery oversight or presumption in the Conduct of our Officers."

Sensing that the men were wavering, and that the British gunnery was shaking their resolve, Prescott climbed up on top of the walls of the redoubt and directed the work from there, strolling back and forth as the round shot whipped past him. One of his captains who understood why he was doing that did likewise. "It had the effect intended," Prescott's son, Judge William Prescott, wrote. "The men soon became indifferent to the fire of the artillery, which, though incessant, did but little injury to them or the works." As the day grew warmer, Prescott exchanged his heavy coat for a loose linen coat called a banyan. Prescott's son would recall seeing the banyan and his father's waistcoat rent with numerous holes made by British bayonets.

Judge Prescott also related a story that, if true, likely happened about this time. As preparations for the fight were under way, General Gage and some of his officers were watching from the Copp's Hill Battery. Among them was Colonel Abijah Willard, who was William Prescott's brother-in-law and who, just a few months before, had tried to dissuade Prescott from joining the American cause.

From Copp's Hill, the British officers could see Prescott moving confidently along the top of the redoubt. Gage handed a telescope to Willard and asked him "to look and see if he knew the person who appeared to have the command of the rebels." Willard looked and told Gage that he knew him well, the man was his brother-in-law, William Prescott, and was sorry to see him there.

"Will he fight?" Gage asked.

"Yes," Willard answered. "He is an old soldier; he will fight as long as a drop of blood remains in his veins; it will be a bloody day, you may depend on it."

To that, Gage replied, "The works must be carried."

Soon after daylight a number of officers approached Prescott and "represented that their men had brought no provisions with them, had been on severe fatigue all night, and were dissatisfied, and in no condition for action." They urged Prescott to call for fresh troops to relive the men in the redoubt, or at least send for reinforcements and provisions.

Prescott would not even consider having his troops relieved. "The men who had raised the works were the best qualified to defend them," he argued. "They had already learned to despise the fire of the enemy. They had the merit of the labor, and should enjoy the honor of the victory." One wonders how dogmatic the men wielding the shovels, thirsty and half starved, felt on that point. Prescott did, however, agree to send for reinforcements and food and water. The first would be a long time in coming; the second and third were never sent.

BRACING FOR THE BLOW

General Israel Putnam spent the night at camp with his regiment. If he was not awake before, the broadside guns of the *Lively* certainly jolted him out of bed, and he hit the ground with his usual unchecked energy. He sent off one of his lieutenants to Artemas Ward's headquarters to find a horse for him to use. By the time the lieutenant returned, Putnam had found a horse on his own and had galloped off to confer with Ward himself.

Arriving in Cambridge, Putnam urged Ward to send reinforcements to Breed's Hill. He did not find the commander in chief overly receptive. Ward considered every point along the Americans' extensive lines vulnerable to attack. Thanks to the boats of the Royal Navy, the British army could launch an assault nearly anywhere. Or they might come over Boston Neck. General Thomas's defenses in Roxbury were none too formidable, his troops thin on the ground and as ill trained and equipped as any in the American army. The cautious Ward did not dare weaken his existing lines to reinforce this entirely new front.

Having done what he could, Old Put mounted up again and raced off for Breed's Hill. He must have been impressed when he reined to a stop by the new-built redoubt. When he had left it the night before, it had been just a grassy field with lines staked out where walls should be. Now it was a genuine fortification, with a breastwork, which had not been part of the original plan, extending northerly from the east wall. The men were still digging when Putnam arrived, the enemy's shot filling the air. The Connecticut general could no doubt see that the men were in bad shape.

He and Prescott conferred on the situation, and Putnam agreed to return to Cambridge and renew his efforts to have reinforcements sent up the hill. Once again he mounted up and rode off toward headquarters. His frenetic activity was reminiscent of his abandoning his plow and charging off in his sweaty, dirt-covered clothes for the Lexington Alarm. One soldier who saw him would write, "General Putnam rode between Charlestown and Cambridge without a coat, in his shirt-sleeves, and an old white felt hat on, to report to General Ward, and to consult upon further operations."

Ward was still reluctant to weaken his lines and felt that the British would most likely strike at Cambridge, where the Americans' stores were located. The British were doing their best to encourage this belief and keep the Americans off balance. Lord Percy was stationed at the lines of Boston Neck on the morning of June 17. He informed his father a few days after the battle that he did not take part but "was only entertained by a pretty smart cannonade, wh[ich] we kept up from there upon Roxbury, in order to amuse the Rebels of that side."

Under the onslaught of Putnam's arguments, Ward began to waver. He sent orders to Colonel John Stark "to send a detachment of two hundred men, with proper officers," to reinforce the men on Breed's Hill. Stark's regiment was in Medford, north of Cambridge and about four miles from Charlestown. Being farthest from Cambridge or Roxbury, Ward no doubt felt they were the most easily spared. Stark, on receiving the orders, organized the detachment and sent them off under the command of Lieutenant Colonel Wyman.

By 9:00 A.M. the men in the redoubt could see a swarm of activity along the Boston waterfront, and they knew that the regulars would be coming soon. Prescott once again called a council of his officers and once again would not hear of having his troops replaced in the redoubt. He did, however, consent to send yet again to headquarters for refreshment and reinforcements. Putnam had been twice, to apparently no avail, so Prescott agreed to send Major John Brooks to make another request.

Brooks was ordered to take one of the artillery horses, one of the few mounts on Breed's Hill, but Captain Samuel Gridley argued that the field pieces would be in danger if he did not have his horses to draw them off. Incredibly, Gridley prevailed, and Brooks headed off on foot, arriving at headquarters around 10:00 A.M.

Ward had not changed his opinion and would not commit anything beyond meager reinforcements to Breed's Hill, but the Committee of Safety was meeting in the same house that Ward was using as a head-quarters, the home of Jonathan Hastings, steward of Harvard College, so Ward decided to turn the question over to the civilian leadership. After some debate, and an impassioned plea by Richard Devens, a member from Charlestown, it was agreed to recommend a more significant rein-forcement be sent.

Once again Ward turned to Stark's New Hampshire men, the regi-ment farthest from Cambridge and least able to help defend headquar-ters, ordering that they all march for Breed's Hill, but Brooks's walking to Cambridge, his relaying the orders to Ward, and their discussions with the Provincial Congress had all taken valuable time. It might have been as late as noon before the express rider clattered out of Cambridge heading for Stark's headquarters in Medford. In the end Stark's entire regiment, with Stark at its head, would make it to the battlefield on time, but just barely.

Captain Ebenezer Bancroft, of Bridge's regiment, was stuck taking part in a court-martial on the morning of June 17 while the rest of his company was entrenching on Breed's Hill. Desperate to be with them, he finally received permission from Ward to go. When Bancroft arrived at the redoubt he found "our men had left work and piled their en-trenching tools in our rear and waited in expectation of reinforcements and refreshments, but neither reached us if any were sent." Some time in midmorning the British guns ceased fire, a short but welcome respite from the constant bombardment.

The men in the redoubt were in bad shape. They had not slept in thirty hours and had been at hard labor for the past twelve. They knew that food, water, and reinforcements were to be had just a few miles away, but none of it was being forwarded to them. Then, around 11:00 A.M., the British guns started in again.

The ships and the Copp's Hill Battery "began to fire as brisk as ever," Peter Brown wrote, "which caus'd many of our young Country people to desert, apprehending the danger in a clearer manner than others who were more diligent in digging, & fortifying ourselves against them." Brown seems to suggest, not surprisingly, that those who were busying themselves with entrenching were not as susceptible to panic as those who had nothing to do but ponder their immediate future.

Putnam by this time had returned to Breed's Hill, racing around on his horse and organizing to the best of his ability. At the redoubt he saw the pile of unused entrenching tools on the ground. "My lads," he said, "these tools must be carried back." Prescott objected, suggesting that anyone detailed to carry the tools away would not return. Putnam was insistent, apparently thinking of beginning a new earthwork on Bunker Hill.

"An order was never obeyed with more readiness," Bancroft recalled. "From every part of the line volunteers ran and some picked up one, some two shovels, mattocks, &c., and hurried over the hill." Bancroft assured those left in the redoubt that their fellow soldiers would return, "though I was by no means confident that they would." In the end it is hard to know how many came back to the redoubt and how many used the tools as a means to desert their post. There were certainly many instances of both.

A small train of artillery, consisting of two guns under the command of Samuel Gridley and another artillery officer, John Callender, had marched with Prescott the night before. Reports indicate that more cannon were sent up in the morning. Samuel Trevett of Marblehead is known to have had charge of one gun. In all the Americans might have deployed as many as six guns of various sizes on the battlefield, but exactly how many there were and where they were positioned is difficult to determine. Nor is it clear how much good they did. Of the guns in the redoubt, Peter Brown wrote, "Our Officers sent time after time for Cannon from Cambridge in the Morning & could get but four, the Captn of which fir'd a few times then swung his Hat three times round to the enemy and ceas'd to fire."

According to Bancroft the artillerymen, who for the most part would not be conspicuous for their bravery, had all snatched up entrenching tools and disappeared. Prescott then turned to him and said, "If you *can* do anything with the cannon I wish you would. I give you charge of them." The redoubt was not constructed with cannon in mind. There were no embrasures or platforms on which to mount the guns. Bancroft ordered the men to start digging the openings through which the guns would aim, which they had to do with their bare hands, since all the entrenching tools had been carried away. To loosen the earth, Bancroft loaded the guns and fired round shot into the walls of the redoubt.

The morning wore on and lapsed into afternoon, the day getting hotter, with the men in the redoubt growing more hungry and thirsty and more filled with uncertainly as the reinforcements dribbled in and the provisions did not come at all. Still they worked as best they could to prepare for the assault. Amos Farnsworth wrote, "We with little loss Continued to Carry on our works till 1 o'Clock when we Discovered a large Body of the Enemy Crossing Charles-River from Boston." For the second time in two months, the redcoats were coming.

Chapter Fifteen

REDCOATS AND
BLUEJACKETS

About four hours after she opened fire, the *Lively*, sloop-of-war, hauled up her anchors, sheeted home topsails, and ghosted along in the light breeze, shifting her position from the Charlestown waterfront to near the Winnisimmet Ferry, where the *Diana* had met her end. From there she had a clear shot right up Breed's Hill toward the American redoubt, and her guns could cover the landing of the British troops at the eastern end of the Charlestown peninsula.

The big men-of-war were too deep to get close to Charlestown, so men were shifted from there to the smaller vessels that were able to work in close to shore. The sixty-eight-gun *Somerset,* with her complement of 520 men, sent 20 of her crew on board the smaller sloop-of-war *Falcon* and 30 on board the armed transport *Symmetry. Falcon* worked her way in close to Charlestown, between the peninsula and the North End of Boston, and lent her firepower to *Lively*. Her journal records, "By Springs on our Cable got our Broad side to Bear on the Rebells."

The "spring" line, attached to the anchor cable and run aft and then into the ship through a port in the stern, allowed the ship to be turned in almost any direction, despite wind or tide. With little room to shift guns laterally, aiming a ship's broadside generally meant aiming the entire ship. "Began to fire with Round Grape & Small Arms," the journal continued.

General Howe and Admiral Graves went aboard the *Somerset* to see if she could be warped in close to Moulton's Point to cover the landing, "but there was not sufficient depth of Water." This would be work for the smaller, more shallow draft vessels. *Symmetry* and a sloop named *Spitfire,* mounting six three-pounder guns, made their way up the Charles River, past Charlestown to the causeway, and there they joined *Glasgow* in raking the neck. Several scows, or gondolas, had also been fitted out, each with a twelve-pounder at the bow and stern, and they were able to get in closer still.

To add to the firepower, Gage ordered four twenty-four-pounders hauled up to Copp's Battery to augment the guns already there. By mid-morning the redoubt and Charlestown Neck were under a crossfire coming from at least seven different directions.

While the naval vessels were jockeying for position, the infantry and marines were preparing to go. In the months since Lexington and Concord, Gage's troop strength had increased, with new regiments sent out from Ireland and others collected from various posts in America. In fact, transports carrying the 35th, 49th, and 63rd regiments and the 17th Regiment of Light Dragoons had arrived so recently that many of those troops were still on board the ships anchored in the harbor, with part of two of the regiments still at sea. By June 17 Gage had around 6,400 men under his command in Boston.

After the fighting on April 19 the flank companies had rejoined their regiments, but on June 5 they had once again been pulled away and formed into two new regiments, one of grenadiers and one of light infantry. This was likely done in anticipation of some move against the rebels, such as the attack on Dorchester Heights planned for June 18. Now it was decided that the two regiments of flank companies would be sent to Charlestown, along with the 2nd Brigade, which consisted of the 5th, 38th, 43rd, and 52nd Regiments. Lieutenant Colonel George Clark was in command of the light infantry, and Lieutenant Colonel James Abercrombie the grenadiers.

The general orders for the morning of June 17 read, "The 10 Eldest Companies of Grenadiers and the 10 Eldest Companies of Light
Infantry . . . the 5th and 38th Regiments to parade at Half after 11 o'clock,
with their arms, Ammunition, Blanketts and the provisions Ordered to
be Cooked this Morning, They will March by Files to the long wharf."

As those troops paraded to the Long Wharf to meet the boats that
would carry them across the river, the 43rd and 52nd regiments and the
remaining flank companies were to march to the North Battery. After
the men heading for Charlestown were embarked in the boats, the
47th Regiment and the 1st Battalion of Marines were also to march to the
North Battery as a reserve and be ready to go when ordered. "The rest of
the Troops," the general orders read, "will be kept in readiness to March
at a Moments Warning."

The British units formed up and marched off by file, black shoes hitting cobbled streets with perfect rhythm, Brown Bess muskets held with
exactness, each company taking its assigned place in the regiment's parade order. Unlike the Americans' mishmash of civilian dress, these men
were perfectly uniformed with white breeches and waistcoats and red
regiment coats, each with its distinctive trim—yellow cuffs and facings
for the 38th Regiment of Foot, dark blue with white lace for the King's
Own, green trim for the 5th Regiment of Foot.

There could be no better example of the difference between the old,
well-established, professional British army and the nebulous mob that
would eventually form itself into the American army than the relative
ease with which each deployed to Bunker Hill. Around the time that the
British troops were marching to the waterfront, their fife and drum
corps playing a lively tune, regimental banners flying, Israel Putnam was
racing to Cambridge in his shirtsleeves and begging Ward to send more
men to Breed's Hill. While the redcoats moved off in their long, straight
columns, their provisions neatly packed in matching white goatskin packs,
canteens and cartridge boxes at their hips, the troops from Massachusetts, New Hampshire, and Connecticut, furiously building their redoubt,
were suffering from hunger and thirst and wondering if they were being
sacrificed by their officers.

Howe had about 1,600 men in the first wave of troops slated to cross over to Charlestown and another 700 waiting in reserve, giving him a total of around 2,300 men immediately available to him. The rest of the army had been ordered ready to move at a moment's notice. "Any man who shall quit his rank on any pretense," the general orders read, "or shall dare to Plunder or Pillage will be Executed without Mercy." That last order Gage may have felt was necessary after the retreat from Lexington.

With regard to where they would come ashore, Howe explained to his brother Richard, "as the shore where it was judged most proper to land was very flat," they had to wait until high water, around 2:00 P.M. "It was, therefore, necessary that no delay should be made in our proceeding." Yet it was seven and a half hours from the time that the general orders were issued until the first of Howe's men stepped out along the Long Wharf to find the ship's boats that would carry them the mile or so to Charlestown. Perhaps, with all the logistics involved in moving a third of the army across the Charles River, where they were expected both to fight and to make camp on the field of victory, seven and a half hours was in Howe's mind a rapid deployment.

Along with this organizational and logistical superiority, however, seems to have come a not so healthy dose of hubris, at least on the part of William Howe. Clinton, on seeing the American works, wanted to strike fast and immediately. He envisioned an attack launched just hours after daybreak, with an amphibious assault that would have cut Charlestown off from the mainland and trapped the rebels there. Clearly such a thing was possible, or a soldier of Clinton's experience would not have suggested it.

Howe apparently did not feel the need for so swift a reaction. He, along with Gage and the others, was not envisioning a fast raid, like the march on Concord, but rather an expedition to take and hold Charlestown. Howe apparently held his enemy in such contempt that he was willing to allow them an additional eight hours to strengthen their defenses and call up reinforcements while the British troops cooked their rations and packed their field equipment and waited on the tide to make their landing spot perfectly accessible.

Howe did not have to land at Moulton's Point, and he did not have to wait on the tide. The Charlestown waterfront had wharves on which the troops could have landed regardless of the height of the water. Indeed, the orientation of the redoubt on Breed's Hill suggests that the Americans expected a landing there, and an enemy advance from the south. American snipers shooting from empty buildings may have made the landing more difficult, but it is unlikely that they could have prevented it. Again, though, Howe preferred to wait.

The leaders of the British forces were still intent on carrying out the plan for taking Dorchester Heights and Charlestown on which they had already fixed, a move that was to have been launched on the 18th. The Americans had simply forced them to take Charlestown first, to "alter our plan and attack on that side," as Burgoyne put it, and to do it a day earlier than they had intended.

Clinton, too, in his memoir suggests that the presence of the Americans on Breed's Hill led to a reordering of plans, but not a change in strategy. In fact, after the fighting on Breed's Hill was over he returned to Boston still expecting to lead his attack on Dorchester Heights the next day, but the carnage of the Battle of Bunker Hill precluded that. "This plan . . . ," he wrote of the attack on Dorchester, "did not take place at all."

Clinton at least was willing to revise his strategy as circumstances dictated, as is seen in his suggestion of a fast attack. Howe apparently did not think that embattled farmers warranted that much consideration. There was no need for excessive hurry, no need for elaborate plans involving a landing on Charlestown Neck.

In the final reckoning, scores of British lives were wasted as men were flung against American defenses that would not have been there if Howe had not waited for his troops to cook their rations and for the tide to come in. Dozens of officers were shot down by American marksmen who would have been still in camp if Howe had moved at once and landed on the docks at Charlestown. The battle might have been over before Ward even sent word for John Stark to march his men to Charlestown. In the final reckoning, Howe realized as much.

The journal of the *Cerberus* recorded, "At Noon the Signal was Made for all Boats of the Squadron to Attend to the landing of the Troops under General Howe." From all over Boston Harbor, and Nantasket Road farther out, the heavy boats were swayed up off the ships' booms and lowered down into the water. Blue-jacketed sailors dropped easily to the thwarts and with practiced ease held their long oars up, waiting for orders.

Command of the squadron of boats was given to a midshipman named Cuthbert Collingwood. In later years Collingwood would command ships of the line in some of the greatest naval actions of the Napoleonic War and win fame as Nelson's second in command at Trafalgar. On that summer day in 1775, his diminutive fleet was meant only to move soldiers across a narrow strip of water. "P M at 1," the flagship *Preston*'s journal read, "The Boats of the Fleet and Transports repaired to the different wharves to embark the Troops and Ferry them over, which was done to the West side of Mystake River."

"MORE CONFUSION AND LESS COMMAND"

From the walls of the redoubt on Breed's Hill, the Americans could likely see the British troops gathering at the North Battery, the swarm of redcoats, bright flags waving, the barrels of their guns glinting in the sun. They certainly could see the flotilla of boats coming from the ships anchored out in the harbor and making for Long Wharf or pulling around Hancock's Wharf for the North Battery just across the river.

With the regulars on the move, it was now all but certain there would be a battle, and it would be on the Charlestown peninsula. The activity in the American camps became more frenzied, if no better organized. John Pitts, a member of the Provincial Congress, would later write to Sam Adams, "To be plain it appears to me there never was more confusion and less command. No one appeared to have any but Col, Prescott whose bravery can never be enough acknowledged and applauded.—General Putnam was employed in collecting the men but there were no officers to lead them."

Once the boats began pulling across from Boston, it was clear they were heading for Moulton's Point, which meant the attack would come from the east. A company of men under Captain Nutting was once again sent to Charlestown to take shelter in the empty buildings and annoy the flanks of the enemy as they marched toward the redoubt. Prescott also sent "Lieut.-col Robinson and Major Woods, each with a detachment, to flank the enemy, who, I have reason to think, behaved with prudence and courage."

At first light Prescott had realized that the British might attack from the direction of Moulton's Point and had ordered the breastwork built to defend against it. Now he could see that the attack would most certainly come from that direction, and he began to realign his forces. "The enemy began to land [at] a north-easterly point from the fort," Prescott wrote, so he "ordered the train [of artillery], with two field-pieces, to go and oppose them, and the Connecticut forces to support them," apparently leaving it up to the artillery and the Connecticut men where best to position themselves to resist the British landing.

The guns and supporting troops moved off toward the rail fence, which was several hundred yards west of the redoubt, running nearly from the banks of the Mystic River up the sloping ground where Bunker Hill merged with Breed's Hill. Prescott seems not to have taken note of where they went, as he came to believe that they had deserted him. Rather than take up a defensive position, he wrote, "the train marched a different course, and I believe those sent to their support followed, I suppose to Bunker Hill." Prescott displayed an understandable bitterness toward the men who deserted him and was quick and prolific in his accusations.

The Connecticut forces at that time consisted only of the 120 men under the very able command of Captain Thomas Knowlton. Prescott gave no specific orders to Knowlton, which suggests that it was Knowlton who saw the advantage of turning the rail fence into another breastwork to prevent a British move around the north of Breed's Hill. The

Connecticut men took their place at the southern end of the rail fence, farthest from the Mystic River and closest to the redoubt, but they were far too few to cover the entire length of the makeshift wall.

A number of men were beginning to congregate on Bunker Hill, within the field of battle but far from any danger. Some of these were the men who had carried off the entrenching tools, or otherwise slipped away from the redoubt. Putnam, as senior officer there, would spend a good deal of his time trying to get the men to build a second defensive work to help cover a retreat. He would also try to push men forward to augment the troops in the redoubt and the rail fence, with mixed results. As the only officer there on horseback, he would also spend time riding from Bunker Hill to Breed's Hill, instructing and inspiring the men there. One private was astounded that in the hail of lead he was never knocked from his horse.

In Medford, four miles away, John Stark received Ward's order for his "whole regiment to proceed to Charlestown, to oppose the British who were landing on Charlestown point." Another regiment of New Hampshire men under the command of Colonel James Reed was also ordered to go. Among Stark's men was a young officer named Henry Dearborn. Dearborn would end the war as a lieutenant colonel after taking part in some of the bloodiest fighting of the conflict. He would serve as secretary of war under Jefferson and see combat again in the War of 1812, though from the vantage point of a senior major general and commander in chief of the Northern Department.

On June 17, though, Henry Dearborn was just a twenty-four-year-old captain, a big, energetic man, but one with no combat experience. He had trained as a doctor, and like many of his contemporaries, such as Nathanael Greene and Henry Knox, who were too young to have served in the French and Indian War, he had made an academic study of military concerns. Now he would get some hands-on training.

Dearborn recalled that "orders were immediately issued for the march of a considerable part of our army to reinforce the detachment at the redoubts on Breed's Hill." Looking back after many years as a professional soldier, he could see how chaotic and amateurish the operation was.

"Such was the imperfect state of discipline," he wrote, "the want of knowledge in military science, and the deficiency of the materials of war, that the movement of troops was extremely irregular and devoid of every thing like concert—each regiment advancing according to the opinions, *feelings,* or caprice of its commander."

The deficiency in equipment, or "materials of war," that Dearborn alluded to would play a large part in the outcome of the day's fighting. The Americans were still struggling to acquire adequate amounts of gunpowder, and the lack of that item was one of the reasons that Ward was not terribly enthusiastic about an all-out fight on Breed's Hill. However, the Americans' needs went well beyond that.

Victory on an eighteenth-century battlefield often depended on an army's rate of fire, and a rapid rate of fire could only be maintained if a soldier was provided with cartridges, which consisted of a premeasured charge of powder and a musket ball wrapped in paper. Every British soldier was provided with these premade cartridges that he carried in a special leather case slung from his shoulder called a cartridge box.

The Americans were not yet set up for this sort of thing. Though the Committee of Safety had been gathering cartridges, none of them seemed to have reached the New Hampshire men. Dearborn wrote, "The regiment being destitute of ammunition, it formed in front of a house occupied as an arsenal, where each man received a *gill* [one-fourth of a pint] *cup* full of powder, fifteen balls and one flint."

That done, the captains marched their companies off to their quarters to roll the powder and balls into cartridges. Most of the muskets were the men's private property, and they were of varying calibers, which meant the balls had to be trimmed to fit. Few of the troops had cartridge boxes, so they put the powder in powder horns and the balls in a shot pouch. Soldiers using a powder in a horn and loose shot could not hope to load as fast as an enemy provided with premade cartridges.

It was around 1:00 P.M. when Stark's and Reed's regiments marched out of camp on their way to Charlestown. Like every other regiment in the American army, they were a mismatched lot. There were virtually no uniforms; every man marched in his civilian coat and breeches, a three-cornered cocked hat or a round-brimmed slouch hat on his head, his personal musket resting on his shoulder. They wore powder horns or shot pouches on shoulder belts, carried blankets rolled and slung over their shoulders, and toted any provisions in an eclectic mix of knapsacks and haversacks.

At Charlestown Neck they halted. Two regiments were in front of them, the troops considering the advisability of crossing while the British gondolas and the *Symmetry* and *Spitfire* were shooting a relentless barrage across the strip of land. Round shot, bar shot, and chain shot screamed low over the road. Stark sent one of his majors forward to ask the commanders of the regiments to move their men aside if they did not intend to cross the neck. The commanders agreed to that, and soon the way was cleared for the New Hampshire men to proceed.

Dearborn's company was in the lead, and so Dearborn found himself marching beside Stark, who "moved with a very deliberate pace." Considering the amount of metal flying through the air, Dearborn suggested they might try quickening the regiment's march, a suggestion that did not go over well.

"With a look peculiar to himself," Dearborn recalled, "he fixed his eyes upon me, and observed with great composure, 'Dearborn, one fresh man in action, is worth ten fatigued ones,' and continued to advance in the same cool and collected manner."

THE FIRST WAVE

A blue flag was the agreed-upon signal for the boats to push off from the Boston waterfront, and around 2:00 P.M., with the tide nearing its crest, it was hoisted aloft. From Long Wharf and from the North Battery the flotilla of bright white painted boats got under way, their long oars going up and down with the flawless rhythm of a man-of-war's boat crew, as if they were connected one to the other.

Each of the lead boats mounted a small cannon in the bow to sweep the shore of any opposition, but they were not needed and likely not

fired. As the fleet of boats pulled across the water, the men-of-war, *Lively,*
Falcon, Glasgow, and the others, stepped up their rate of fire, pouring
shot into the redoubt. One observer noted, "It was the heaviest cannonade previous to the landing." Such a bombardment might well have
stopped any American attempt to oppose the landing, if the Americans
had any intention of opposing it, which they did not. With their exhausted and disorganized troops and odd assortment of artillery, there
was not much the Americans could do to stop the British from coming
ashore.

One by one the boats pushed up to the point. The sailors unshipped
oars and scrambled ashore, bare feet splashing in the warm river water,
pulling the boats farther up so the red-coated troops could clamber out.
Lieutenants and noncommissioned officers called out orders for the
men to form up, shouting to be heard over the concussion of the guns.
Admiral Graves wrote that his ships covered the landing "and continued firing so long as they could annoy the Enemy without injuring our
own Troops."

The entire operation was carried out with a professional efficiency.
Brigadier General Valentine Jones, who had "seen many actions," was
moved by the "solemn procession preparative to this, in embarking the
troops in the boats, the order in which they were rowed across the harbour, their alertness in making good their landing, their instantly forming in front of the enemy."

The boats could only carry about 1,100 of the 1,550 infantry that made
up Howe's initial force. First over were the ten companies of the grenadiers and light infantry, along with the 5th and 38th regiments. After
they were landed the boats pulled back for the 43rd and 52nd regiments,
along with the artillery. There were a dozen guns brought over, four light
twelve-pounders (a "light" twelve weighed 2,900 pounds), four light sixes,
and four 5½-inch howitzers, and with them the blue-coated officers and
men of the Royal Artillery.

William Howe went across with the second embarkation. With him
was Brigadier General Robert Pigot. Pigot was a small man but a bold
and intelligent officer who would be conspicuous for his bravery that day.

As commanding officer of the 2nd Brigade he would serve as Howe's second in command.

Incredibly, it was only now, when Howe came ashore on Moulton's Point, that he finally got a look at what he was up against. At any time in the past ten hours he might have had a boat row him safely around the point and into the Mystic River, where he could have seen all of the American preparations, but he never did. Perhaps he felt that such reconnaissance, like Clinton's elaborate plan of attack, was not warranted when facing so unprofessional an enemy.

In the aftermath of the battle, much of the blame for these failures would fall to Gage, not Howe. It was Gage who would be recalled, his reputation in tatters, while Howe was promoted to command of the army. Certainly Gage, as commander in chief, bore the ultimate responsibility. However, Gage appears to have left the actual planning and execution of the fight entirely to Howe. After the initial meeting of officers and the issuance of general orders detailing the men to be sent to Charlestown, there is no indication that Gage exercised any further control over the deployment of the men. Howe had free rein, and the decisions made at Bunker Hill were his.

As Major General Howe came ashore on the eastern end of the Charlestown peninsula, he could see details of the American lines that were not visible from Boston. What had appeared as a redan when viewed from the south he could now see was in fact an entire redoubt, with a breastwork extending north one hundred feet from the small fort and running down the slope of the hill toward the river. His plan of attack had involved a flanking move along the banks of the Mystic River that would envelop the redan. Now he could see that that way was blocked both by the breastwork and by a rail fence farther west. If he observed the fence through a glass, which he likely did, he would have seen that it had been strengthened with additional rails, and the gaps filled in with something he might have recognized as straw. He certainly could see that dozens of men, perhaps hundreds, were rushing to take up position behind it.

One of Howe's young officers was twenty-year-old Francis, Lord

Rawdon, a lieutenant in the grenadier company of the 5th Regiment of Foot. Rawdon was another one who would prove his worth on the battlefield that day; as Burgoyne wrote after, "Lord Rawdon behaved to a charm; his name was established for life." On that June day, he would take part in the first set-piece battle of the American Revolution. Six years later, his health imperiled by his brilliant but exhausting work commanding the British forces in the South, Rawdon set sail for England. Soon after, the ship he was aboard was captured by the French fleet sailing north to blockade Lord Cornwallis at Yorktown. From the deck of a French man-of-war Rawdon would witness the end of the revolution in the former colonies.

As Rawdon came ashore by Moulton's Point and formed up with his grenadiers, sweat running down his face from under his tall bearskin cap, the young lieutenant surveyed the American defenses that he, too, was seeing complete for the first time. He later wrote to his uncle:

> The work we had seen from Boston was upon the heights just above this town, but upon approaching it we perceived that it was continued quite to the bottom of the hill on the side where we landed. We had halted for some time till our cannon came up, during which time we perceived great numbers of the enemy marching into their works. Our cannon fired upon the entrenchment for some time, but it was so strong that our balls had no effect upon it, and their men kept so close behind it that they were in no danger.

As Howe considered the situation, he realized that the Mystic River, not the Charles, was the point where the gunboats could be most effective. For all the iron they had been blasting at Charlestown Neck, they had done little to actually prevent anyone with nerve enough from crossing, chiefly because the causeway prevented the gunboats from getting close.

Among the various shallow draft gunboats were the "Gondolas" that Lieutenant Barker described as "large, flat boats, sides raised and musquet proof." They had been sent by Clinton against Charlestown Neck, and now Howe requested that they be sent around Moulton's Point to the Mystic River and the north side of the Charlestown peninsula.

Had the gondolas made it into the Mystic, they would have changed everything. They could have enfiladed the men at the rail fence and come to within a few dozen yards of Charlestown Neck from the north. As Barker put it, "They would have taken a part of the Rebels intrenchment in flank, and in their retreat wou'd have cut off numbers."

Unfortunately, when the artillery officer commanding the gondolas got the word to move, the tide was still flooding in the Charlestown River. The unwieldy boats were barely able to buck the current. By the time they got around Moulton's Point the tide had changed, the Mystic River was ebbing, and the boats were still fighting the current. "He quitted the first position where he was doing great service," Clinton grumbled, "and both tides being against him could not get to the second his service therefore was wanting."

Howe came in for considerable and justified criticism for not getting the gunboats into the Mystic River. A few weeks later, a British officer who had fought at Bunker Hill wrote a scathing criticism of the manner in which the fight was carried out. "We went to battle without even reconnoitering the position of the enemy," he wrote. The *Symmetry,* he argued, might have been towed around behind the American lines and brought within a musket shot of the wholly unprotected American left flank, "had we only wanted to drive them from their ground, without the loss of a man."

As the second embarkation of troops came ashore, General Howe was with them. Given the short time he had been in America, it was likely the first time he had set foot on the Charlestown peninsula. He reported that he "went on shore with Brig. General Pigot, and formed my little Corps in three lines, upon a rising spot about 100 yards from the beach." The rising spot, where Howe's right wing formed, was Moulton's Hill, or Morton's Hill. Howe then sent four companies of light infantry out a few hundred feet ahead. The left wing, made up of the part of Pigot's 2nd Battalion that had come over and the 5th and the 38th regiments, moved off toward Charlestown and the base of Breed's Hill. Between these lines the artillery was brought up to play on the redoubt.

As he took his first good look at the American lines, "seeing that they were pouring in all the strength they could collect," Howe understood that he needed more men. The 47th Regiment and the 1st Battalion of Marines, as well as some of the flank companies, had been left at the North Battery as reserves. Howe sent word to Gage that he wanted those troops sent over immediately. As that was happening, some of Howe's men dug into the provisions they had cooked that morning and had their dinner in the tall grass, under the clear June sky, and waited for the fighting to begin.

REINFORCEMENTS AND RESERVES

None of John Stark's New Hampshire men were killed as they marched steadily through the flying metal at Charlestown Neck, and soon they reached the top of Bunker Hill, where Putnam was in command. They paused there while the rear of the regiment caught up and Stark surveyed the scene.

As a Connecticut officer, Putnam had no authority over Stark, and it does not appear that Stark asked his advice as to where to station his troops, which would be in keeping with the New Hampshire man's character. From the top of Bunker Hill Stark could see the redoubt and the rail fence and possibly the British troops drawn up on Moulton's Point. He made his decision. He turned to his men, gave a "short, animated address; then directed them to give three cheers." That done, he led them down to the left to take up a position behind the rail fence, between Knowlton's men near the top of the hill and the Mystic River.

While waiting for the enemy to advance, Stark had the men strengthen the rail fence by pulling down other fences—and there were plenty of them—and adding the rails to their makeshift breastwork. The grass had been recently cut, and the men gathered up hay and stuffed it into the spaces between the rails, "which had the appearance of a breastwork, but was in fact no real cover to the men."

Where the pasture ran down to the river, it terminated in a steep bank, dropping down four or five feet to a beach that ran along the water's edge. The rail fence only went to the edge of the pasture, meaning anyone walking along the beach had an unobstructed passage around the end. Stark could see that this was a potential source of trouble, so he had his men pull apart an old stone wall and pile the stones on the beach from the end of the rail fence to the water. Behind this low stone breastwork he stationed three ranks of men.

In the end, Stark and the others had about an hour to improve their defensive position while Howe waited for his reinforcements. During that time more and more troops made their way over the neck and up Bunker Hill. Putnam had command there, riding back and forth between the hill and the rail fence, urging men to take their place along the makeshift wall. Dozens, perhaps hundreds, of men joined Stark, Knowlton, Reed, and the others facing the British landing to the east. Many others could not summon the nerve to leave the relative safety of Bunker Hill and march into the hail of iron beyond.

As the British troops came ashore and prepared themselves to advance, the pitch of alarm in the American camps grew more shrill. Whether Ward issued orders for more regiments to rush to Breed's Hill is unclear, but the word spread fast. Around 10:00 A.M. Lieutenant Colonel Experience Storrs had gone off from where the Connecticut troops were encamped near Cambridge to Bunker Hill to find Putnam "who has the command" (Storrs, an officer in Putnam's regiment, naturally considered Putnam the commanding officer). There was no great sense of urgency then. "Some shot whistled around us," Storrs wrote in his diary. "Tarried there a spell and returned to have my company in readiness to relieve them."

By midday that sense of calm was gone. Storrs recorded, "At noon orders came to turn out immediately, and that the regulars were landed at sundry places." Unfortunately, at the regiment's headquarters, Storrs received orders to march his men to one of the other works, called Fort Number One, near the river in Cambridge, and not Breed's Hill. When no redcoats appeared in Cambridge, Storrs abandoned Fort Number

One and was able to get to Charlestown in time to cover the Americans' retreat.

Connecticut lieutenant Samuel Blachley Webb wrote, "About one O'clock P. M. we that were at Cambridge heard that the regulars were Landing from their Floating batteries, & the alarm was sounded & we ordered to march directly down to the Fort at Charlestown."

Captain John Chester had just finished dinner when he heard the alarms. The night before, a subaltern, a sergeant, and thirty men had been drafted from Chester's company, part of Colonel Joseph Spencer's Connecticut regiment, to entrench. Chester was not one of them, and so he had remained in camp.

"I was walking out from my lodgings," he recalled, "quite calm and composed, when all at once the drums beat to arms, and bells rang, and a great noise in Cambridge." Captain Israel Putnam, oldest son of the general, came pounding up on horseback.

"What is the matter?" Chester asked.

"Have you not heard?" Putnam replied. "Why, the regulars are landing at Charlestown, and father says you must all meet, and march immediately to Bunker Hill to oppose the enemy."

Chester raced off to snatch up his gun and his ammunition and met up with his company. Spencer's regiment was apparently one of the few with uniforms, which, according to Chester, consisted of blue coats with red facings. The men did not care to make themselves conspicuous to the enemy, so they pulled their "frocks" and "trowsers" over their uniforms and marched off to battle.

Another man who turned out at the alarm was Dr. Joseph Warren. Warren had been taking part in the ongoing Committee of Safety work at the Hastings House in Cambridge, but on the morning of June 17 he was suffering with one of the disabling headaches to which he was prone. He had just found a bed and lain down to sleep it off when word of the alarm reached him. At that, Warren rose immediately, claiming that his headache was gone and that he intended to join the troops at Charlestown.

There are any number of stories about the many people who tried to dissuade him from going, "alleging that his Life was too much consequence to be exposed on the occasion." One story suggests that, to calm everyone's fear, Warren pretended to go to Roxbury before heading off for Charlestown.

On the road from Cambridge to Charlestown, Warren met up with a few friends, including one of his students. He must have arrived at Charlestown Neck not long before the start of the fighting, at a moment when the shot from the British vessels was really flying across the neck. Warren made it unscathed through that gauntlet and up Bunker Hill on the far side.

At the top of Bunker Hill, Warren met up with Israel Putnam. Most accounts of this meeting were written long after the event. In most, Putnam expresses sorrow at seeing Warren there, because "from appearances we shall have a sharp time of it."

With his promotion, Warren now outranked Putnam, and Putnam informed the doctor that he would "receive your orders with pleasure." Warren had not come with the intention of taking command, though, and, his rank aside, he was insightful enough to understand there was nothing he could tell a man like Putnam or Prescott about how to fight a battle. "I came only as a volunteer," Warren was alleged to have replied. "I know nothing of your dispositions, and will not interfere with them; tell me where I can be most useful."

Putnam directed Warren to the redoubt, and Warren crossed over the grassy hills and through the sally port. The walls of the redoubt were dried to a powder in the sun, the men within tense as they clutched their odd mix of muskets and looked out at the gathering enemy. Warren in his fine clothes made a stark contrast to the men in their homespun coats and filthy and sweat-stained shirts and waistcoats, but his presence was greeted with enthusiasm. The willingness of this gentleman doctor and political leader to stand with the troops in harm's way was a great boost to their flagging morale.

Prescott greeted him and, like Putnam, offered to turn over command, but again Warren insisted he was a volunteer, there only to help in whatever manner he could. With that, Dr. Joseph Warren, president of the Provincial Congress, chairman of the Committee of Safety, confidant of Sam Adams and John Adams and John Hancock, took his place at the wall of the redoubt.

Joseph Warren was one of the most active of the political leaders in Boston. The fact that England and her colonies had come to the point where their differences could now only be solved at the end of a gun was as much his doing as anyone's. And while many of his fellow leaders were risking arrest for treason in Philadelphia, Warren alone among them was risking death at the hands of the British regulars. Below him and off to the east Howe and his men were waiting for their reserves to cross the Charles River, while Warren and the new-minted soldiers all along the American lines waited for the deadly red columns to advance.

Chapter Sixteen

THE BATTLE OF BUNKER HILL

Howe intended to hit the American defenses from two directions. On the British right, he would push ahead with the grenadiers and the light infantry along the shore of the Mystic River toward the rail fence northwest of the redoubt. He would drive the defenders from the fence, then circle around behind the redoubt. Meanwhile Pigot's troops would come in between the town of Charlestown and the redoubt and assault the works from the front.

Regiments from Brigadier General Robert Pigot's 2nd Brigade had already pushed toward Charlestown. The 38th had secured themselves behind a stone wall halfway up the slope toward the redoubt. As they waited for the reserves to come across from Boston, they began taking fire from the American troops shooting at them from the deserted town. If the Americans were allowed to remain there, the British column would have them right on their flanks as they advanced toward the redoubt, which could be disastrous.

Howe was considering these difficulties when Admiral Graves came ashore at Moulton's Point "to be near General Howe, for the sake of seeing whether any further aide could be given." Howe complained to the admiral of "the mischief his left Wing sustained by the fire from Charles

Town." Graves, who for some time had been eager to burn Charlestown, asked Gage if he would like the town put to the torch. Howe answered, *"Yes."*

That was enough for Graves. In fact, the admiral had already made plans for burning Charlestown, having ordered his ships to prepare cannonballs heated until they glowed red hot for firing into the wooden buildings. Now he sent word to those ships to fire away, and also sent word to the Copp's Hill Battery (the former Admiral's Battery) to hit the town with special shells called "carcasses," iron balls filled with inflammable material designed to set their targets on fire.

Henry Clinton and John Burgoyne were at the Copp's Hill Battery. It was there, as Burgoyne wrote, that "Clinton and myself took our stand (for we had not any fixed post)." Their official duty was to command the battery. Clinton had also been instructed to "watch General Howe's corps and if you observe the smallest occasion to reinforce him," send word to the 47th Regiment and 1st Marine Battalion waiting in reserve. Of course, Howe had sent for those reserves even before the fighting started.

From Copp's Hill, the major generals had an extremely good view of the battlefield, with all of the Charlestown peninsula, from the neck to Moulton's Point, spread out before them. The three main hills were all but devoid of cover, so there was little to interfere with their observations. They could not, of course, see anything on the far side of the hills, so the rail fence and all of the action that took place on the British right were lost to them. Still, it was about as good a view of a battle as one might get before the advent of aircraft.

Burgoyne and Clinton were not alone in taking advantage of this quirk of geography. Brigadier General Valentine Jones wrote to a friend, "The rest of the army, that had no share in the action, the sailors on board the ships of war and transports, the inhabitants from the rising grounds, and from windows and the tops of houses, were spectators, and beheld with astonishment, true British valour."

From the battery, Burgoyne and Clinton watched Howe and Pigot deploy their men. "Howe's disposition was extremely soldierlike," Burgoyne wrote. "In my opinion it was perfect." From their vantage they could see the left wing under Pigot, consisting of the 38th and the 43rd regiments, swinging around the southern slope of Breed's Hill as it advanced toward the gap between the town and the redoubt. They could also see that the advance was not as smooth as they might have wished, but rather the men "met with a thousand impediments from strong fences, and were much exposed." Those fences would be the death of many redcoats that day.

With the noise and the smoke from the men-of-war and the firing of the battery on which they stood, the major generals did not realize that Pigot was taking fire from the empty buildings. "They [Pigot's men] were also very much hurt by the musketry from Charlestown, though Clinton and I did not perceive it," Burgoyne wrote. They only realized the problem when a boat arrived at the foot of the battery with word from Howe that "desired us to set fire to the town, which was immediately done."

The guns of the battery opened up with carcasses on Charlestown, just over 1,500 feet away, while Graves's ships poured heated shot into the buildings. William Cockran, who was on Copp's Hill at the time, observed that the first carcass "set fire to one of the old houses just above the ferryways; from that the meeting-house and several other houses were set on fire by carcasses." Cockran could not have known about the red-hot shot from the ships, but he did see men land from boats and set fire to the easternmost houses, where the buildings were more spread out and less likely to catch on their own.

The structures in Charlestown were mostly wood-frame and closely packed, huddled as they were on one of the few flat spots on the peninsula. The weather was hot and unusually dry, near drought conditions. The town took fire fast, one building after the other, and in less time than it took for Howe's reserves to cross the Charles River and land it was fully engulfed. A roiling cloud of black smoke lifted up from the brilliant destruction and rolled off northeast in the light afternoon breeze. It was suggested by some that the purpose of the fire was to blind the defenders in the redoubt with the smoke, but in fact the smoke was more of a problem for the British troops than the Americans.

Howe's decision to burn Charlestown was a reasonable one, given that it was abandoned, the Americans were using the buildings for shelter as they fired on his troops, and it presented a grave threat to his men as they advanced. Still, it was a sure bet that the Americans would not see it that way. Amos Farnsworth, for one, wrote that the town was "almost all laid in ashes by the Barbarity and wanton Cruelty of that infernal Villain Thomas Gage."

It was not long after that that the reserves reached Charlestown. They consisted of the 47th Regiment and the 1st Battalion of Marines as well as some of the flank companies who had been left at the North Battery. They did not land at Moulton's Point but rather at a point halfway between Charlestown and the first landing place, closer to where Pigot's left wing had advanced. Now, at last, nearly twelve hours after the first gun from *Lively*'s broadside announced the American works on Breed's Hill, the British were ready to attack.

THE AMERICAN POSTS

For the Americans, the waiting must have been intolerable. Certainly there were still things to do. Stark's and Knowlton's men likely worked at strengthening the rail fence until half an hour or so before the start of the fighting. Troops sent from Cambridge continued to arrive and take their places, both within the redoubt and along the breastwork and the rail fence. American artillery under the command of Major Scarborough Gridley, Captain Samuel Trevett, and Captain John Callender kept up a steady bombardment of Howe's troops from behind the rail fence. Contemporary maps show two American guns near the north end of the fence, close to the Mystic River, and others closer to the southern end. Some might have been positioned in the gap between the end of the rail fence and the breastwork, where the flèches were positioned. For all that activity, though, most of the American troops could only wait and watch the British prepare.

From the rail fence, particularly toward the Mystic River on the

American left, the view would have been limited. The troops there might have seen the loaded boats pulling steadily up the Charles River, dozens of white boats with rows of upright, scarlet-clad soldiers amidships, muskets held straight up, barrels glinting. They might have seen the boats disappear around the bulk of Moulton's Hill and wondered where they would come ashore.

Then, soon after and only eight hundred yards away, the perfect lines of redcoats appeared on the crest of Moulton's Hill, forming up for an advance. No doubt the men behind the rail fence tried to swallow with parched throats, their palms slick with sweat on the wooden stocks of their muskets. Many of them, particularly the men from New Hampshire and Connecticut, had likely never before seen British troops lined up in battle array.

They were braced for an attack, but it did not come. They did not know, of course, that William Howe had looked on their defenses and decided to call in his reserves, and because Howe was waiting for the new men to arrive, they, too, were waiting. The Americans were not about to leave their defensive works and meet the British on the open ground. The opening move would have to come when Howe decided to advance. So the Americans watched, and the fear built.

Those men in the redoubt would have seen it all. They could see the boats landing at Moulton's Point, the British troops coming ashore. They watched as the enemy formed in three lines on Moulton's Hill while the left wing pushed on toward Charlestown and the redoubt. In the cacophony of gunfire from the British ships and battery they would not have distinguished the sound of the carcasses or the heated shot slamming into the wood buildings of the town, but they did see the men sent ashore to make sure everything burned. Prescott reported to John Adams that "a party of the enemy landed and fired the town." Soon enough they saw the flames and the dark smoke rising from the doomed village.

Like the men at the rail fence, they waited for the British to advance, and they did not know why.

The British forces were led the way an eighteenth-century army was supposed to be led. Howe was in command. He decided on the disposition of his troops, and the order and manner in which they would attack. His strategy was carried out by Brigadier General Pigot and the colonels, majors, captains, lieutenants, ensigns, and sergeants under him. Once the fighting started, of course, that perfect order would break down, but still the firmest control possible would be maintained to see that the army moved according to Howe's will.

The Americans had no real order to begin with. The field, by default, not by planning, was divided up into three separate commands. General Israel Putnam was on Bunker Hill. He was the only general officer there, but he also had no official role, not having been given orders to take command of anything.

William Prescott commanded the men in the redoubt and those standing behind the breastwork. He had with him the remains of the 1,200 men who had initially marched to Bunker Hill, save for Knowlton's Connecticut troops, who had gone off to the rail fence, those he had sent into the town of Charlestown, and those who had deserted, carrying off entrenching tools or just slipping away. Prescott had lost a lot of men from the redoubt, but he had also gained some, having been reinforced by a smattering of Massachusetts companies under the command of Colonels Little, Nixon, Woodbridge, and Brewer and Major Moore.

It is difficult to know just how many men were in the redoubt. Prescott, in his letter to Adams, wrote, "I was now left with perhaps one hundred and fifty men in the fort," which seems an incredibly small number. Peter Brown wrote of "about 700 of us left, not deserted." That would seem a great disparity, but Prescott is specifically referring to men in the redoubt, whereas Brown might be referring to the men in the redoubt and those lining the hundred-yard-long breastwork, which would bear much of the brunt of the British attack.

The redoubt itself was a simple affair, four walls surrounding an open area about 130 feet square. Gridley would have marked the redoubt out in the tall grass, but the grass was soon gone, the sod dug up for material to build the walls, the interior space excavated to better shelter the men. The walls were five or six feet in height and made of brown, fresh-turned earth that grew dusty under the sun and relentless heat. On the interior of the works, the walls would have been as vertical as they could be made, and on the outside they sloped down to give the ramparts thickness at the base and make them more stable. A trench likely ran along the outside base of the walls from which the material for the redoubt was dug, and that would add one more minor obstacle in the way of any attackers trying to scale the walls.

To the west, and far less elaborate, the rail fence represented the third focal point of the fight. In many ways it was the most crucial. It was the presence of that minor breastwork that gave Howe pause and caused him to call in his reserves. Yet the rail fence was the most ad hoc of all the American defenses. Dearborn wrote that his position there was "more the result of accident than any regularity of formation."

Captain John Chester suggested that it was "our officers in command," meaning, presumably, Prescott and his officers, who realized that the British intended to flank the redoubt and so "ordered a large body of men (chiefly Connecticut) to leave the fort, and march down and oppose the right wing." Those men were the troops under Knowlton's command who had been sent to oppose the British landing and who Prescott actually thought had deserted. Chester says that the Connecticut troops "had time to form somewhat regularly behind a fence half of stone and two rayles of wood."

Colonel Prescott, focused on the defense of the redoubt, knew little of the strategic situation beyond his earthen walls. He received no word, no instructions, intelligence, or even reassurance, from Ward or any of the other officers in command at Cambridge. With regard to the other defenses, he wrote to Adams, "There was a party of Hampshire, in conjunction with some other forces, lined a fence at the distance of three score rods back of the fort, partly to the north." From this it is clear that Prescott had little knowledge and no command of what was taking place at the rail fence.

John Stark was the closest thing to a commanding officer at the fence, and there is no indication that he ever spoke to Prescott during the course of the day. His New Hampshire men were at the northern end of the line closest to the Mystic River. Next to them was another, smaller

New Hampshire regiment under the command of Colonel James Reed. Some Massachusetts troops had apparently taken post at the rail fence as well, and at the southern end were Knowlton's Connecticut men and apparently artillery under the command of Captain John Callender, though the location and activity of the American guns that day is very hard to trace.

Also at the rail fence was sixty-nine-year-old Seth Pomeroy, who, like Joseph Warren, was a major general serving as a volunteer without command. He had served with engineer Richard Gridley in the reduction of Louisburg in 1745 and as a lieutenant colonel in the Lake Champlain region during the French and Indian War. When the Committee of Safety began to organize the Massachusetts army, they named Pomeroy as major general, though he had not yet taken any active role. Now, musket in hand, he stood with the amateur soldiers under John Stark's command.

The veterans of the French and Indian War, Putnam, Prescott, and Stark, knew a few things about combat. They understood, for instance, the tendency of soldiers to shoot high, so their bullets passed safely over the enemy's head. Any number of battlefield accounts speak to this tendency. Prescott's son recalled his father's warning the men to "take good aim, and be particularly careful not to shoot over their heads; aim at their *hips*." Similar instructions were given emphatically by the other officers.

The veteran commanders understood as well that panicked men, frightened by the disciplined and seemingly unstoppable British lines, would fire at long range and waste their best chance to do real damage. The men were admonished to hold their fire until they were given the order. Some accounts suggest Stark placed a mark on the beach eight or ten rods, or about one hundred and fifty feet, from the hastily built stone wall and ordered his men not to fire until the redcoats had reached that point. The men "on the bank immediately under his eye, were directed to reserve their fire until they could see the enemy's half gaiters."

Israel Putnam was was all over the place. He was at the rail fence some time before the start of the action and may have been there during part of the fighting. One soldier in Colonel Little's regiment recalled that "Gen. Putnam . . . was riding to and fro in all parts of the line, encouraging the men, pressing them forward, and giving orders to the officers. He did not stop long in any one place." Putnam by many accounts was riding back and forth behind the rail fence, giving orders and encouragement. He, like the others, instructed the men to hold their fire and to shoot low.

Private Philip Johnson recalled, many years later (and, indeed, most of the testimony from the men at Breed's Hill was taken many years later), that Putnam rode up to where he was standing at the rail fence just before the battle. "Men, you know you are all marksmen, you can take a squirrel from the tallest tree," Putnam called. "Don't fire till you see the whites of their eyes."

Others would claim to have heard that same order, and it is certainly possible that Putnam said it. It would not have been original to him. It was an expression in use at the time, somewhat standard advice to soldiers before a battle, which makes it even more likely that Putnam employed the phrase. Either way, the words would work their way into the nation's historical imagination and become a standard and well-known part of Bunker Hill lore, even if few Americans today could name the man who was supposed to have said them. Israel Putnam's "Don't fire until you see the whites of their eyes!" takes its permanent seat beside Paul Revere's "The British are coming!" (which is most certainly a misquote).

Because of the regularity of the British army, it is fairly simple to arrive at a dependable estimate of the number of troops involved and see that it lines up closely with Howe's given number of 2,300.

Because the Americans' situation was so chaotic, it is almost impossible to get an accurate idea of their troop numbers. The report of the Committee of Safety said 1,500 Americans fought in the battle, but that is almost certainly too low. British sources tend to greatly exaggerate the number. A careful analysis of the regiments known to have been involved and the number of American casualties suggests that 2,500 to 3,500 is a reasonable estimate of the men on the American side. This would include the men at the redoubt, the breastwork, and the rail fence and the many hundreds who poured over Bunker Hill for the battle's final act. Those men, many of them in combat for the first time, men who had left their farms or their trade only months or maybe weeks before, stood ready for the British to roll forward. Finally they did.

THE RAIL FENCE

"Gentlemen," Howe said to his men, just before the lines began their advance, "I am very happy in having the honour of commanding so fine a body of men: I do not in the least doubt, but that you will behave like Englishmen, and as becometh good soldiers."

The speech was recorded and later published by an officer who called himself Lieutenant John Clarke of the marines, and who was apparently at the battle, though his identity is a little hard to pin down. It is unclear whether Howe really gave the speech—no one else mentions it—but Clarke does credit Howe with saying, "I shall not desire one of you to go a step farther than where I go myself at your head." Even if Howe did not say it, the sentiment was certainly his. High-ranking, wealthy, and influential as he was, he would indeed lead his men from the front.

The British troops were eager to go, the waiting no doubt wearing on them as it was on the Americans. "Our men at last grew impatient," wrote Rawdon of the grenadiers, "and all crying out 'Push on! push on!' advanced with infinite spirit to attack the works with their small arms."

Howe now had his reserves, consisting of the marines and the 47th Regiment. Because they had landed farther to the west, they formed up on the left of the 38th and 43rd regiments, making the far left wing of Pigot's line. Howe was ready to move. It was somewhere around 3:30 or 4:00 P.M. He changed the disposition of the men from three lines into two, with Pigot still in command of the left wing and Howe of the right. "We began the attack by a sharp cannonade from our field pieces and two Howitzers," he wrote, "the lines advancing slowly, and frequently halting to give time for the artillery to fire."

William Howe's object was the rail fence. He was sticking with his original plan, which was to turn the flank of the redoubt and come up behind, trapping the men inside between his and Pigot's lines. Only now he would have to get through the rail fence first. Luckily, he had the elite flank companies on whom he could depend for a bold assault.

The light infantry companies, totaling around 400 men, were ordered down to the beach that ran along the Mystic River. They would advance in a column of four lines under the protection of the bank while the grenadiers, backed up by the 5th and 52nd regiments, would march along the edge of the field. The 5th Regiment and the 52nd, the Oxfordshire Light Infantry, would ascend Breed's Hill and charge the breastwork while the grenadiers hit the rail fence head-on. The light infantry on the beach would fight their way around the end of the fence, coming up on the rebels' flank and rear, where they could roll up the American line. Caught between the two, the rebels would be routed, and Howe's right wing would swing around and fall on the back of the redoubt.

It was not a bad approach. It might have worked, too, if the Americans had proven to be as easily driven from their defenses as the British assumed they would be.

Off on the left wing, Pigot's troops, consisting of the 38th and the 43rd regiments backed up by the newly arrived 47th and the 1st Battalion of Marines, also began their approach. In the space between the two wings the artillery advanced, firing at the redoubt just three hundred yards away, then limbering up and moving on through the tall grass, uphill, toward the American defenses, the red-coated men keeping pace.

Pigot's troops opened up first, firing from some distance, possibly to hold the attention of the redoubt and the breastwork while Howe moved against the rail fence. Neither their musket fire nor the fire from the artillery had any effect on the redoubt. The Americans were "entrenched up to their chins" and fairly safe as long as the enemy remained a few hundred yards off. They recalled their orders and held their fire, letting the British approach.

On the British right, Howe's men were also advancing slowly and methodically, keeping pace with the artillery. The day was hot, and the men

were wearing wool regimental coats and waistcoats and carrying knapsacks, muskets, ammunition, and gear that all told weighed around 125
pounds. The grenadiers wore their high bearskin caps.

It was slow going. "The intermediate space between the two armies
was cut by fences, formed of strong posts and close railings, very high,
and which could not be broken readily," Howe complained. "Had they
not been in our way, the rebels would have been quickly forced upon
their left, without any great loss on our side." That conclusion is open to
debate. Certainly the rail fences were not interfering with the light infantry on the beach.

Leading the column of light infantry was the company of the 23rd
Regiment of Foot, the famed Royal Welsh Fusiliers. They had the reputation of being the hardest-fighting regiment in the army, and so the punishment that they would receive that day would be particularly gratifying
to the Americans. The Fusiliers had performed heroically at the Battle
of Minden in 1759, the decisive Anglo-German victory over the French
during the Seven Years' War. Minden had been a bloodbath, the carnage
shocking. It would often be used as an example when describing the
aftermath of Bunker Hill.

The troops in Howe's right wing did not fire their guns as they advanced. In fact, they were not to fire at all. Rather, they were "set forward
to the attack with bayonets." They were to march relentlessly ahead,
through the Americans' small-arms fire, and never pause to shoot back
but rather charge and overwhelm the enemy lines with their wicked,
needle-sharp weapons, the terror of the militia. American guns, made
for civilian use, were not fitted for bayonets. Dearborn recalled that the
Americans "did not carry into the field fifty bayonets. In my company
there was but one."

Struggling over the fences, the grenadiers swept forward, while the
light infantry continued their advance along the beach. They approached
within one hundred feet, then fifty feet. The grim faces of the enemy
under mismatched hats were visible over the makeshift, straw-filled rail
fence. Their muskets, resting on the upper rail, were steady.

The Americans showed extraordinary discipline. No one panicked;

no one fired early as the lines of redcoats came closer. Finally, as the British struggled over the last fence between themselves and the Americans and readied for what would have been an unstoppable bayonet charge, the order came to fire.

The muskets, so long prepared, roared out as one. A great wall of lead blasted across the short distance, slammed into the British troops, and sent them reeling, stopping their advance dead. The front ranks were mowed down as if the hand of God had swept them away. They did not break and run, but neither did they go on. The grenadiers were hung up on a rail fence, and as they struggled to get over they were blasted again and again. The light infantry were shot down as they came, each rank exposed as the ones before were blown away.

Rawdon was stunned, but he pushed on to the last. He wrote that the rebels "poured in so heavy a fire upon us that the oldest officers say they never saw a sharper action. They kept up this fire till we were within ten yards of them; nay, they even knocked down my captain, close behind me, after we got into the ditch of the entrenchment."

The grenadiers began to fire back. It was not what they were supposed to do, but they could not advance into the hail of American bullets, and they were not yet panicked enough to run. Howe recalled that "under a heavy fire, well kept up by the Rebels, they began firing, and by crowding fell into disorder, and in this state the 2d line mixed with them."

Almost at once the entire attack devolved into bloody chaos. The light infantry were shot down by Stark's three-deep defenders at the makeshift stone wall. The grenadiers were bunching up, getting in each others' way, uselessly returning fire as they were butchered by the relentless American volleys. "The Light Infantry at the same time being repulsed," Howe wrote, "there was a moment that I never felt before." That new feeling was, no doubt, panic—not fear for his own personal safety, but the horrible realization that he had led his men into a disaster.

It did not last long. Even the vaunted flank companies could not stand for any time in that withering fire. Within moments of their advance being halted, the grenadiers and the light infantry broke and ran, racing back the way they had come, leaving casualties strewn behind them. Dearborn recalled, "The dead lay as thick as sheep in a foal."

The redcoats retreated until they were beyond the range of the American guns. Some reports suggest they fled clean back to the boats and even climbed aboard, but that is not likely. In the American lines, many of the provincial troops, exalting at what they had done, no doubt delirious at finding themselves still alive and even victorious, wanted to leap the rail fence and pursue the fleeing redcoats, and only by "the prudence of the officers they were prevented lea[ving s]o advantageous a post."

For all the myriad difficulties the American army had throughout the war in finding competent officers, those at Bunker Hill displayed an amazing calm and professionalism and effectively curbed the worst tendencies of the men. It is certainly to the discipline and leadership of veterans such as Stark and Prescott, and men such as Knowlton, new to the service but with a natural ability, that the credit for the Americans' unexpected bold stance must go.

THE BRITISH LEFT

John Burgoyne, watching the action from the Copp's Hill Battery across the Charles River, was stunned by the scene laid out before him. Pigot's men were sweeping up the hill, American reinforcements from Bunker Hill were racing into the fight, Charlestown was fully involved—all this playing out on the grassy fields under the perfect June sky. To his nephew Lord Stanley he wrote:

> And now ensued one of the greatest scenes of war that can be conceived, if we look to the height. Howe's corps, ascending the hill in the face of intrenchments, and in a very disadvantageous ground, was much engaged; and to the left, the enemy poured in fresh troops by the thousands over the land; and in the arms of the sea, our ships and floating batteries cannoned them; straight before us a large and noble town in one blaze: the church-steeples, being

made of timber, were great pyramids of fire above the rest; behind
us, the church-steeples and heights of our camp covered with spectators. The enemy all anxious suspense; the roar of the cannon,
mortars, musketry; the crash of churches, ships upon the stocks,
and whole streets falling together in ruin, to fill the ear; the storm
of the redoubts, with the objects above described, to fill the eye; and
the reflection that, perhaps, a defeat was a final loss to the British
empire in America, to fill the mind,—made the whole a picture,
and complication of horror and importance, beyond any thing that
came to my lot to be a witness to.

Burgoyne could not see the rail fence from his vantage, but he would
still have plenty of opportunity to see a stubborn rebel defense, and British troops breaking and running in the face of American fire. Pigot's
wing was advancing, and they were about to get as harshly mauled as
Howe's.

Charlestown had likely been burning for close to an hour before Pigot
made his first real advance against the redoubt, but the fire apparently
had not spread far enough to drive all the rebels from the houses. "Upon
the left," Howe wrote, "Pigott met with the same obstruction from the
fences, and also had the troops in the houses to combat with, before he
could proceed to assail the redoubt."

The rebel troops in Charlestown, according to Howe, were by themselves enough to give Pigot "sufficient employment." It was not long,
however, before the fire drove them from their posts. It is not entirely
clear where they went, but to the west of the redoubt, about halfway between the redoubt and Charleston, stood a few buildings and a stand of
trees, and it seems likely the troops from the burning town retired to that
place, where they continued to annoy Pigot's left flank. A contemporary
map of the battle shows the structures and the trees and indicates that a
part of the marine battalion and the 47th Regiment were sent there "to
Silence the fire of a barn."

Those men driven from Charlestown, however, would not be a threat
until Pigot's wing enveloped the redoubt. With Charlestown burning

and the immediate danger to the flank gone, Pigot was ready to begin his advance against the redoubt.

The regiments that made up the left wing were formed in ranks and spread in a semicircle around Breed's Hill. Peter Brown, watching from over the dirt rampart, wrote, "The enemy landed, fronted before us, and form'd themselves in an oblong square in order to surround, which they did in part." The 47th Regiment and the 1st Battalion of Marines under the command of Major John Pitcairn, who had done such good service at the Battle of Lexington and Concord, advanced toward the southern face of the redoubt. To the east, and marching toward the eastern wall and the breastwork, were the 43rd and 38th regiments. As Howe's line moved forward, the 5th and the 52nd followed behind the flank companies and advanced on the breastwork as well. Up the hill they went, bearing packs and muskets, parting the knee-high grass like a great ship moving through the sea. The Americans held their fire, as they had at the rail fence.

Brown wrote, "After they were well form'd they advanced towards us in order to swallow us up, but they found a Choaky mouthful of us, 'tho we could do nothing with our small arms as yet for distance." The men in the redoubt may have been better protected than those at the rail fence, but they were also facing a more formidable-looking advance, a veritable wall of redcoats stretching from the southern face of the redoubt all the way around to the breastwork. The four regiments weren't just coming straight at them, they were threatening to half envelop the redoubt and its meager 150 defenders within the walls.

"It was an awful moment," Captain Bancroft recalled. The men in the redoubt were starting to look around for reinforcements they hoped would come, or the return of the men who had carried off the entrenching tools. No doubt they could see the gathering of troops on Bunker Hill, upwards of a thousand of them, who were making no effort to come to the aid of the men on the lines. Those men who had been on Breed's Hill all night, and under fire since four o'clock that morning, "had got hardened to the noise of cannon," Captain John Chester wrote, "but those that came up as recruits were evidently most terribly frightened, many of them, and did not march up with that true courage that their cause ought to have inspired them with." Patriotic zeal, apparently, only went so far.

The troops in the redoubt began to move away from the eastern wall, where the assault would come, shrinking from the advancing enemy, threatening to abandon the fort as their panic overtook them. "This, in my opinion, was the very crisis of the day, the moment on which every-thing depended," Bancroft wrote. It was also a moment when Prescott again showed his leadership. He hurried over to the men and "repre-sented with earnestness that they must not go off, that if they did, all would go." They could not, he told them, just abandon a fortification they were all night in building. Prescott's words struck the right note, and the men returned to the walls of the redoubt, standing on the earthen platform, peering over the dusty ramparts at the relentless red line before them.

Among those men, of course, was Dr. Joseph Warren, conspicuous in his fine clothes, his hair held in place with the same sort of pins that had been shot clean away at Lexington. True to his word, he seems not to have exercised any command in the redoubt. None of the contemporary accounts mention him, and the later simply mention his presence. As significant as Warren had been in fomenting the very revolution that was being fought that day, on Breed's Hill he was just another musket at the wall.

As the British came on, Prescott gave his final instructions. Knowing that if the officers were killed it would throw the men into confusion, he told his troops "to take particular notice of the fine coats, and to aim as low as the waistband, and not to fire till ordered." With that, the rebels waited and the redcoats advanced.

Chapter Seventeen

ATTACK AND
REPULSE

Pigot's attack on the redoubt and Howe's assault on the rail fence took place at nearly the same time, and with nearly the same results. The British left wing advanced slowly and, like Howe's men, "met with a thousand impediments from strong fences." They paused on occasion to let the artillery catch up and fire at the redoubt. Unlike Howe's men, who were supposed to look only to the bayonet, Pigot's lines fired an occasional volley of small arms at the redoubt before moving on.

The Americans for the most part held back. "A firing of eight or ten guns commenced before orders, at the left of the redoubt," Bancroft wrote, "but was immediately stopped." Like Stark, Prescott wanted that first volley to be a devastating blow, delivered when the British were well within range.

It worked. Pigot's lines had advanced to within fifty or sixty feet when Prescott finally gave the word. Seven hundred muskets went off at once, a wall of flame from the breastwork and the redoubt. "Our first fire was shockingly fatal," Bancroft wrote. "There was scarcely a shot but told. The enemy were thrown into confusion and retreated a short distance. Their lines were broken."

The British left, like the right, was stopped dead by the onslaught of musket fire. Judge Prescott wrote that there was "a simultaneous discharge from the redoubt and breastwork, and nearly the whole front rank of the enemy fell, and the whole body was brought to a stand for an instant." The officers rallied the men to fire back, but they could not advance against the terrific volleys from the breastwork and the redoubt.

The 52nd Regiment, the Oxfordshire Light Infantry, had become entangled in some of the man-made obstacles. "About one hundred yards from the [redoubt]," wrote General Martin Hunter, who had been an ensign with the 52nd that day, "they were stopped by some brick-kilns and enclosures, and exposed for some time to the whole of its fire; and it was here that so many men were lost."

"On the left Pigot was staggered and actually retreated," wrote an officer who took part in the attack. "Observe our men were not driven back, they actually retreated by orders: great pains have been taken to huddle up this matter." With the recriminations that followed the battle, the British officers likely accused the men of retreating without orders, which the anonymous but seemingly well-informed writer suggests is not quite the truth. The British returned fire, but it was high and ineffectual, and few men within the redoubt were hurt. That is hardly an indictment of British marksmanship. The Americans were shielded by the ramparts with only their heads showing, a difficult shot even for men trained to shoot at individual targets, which the redcoats were not. Nor were they in a situation where they could be expected to take calm and careful aim. The Americans, on the other hand, could hardly miss. One man in the redoubt would later say, "There was no need of waiting for a chance to fire, for, as soon as you had loaded, there was always a mark at hand, and as near as you pleased."

Pigot certainly intended to take the redoubt with the bayonet, just as Howe had planned on using that weapon to drive the Americans from the rail fence. It was standard military practice of the time to fire a volley and then rush the lines with those stiletto-sharp, three-sided seventeen inches of steel, which, at the end of a five-foot musket with nine pounds of weight behind it, was terribly hard to parry. The British officers understood that the bayonet would be particularly effective against the Americans, who were not equipped with them and who lacked the training and disciple to withstand a bayonet charge. Against the relentless storm of bullets, though, the redcoats could not charge, could not even move forward.

It is unclear how long Pigot's lines stood before the breastwork and endured the rebels' volleys. Longer than Howe's men had at the rail fence, it seems, but still not terribly long, and soon they retreated back down Breed's Hill. Most sources suggest the retreat was done hastily, but it was not the panicked rout of Howe's flank companies. Pigot's troops fell back in a more orderly fashion and regrouped. As much as they dreaded the thought, they certainly knew that they would be advancing again.

If Pigot's assault on the redoubt had one benefit to the entrenched Americans, it was that it forced the British artillery to fall silent. As the lines of redcoats advanced up Breed's Hill, the guns on board the men-of-war and the gunboats and at Copp's Hill Battery broke off their fire for the first time since 4:00 A.M. Despite the roar of the flames from Charlestown, there must have been an odd stillness when that undercurrent of sound, which had been nearly constant for the past twelve hours, was suddenly gone.

The sound of big guns, however, was still heard on the field. British and Americans both went to great lengths to make sure their troops were supported by artillery, though it did not do much good for either army.

Howe positioned the British guns between his and Pigot's wings to advance with the infantry. It is likely that just the four six-pounders and the howitzers were sent forward, and not the twelve-pounders. A twelve weighed somewhere around three-quarters of a ton. A six-pounder weighed around a thousand pounds less. The guns were mounted on field carriages with tall, spoked wheels to facilitate moving over uneven ground. Generally the guns were pulled by horses, but there is no indication that Howe had draft animals of any kind. Without them the task of hauling the massive guns uphill over broken and often swampy ground fell to the artillerymen using drag ropes.

Lieutenant Barker was in Pigot's left wing. He recorded in his diary, "As soon as landed we march'd up to near the Redoubt and waited for the Artillery, which when it came up kept a smart fire upon the Redoubt for some time but without making any Breach." It was an odd way for the troops to proceed. Standard practice at the time, developed by Howe's mentor General James Wolfe, called for troops attacking an entrenched enemy to move swiftly. Perhaps it was Howe's plan to divert the Americans' attention to the redoubt while the light infantry turned the flank at the rail fence.

Whatever he had in mind, things did not go smoothly for Howe's artillery. About three hundred yards from where they started on Moulton's Hill, the guns became mired in swampy ground and could not advance. A detailed map of the battle, done by British soldier Henry De Berniere, indicates a swampy area between Moulton Hill and Breed's Hill, which he notes was the place where the guns were "Stopt by the Marsh."

With considerable effort they were hauled free and continued to advance up Breed's Hill with the infantry. Then, as the troops neared the redoubt, the artillery stopped firing. When Howe inquired as to the problem he "was told they got twelve pound balls to six pounders, but they had grape shot." Somehow the wrong ammunition had been sent with the guns. Howe "ordered them forward and to fire grape." Grape shot was most effective against troops in the open, not against the walls of a redoubt, but Howe judged it better than nothing.

The issue of the mismatched ammunition caused a minor scandal. Responsibility for the guns fell to artillery colonel Samuel Cleaveland. One officer wrote of Cleaveland, "The wretched blunder of the oversized balls sprung from the dotage of an officer of rank in that corps, who spends his whole time in dallying with the schoolmaster's daughters. God knows he is old enough—he is no Sampson—yet he must have his Delilah."

Cleaveland placed the blame elsewhere. "At Bunkers Hill I sent 66 Rounds to each Gun," he wrote. "Not more than half was fired, but the men sent on purpose to carry the Boxes of Ammunition after the Cannon went a Plundering." He went on to complain that he could not be everywhere at once, and that it was hardly fair that any mistake made was assigned to him.

General Gage saw in the incident the possibility of sabotage. The schoolmaster with whose daughters Cleaveland was accused of "dallying" also had two sons. One was James Lovell, a known Whig and Patriot and later delegate to the Continental Congress. The other, Benjamin Lovell, was the clerk of artillery stores. Gage suspected that Benjamin had been influenced by his brother to send the wrong shot, but he had no proof. Benjamin was discharged from his office, as was the conductor of stores. James would later be arrested as a dissident and held at Halifax as a prisoner until he was exchanged for Loyalist Philip Skene.

The movements of the American artillery are more difficult to follow. As Howe was landing, Prescott sent the guns under Callender's command off to oppose them, accompanied by Knowlton's Connecticut men. Peter Brown wrote that "when our officers saw that the regulars intended to land, they ordered the artillery to go out of the fort and prevent their landing, if possible; from whence the artillery captain took his field-pieces, and went right home to Cambridge fast as he could—for which he is now confined, and we expect he will be shot for it."

Brown, like Prescott, assumed the gunners deserted with their guns, and while much of what Brown relates is correct, there is quite a bit he did not know. Callender, Gridley, and Trevett did make a stand in opposition to the British landing. Some of the American artillery appears to have been in position to fire on Pigot's troops, perhaps at the breastwork. Barker, with the left wing, writes, "The Americans fired a few Cannon but did no harm." Barker's assessment that the American guns did no harm seems to have been the universal opinion.

The American artillery did not remain long in the field, however. Gridley drew his guns off, later taking post near the neck to cover the retreat, before abandoning them altogether. As the fighting progressed, Callender apparently had enough, limbered up his guns, and headed for Bunker Hill and presumably safety.

On reaching Bunker Hill, Callender encountered Putnam, who was on horseback. Putnam ordered Callender to return, but the artilleryman refused, claiming that he was out of cartridges. According to testimony before a committee of the Provincial Congress, "The General dismounted and examined his boxes, and found a considerable number of cartridges, upon which he ordered him back; he refused, until the General threatened him with immediate death, upon which he returned up the hill again, but soon deserted his post and left the cannon."

Putnam would later recommend that either Callender or Gridley be put to death for their actions. Samuel Trevett was the only artillery officer to end the day with his reputation intact. He fought to the last and was able to bring one of the two guns under his command off the field, the only one of the six American guns engaged that was not captured by the British.

In the aftermath of the battle, Scarborough Gridley was tried at court-martial and found guilty of "being deficient in his duty." He was dismissed from the Massachusetts service, but with the proviso that "on account of his inexperience and youth, and the great confusion that attended that day's transactions in general," he was not considered ineligible for a commission in the Continental Army.

Callender was also court-martialed, the first trial to take place as a result of the action at Breed's Hill. He was found guilty of disobeying orders and alleged cowardice and dismissed from the service, without the possibility of a continental commission. Callender felt the sentence was unjust, however, and continued to serve in the army as a volunteer. The next year, at the Battle of Brooklyn, he fought with such courage that his commission was restored and Washington ordered the sentence of cowardice to be erased from the orderly book. Callender served with honor for the remainder of the war, including a year as a British prisoner.

The desertion of the artillery served as yet another excuse for the shirkers milling around on Bunker Hill to avoid joining the fight. The "re-enforcements, ordered up the hill, could not be prevailed upon to go," the committee found; "the plea was, the Artillery was gone, and they stood no chance for their lives in such circumstances." A weak argument indeed given how little the artillery accomplished.

Ironically, the Americans suffered the same problem the British did with the wrong-sized cartridges and cannonballs sent with the guns. A number of later stories suggest artillery officers used this as an excuse to abandon their posts. Some accounts have Putnam pointing out that the cartridges could be broken open and the loose powder poured down the barrel, and the guns loaded with handfuls of musket balls rather than the oversized round shot. This would have been an inefficient way to load the guns, nor would the musket balls have delivered the impact that round shot would, but it would likely have been better than nothing.

Artillery was the most scientific and complicated of battlefield duties, and it took great discipline to service and protect a cannon and its attendant gear in the face of an advancing enemy. It is hardly a surprise that the nascent American army failed so terribly on this front.

THE SECOND ADVANCE

General William Howe's right wing was shattered by the American fire and sent running to safety, a thing that no British troops, and certainly not the grenadiers and light infantry, would have imagined happening to them at the hands of Americans. Still, they were most certainly not defeated, and Howe ordered them to prepare for another attempt. "Here the officers were observed, by the spectators on the opposite shore," read the official report of the Committee of Safety, "to run down to them [the troops] using the most passionate gestures, and pushing the men forward with their swords." With shouts and prodding from the officers, the flank companies were formed up again and "marched up, with apparent reluctance, toward the intrenchment."

This time the light infantry were not sent down to the beach, where they had been so severely mauled by Stark's men, but rather joined the grenadiers on the sloping fields above the riverbanks. Once again the long red lines advanced through the high grass toward the fence and the American muskets resting on its upper rails. Once again the Americans waited with impressive discipline as the enemy approached and then, when they were within easy musket range, opened up on them. This second assault was as fatal as the first.

"As we approached, an incessant stream of fire poured from the rebel lines," one officer wrote.

It seemed a continued sheet of fire for near thirty minutes. Our light infantry were served up in companies against the grass fence, without being able to penetrate; indeed how could we penetrate, most of our grenadiers and light-infantry the moment of presenting themselves lost three-fourths, and many nine-tenths of their men. Some had only eight and nine men a company left, some only three four and five.

Once again the British were shot down as they came, though they appear to have stood their ground more firmly on the second advance than they had on the first, perhaps because they were not surprised this time by the fury of the American defense. They understood now that the Americans would not flee at the mere sight of their bayonets, but still they tried to get around the American left flank where it met the Mystic River. Dearborn recalled, "Several attempts were made to turn our left, but the troops having thrown up a slight stone wall on the bank of the river and laying down behind it, gave such a deadly fire, as cut down almost every man of the party opposed them."

The soldiers of the flank companies were shot down by the American guns, but the officers were handled even more roughly, their losses proportionally much higher than those of the rank and file. This was no accident. The Americans were selecting their targets. "'Tis astonishing what a number of officers were hit on this occasion," wrote Adjutant John Waller of the marines, "but the officers were particularly aimed at."

Howe's aides-de-camp were shot down around him. On several occasions he found himself the only man left standing from what had been a group of officers. It is indeed somewhat miraculous that the major general himself came through unhurt. As befitted a man of Howe's station, he had on the field a servant who "attended the whole time with wine and other necessities for the refreshment of the general," until the wine bottle was shot out of his hand.

Howe's lines were being decimated from the front, and they were likely being enfiladed on their left flank as well. Up the slopes of Breed's Hill, in the two-hundred-yard gap between the end of the breastwork and the beginning of the rail fence, there were the three little flèches shown on De Berniere's map (others described a post and rail fence running along that gap). American troops were posted at these makeshift defenses, described by De Berniere as the "Place, from whence the Grenadiers received a very heavy fire." American artillery might have been posted there as well. Caught between two fires, unable to turn the enemy's flank or bring their bayonets to bear, the British could not stand for long.

Nor did they. The regulars "were compelled a second time to retreat with precipitation and great confusion," that is to say they were sent racing back again, out of range of the deadly American muskets. There was no standing up to those relentless volleys. Quite unconsciously, the Americans had hit on exactly the best mode of regulating their fire: that was not to try to regulate it at all. Rather than calling out orders for loading and firing, as was done in European armies, each platoon officer handled his own musket and let his men do the same, "but never without a sure aim at some particular object," usually an officer's midriff.

Henry Dearborn, writing years later and with considerable military experience under his belt, felt that this approach was "more destructive than any mode which could have been adopted with troops who were not inured to discipline." The American troops may have had no training, but they were "familiar with the use of arms, from boyhood . . . each having his peculiar manner of loading and firing, which had been practiced upon for years, with the same gun." The most effective policy was to let each man do as he was accustomed to doing.

After the fighting began in earnest, there was likely no communication or coordination between Howe's right wing and Pigot's left, but still the two sections of the army seemed to be moving in coordination, with Pigot's second advance taking place at about the same time as Howe's.

Pigot's men had not retreated quite as far from the enemy as Howe's had, and they remained close enough as they re-formed that "a scattering fire was still kept up" by the men in the redoubt. Prescott was beginning to worry about his supply of ammunition, though. "After a considerable time," he wrote, "finding our ammunition was almost spent, I commanded a cessation" of firing. They had been waiting all morning for reinforcements and supplies and none had come, and they certainly would not be coming now. The rebels on Breed's Hill could expect to have no more ammunition than what they currently had with them.

Meanwhile, Pigot and his officers formed the men back into their ranks and once again advanced up Breed's Hill, marching straight toward the murderous musket fire of Dr. Joseph Warren, Amos Farnsworth, Peter Brown, and the others from the redoubt and the breastwork. A local newspaper published a description, based on eyewitness testimony, that read, "As fast as the front man was shot down, the next stepped forward to take his place, but our men dropped them so fast they were a long time coming up. It was surprising how they would step over their dead bodies, as though they had been logs of wood."

Once again Pigot's lines stood for as long as they could in the hail of bullets, returning fire but unable to reach the redoubt to bring their bayonets into play. Amos Farnsworth wrote, "We within the intrenchment, and at a Breast Work without, sustained the Enemy's Attacks with [g]reat Bravery and Resolution, kild and wounded great Numbers, and repulsed them several times."

As Pigot's lines wrapped around the south and west walls of the redoubt, the left flank began to take fire from the barns and the stands of trees where the men driven from Charlestown had taken refuge. Once again the British troops found themselves harassed by an unseen enemy. They were apparently effective enough in this that Pigot felt compelled to send part of the marines and the 47th Regiment to drive them off.

As much to save ammunition as to stagger the redcoats, Prescott ordered his men to hold off firing "till the enemy advanced to within thirty yards, when we gave them such a hot fire that they were obliged to retire nearly one hundred and fifty yards before they could rally and come again on the attack."

With the second failed assault, Pigot's men fell back beyond musket range, the officers no doubt thinking that it was time to reevaluate the operation. Watching from the Copp's Hill Battery, Burgoyne and Clinton could see that things were going badly. "A moment of the day was critical," Burgoyne wrote. "Howe's left was staggered." In addition, American reinforcements were starting to arrive, men who were actually willing to cross the half mile from Bunker Hill to Breed's and put themselves in the middle of the bloody fighting taking place there.

Others reached Bunker Hill and would go no farther. Massachusetts colonel Samuel Gerrish managed to get his men to the crest of Bunker Hill and then lost his nerve, claiming that exhaustion prevented him from going on. His adjutant, a Dane named Christian Febiger, led part of the regiment into the battle, but most of them lingered behind with their colonel. For his behavior, Gerrish was court-martialed, found guilty of cowardice, and cashiered.

From their vantage point on Copp's Hill, Burgoyne, Clinton, and the others could see the thousand or so American troops loitering on Bunker Hill. From where the British generals stood, the men appeared to be reinforcements. If those men joined the fight, there was a good chance that Howe would be routed.

Howe also understood that he had come to a critical juncture, a point where everything could collapse around him. It was supposed to have been an easy victory. Defeat would be utterly humiliating, intolerable. He sent a note off to Boston for reinforcements. The request made its way to Clinton, who was looking out to see if more men were needed. In a scrawled note to himself, Clinton wrote, "Enimy appeared in great force, [Howe] desired reinforcement, and orders me at embark 2 marines and another Batt[alio]n." Clinton ordered the 2nd Marine Battalion and the 63rd Regiment to cross over to Charlestown.

There was no time to wait for the reinforcements, however. More rebel troops were coming over from Bunker Hill, and the British regulars would not benefit from standing around contemplating another assault on the enemy's works. It was time to go.

None of Howe's letters admit to the beating his men took at the rebels' hands. Even in the most honest of them he only talks of the light infantry being "repulsed." He never mentions that his two failures led him to change his approach on the third assault, but the disposition of the troops makes it clear that he did just that. Howe was finished with flinging his men against the rail fence. He had done it twice, and it had resulted in the day's worst carnage. The grenadier company of the 52nd, for example, suffered a casualty rate of 100 percent.

American observers across the Mystic River witnessed the preparations for the final push. "The ministerial army now made a decisive effort," Joseph Palmer wrote in his report to the committee of safety. "The fire from the ships and batteries, as well as from the cannon in the front of their army was redoubled. The officers, in the rear of their army, were observed to goad forward the men with renewed exertions, and they attacked the redoubt on three sides at once."

According to one later source, Howe "wisely gave orders for the troops to disencumber themselves of their knapsacks." A British officer, wounded in the fighting and suffering from "severe shivering," complained, "Our blankets had been flung away during the engagement." The rank and file were undoubtedly grateful to shed their loads. Freed of those burdens, they moved out across the open ground, the light infantry and the grenadiers marching along the river banks, the 5th and 52nd regiments once again sweeping up the northeastern slopes of Breed's Hill.

Howe's redcoats advanced toward the rail fence, "the ground . . . covered with the dead and wounded." They did not make a frontal assault this time; rather, "a few small detached parties again advanced, which kept up a distant, ineffectual, scattering fire" on the rail fence. These troops were only there to keep the men at the rail fence occupied, while the real attack was launched against the redoubt.

On Howe's left, the 5th and 52nd regiments wheeled to the left and headed up the side of Breed's Hill, toward the gap between the breastwork and the rail fence, the gap protected by the insubstantial fence or the three flèches. Rather than going around the rail fence, they were going in front of it. Rather than hitting one of the most strongly defended points on the American line, Howe had found the weak spot. If he pushed through, he would come in behind the breastwork and it would be the end.

Pigot also understood that another assault had to be made, that it could not wait. He gathered his men up and formed them in their lines. Inside the walls of the redoubt, the Americans were scrambling for every grain of gunpowder they could find. When a few artillery cartridges were discovered, Prescott had them torn open and the powder distributed to the men, "exhorting them not to waste a kernal of it, but to make it certain that every shot should *tell*." If Pigot had known how desperately low on ammunition the Americans were, he would have been more sanguine about this new assault.

It was somewhere around 4:30 or 5:00 P.M. The Battle of Bunker Hill had been going on for about fifty minutes when the long red line rolled forward for the third time.

"GOOD GOD HOW THE BALLS FLEW"

Captain John Chester of Spencer's Connecticut regiment had marched his company off for Bunker Hill as soon as he got the word from Daniel Putnam (and after his men made the pointless effort of pulling their frocks over their uniform coats). The battle was raging as they hurried down the road. Chester's friend and fellow soldier Lieutenant Samuel Blachley Webb wrote to his brother, "On our March down we met many of our worthy friends wounded sweltering in their Blood,—carried on the Shoulders of their fellow Soldiers—judge you what must be our feelings at this shocking Spectacle."

Despite the unnerving sight of the wounded, "the orders were, *press on, press on*." Charlestown Neck was still under a terrible cannonade as the ships and floating batteries tried to prevent reinforcements from crossing. "Chain Shot, Ring Shot & Double headed Shot flew as thick as Hail Stones" as Chester's company made its way across. Several men were wounded in the crossfire, but none killed, as the troops reached the far side and made their way up Bunker Hill.

The Connecticut men reached the top of the hill as the battle was approaching its high point, probably just as Howe was beginning his third advance against the rail fence. Despite all the unpleasant shocks they had had on the march to the battlefield, they were stunned to step up over the crest of Bunker Hill and into the thick of the fighting. "When we mounted the Summit, where the Engagement was," Webb wrote, "—good God how the Balls flew.—I freely Acknowledge I never had such a tremor come over me before."

Spencer's regiment was not the only one hurrying to the battle. Among the others hurrying to the fight were companies of Connecticut troops under the command of John Clark and William Coit. Coit would soon give up the army for command of an armed schooner commissioned by George Washington and would enjoy the distinction of being the first American captain to capture a vessel flying the British flag.

As the fresh troops got into the fight, unit cohesion broke down almost immediately, and what Chester found was chaos. "When we arrived there was not a company with us in any kind of order," he wrote. The troops "were scattered, some behind rocks and hay-cocks, and thirty men, perhaps, behind an apple tree, and frequently twenty men round a wounded man, retreating, when not more than three or four could touch him to advantage."

Men were streaming off the battlefield past Chester's company. Some claimed they had been given leave "because they had been all night and day on fatigue, without sleep, victuals, or drink." There were certainly men in that circumstance, though it is unlikely they had been given permission to go. Some said they had no officer to lead them, which was often true; many officers, such as Gridley and Gerrish, had given shameful displays of cowardice. Others had no excuse at all. One company of men was marching off with an officer at their head, and when Chester asked the reason they ignored him. Chester then ordered his men to cock their weapons and assured the retreating company that they would all be shot if they did not return to the fight, which they did.

Chester led his men down the far side of Bunker Hill toward the action, as "the small as well as cannon shot were incessantly whistling by us." They took up position at a stone wall somewhere behind the redoubt, from where they were able to hammer the British with musket fire. "Here we lost our regularity, as every company had done before us," Chester wrote, "and fought as they did, every man loading and firing as fast as he could."

They were not at the wall long, maybe six minutes, delivering their volleys. Webb wrote, "The Regulars fell in great plenty, but to do them Justice they keep a front and stood their ground nobly." The 5th and 52nd regiments were now advancing up the north side of Breed's Hill, General Howe conspicuous in the lead.

Howe's regiments had artillery with them, and they set the guns to work as they neared the top of the hill. "The artillery was directed to the opening between the breastwork and the rail fence," Judge Prescott wrote. "From the position they took, they raked the breastwork, drove the men into the redoubt, and did much execution within it." Howe had managed to flank the redoubt at last, pushing through the two-hundred-yard gap between the breastwork and the rail fence. The Americans at the flèches were either driven off or were too far from Howe's flank to do much damage as the redcoats came in behind the men at the breastwork and rolled up the line, with cannon fire leading the way.

On the other two sides, Pigot's men were also making their third assault on the redoubt. Marine adjutant Waller wrote, "When we came immediately under the work, we were checked by the severe fire of the enemy, but did not retreat an inch." The Americans were firing the last of their ammunition in a desperate attempt to stave off the British assault. Redcoats were shot down as they prepared for the bayonet charge that would end it.

"We were now in confusion," Waller wrote, "after being broke several times in getting over the rails, &c." Under the fire of the enemy, Waller and the other officers prepared the troops for another assault. Leading the marines was Major Pitcairn. The veteran officer had made it to the last ditch on Breed's Hill when an American volley struck him down. "Major Pitcairne was killed close by me," Waller wrote, "with a captain, a subaltern, also a sergeant, and many of the privates."

Any number of Americans claimed to have fired the shot that killed Pitcairn, though credit most often goes to a man named Salem Prince, one of the many free black men fighting with the Americans that day. By some accounts, Pitcairn had already been wounded twice and had just called out to his men, "Now for the glory of the marines!" when four balls slammed into him.

Pitcairn was mortally wounded, but not killed on the spot, as Waller thought. His son, who was also on the field, carried him down to a waiting boat, and he was taken back to Boston. The wounds were too much, however, and he soon succumbed. Pitcairn was a skilled officer and much loved. His loss was devastating to the British forces in America.

Deprived of Pitcairn's leadership, Waller and the other officers raced back and forth getting the men in position "in order that we might advance with our bayonets to the parapet." He ordered the men to stop firing, as it was preventing them from getting ready for the assault. "When we had got in tolerable order," he wrote, "we rushed on, leaped the ditch, and climbed the parapet, under a most sore and heavy fire."

The fire was dying out, however. According to Prescott, "Our ammunition being nearly exhausted, [we] could keep up only a scattering fire. The enemy being numerous, surrounded our little fort, began to mount our lines and enter the fort with their bayonets." Some of the men began to throw rocks at the onrushing enemy. Private Perkins of Newburyport "fir'd away all his Cartridges & having some loose Powder in his Pocket he was oblig'd to Strip & tore off some part of his shirt to make wadding."

The redoubt was surrounded on three sides. Redcoats were scaling the walls and pouring in through the sally port with bayonets fixed. Captain George Harris of the 5th Regiment of Foot was one of the first on the wall. "I had twice mounted," he wrote, "encouraging the men to follow me, and was ascending a third time when a ball grazed the top of my head." Knocked out cold, Harris fell back into the arms of Lieutenant Francis, Lord Rawdon, who was right behind him. Rawdon, thinking Harris was dead, began to haul his body off so it would not be trampled. The motion revived the captain, who pleaded, "For God's sake, let me die in peace!"

Instead, Rawdon ordered four soldiers to carry Harris off to a place of safety. The captain made it back to Boston where a surgeon trepanned the wound, that is, removed a part of the skull. Not only did Harris live, but with the aid of looking-glasses he had "a view of his own brains."

As Harris was carried from the field, British troops rushed up the sloped sides of the redoubt, driving off the defenders. The Americans at the breastwork had been driven into the redoubt by the advance of Howe's troops and artillery, and now the space was crowded with men. Marine adjutant Waller gives a vivid description:

> Two companies of the first battalion of marines, and part of the 47th regiment, were the first that mounted the breastwork . . . I was with those two companies who drove their bayonets into all that opposed them. Nothing could be more shocking than the carnage that followed the storming [of] this work. We tumbled over the dead to get at the living, who were crowding out of the gorge of the redoubt.

"The day was over," Bancroft recalled, "and we had nothing more but to retreat as well as we could." Amos Farnsworth noted in his diary, "I Did not leave the Intrenchment untill the Enemy got in[.] I then Retreated ten or Fifteen rods, then receved a wound in my rite arm the bawl gowing through a little below my Elbow."

The first half of Peter Brown's letter is quite matter-of-fact, but as he relates the end of the battle he increasingly mentions God's mercy, as if realizing, as he wrote, the miraculous nature of his survival. "Oh may I never forget Gods distinguishing Mercy to me," he wrote, "in sparing my Life, when they fell on my right hand, and on my left, and close by me, they were to the eye of reason no more expos'd than myself.—When the Arrows of death flew thick around me, I was preserv'd while others were suffer'd to fall a prey to our Cruel enemies."

Brown, however, adhered to the philosophy that God helps those who help themselves: "I was in the fort when the enemy came in, Jump'd over the wall and ran half a Mile, where balls flew like hail stones and Cannon roar'd like thunder, but tho I escap'd then it may be my turn next."

As the redcoats came over the wall, the Americans poured out of the sally port or over the ramparts on the opposite sides. The redoubt was all but surrounded, jammed with struggling men inside and out, bayonet-wielding British troops and Americans swinging muskets like clubs. The dust rose in clouds, making it difficult to see. Any control that the officers had formerly exercised was gone, as the melee devolved into a fight that was every man for himself. In the confusion of those last, desperate moments, few were aware of what was happening beyond their immediate situation. It was then, during the last frantic struggle, as the American troops abandoned the redoubt, that Dr. Joseph Warren was killed.

There were no witnesses. Indeed, it was several days before the Americans knew for certain that he had been killed, leading the Provincial Congress the following Monday to elect a president "in the room of the Hon. Joseph Warren, Esq., supposed to be killed in the late battle." Warren had stood his place at the earthen wall through the repeated assaults of Pigot's left wing, firing away all of his ammunition. As the American troops were finally driven from the defenses, Warren hung back, one of the last to leave the works.

Warren managed to get clear of the redoubt, either through the sally port or over the wall, and with a handful of Americans made a fighting retreat. As he and the others abandoned the redoubt, they likely ran straight into the 5th and 52nd regiments, who had driven the men in from the breastwork. Brown's letter and Farnsworth's diary make clear the British were firing a hail of lead at the retreating Americans. Warren was apparently trying to rally the American troops, sword in hand, for a rearguard action. That stubborn resistance, and his fine clothes and his powdered and curled hair, would have made him conspicuous in those final moments.

Any number of romantic tales soon attached themselves to Warren's death, stories of last words uttered by the dying hero, of officers both British and American trying to prevent his being killed, but there is little evidence that any of them are true. Warren's death seems to have gone as unnoted at the time as was his presence during the battle. According to the most likely account, Warren was sixty yards from the redoubt when he was recognized by a British officer. The officer snatched a musket from a soldier beside him and shot Warren in the right side of the head, killing him instantly.

With the Americans giving up the redoubt, the Battle of Bunker Hill was in its final moments. The reinforcements that Clinton had sent over, the 2nd Marine Battalion and the 63rd Regiment, landed just before that, as the final assault was taking place. From Copp's Hill, Clinton could see that the newly arrived troops were in confusion, not sure where to go. He "desired General Burgoyne, who was with me, to save me harmless to General Gage for going without his orders," found a boat and crew, and headed off for Charlestown.

American troops fired on Clinton's boat as it pulled across the river, wounding two men before Clinton could get ashore. Once he was there, the major general took charge of the men and rallied a number of wounded who had come down to the landing to get away from the fight. He led them back up the hill, and they "advanced in column, with as much parade as possible to impose on the enemy." Howe later thanked Clinton for his efforts, and in England he was praised and even re-warded for his initiative. In truth, the fighting had all but ended by the time he arrived, and his contribution did not amount to much.

Bancroft made it out of the redoubt, but just barely. The sally port was "completely filled with British soldiers" by the time he figured he should make his escape. With his long musket, which he had taken from the French in the previous war, held horizontally in front of him, he charged the enemy, knocking them aside until someone grabbed the gun from him. He then leaped up on the men blocking his path and launched him-self forward, coming down on a British soldier and landing with his feet on the ground. The butt of a musket was swung at his head and missed, but connected with his shoulder as others tried to grab him by the arms. He shook them off and dashed for the sally port, striking the last man across the throat as he cleared the redoubt and ran for Bunker Hill.

"A shower of shot was falling all around me as I ran down the hill," he recalled. Bullets plucked at his clothes. His hat was shot from his head, and a musket ball took off his left forefinger, but he did not stop running until he was over Charlestown Neck.

Once Howe had made an attack on the breastwork and the redoubt, the rail fence became an isolated part of the field, the men there cut off from the rest of the action. As with Prescott's men, their ammunition was all but expended, and they could not have stood much longer against the enemy. As the redoubt was abandoned and the troops who had been posted there streamed past on their retreat toward Bunker Hill, the men at the rail fence abandoned their post as well. There was no longer a semblance of order. "The whole of our line immediately gave way," Henry Dearborn wrote, "and retreated with rapidity and disorder toward Bunker's Hill."

Despite Dearborn's characterizing the retreat as a panicked rout, the troops at the rail fence managed to once again stop the advance of the British lines. According to the report from the Committee of Safety, the men retreating from the redoubt would have been cut off by the redcoats, had they not been "checked by a party of the provincials, who fought with the utmost bravery."

Behind the dubious protection of the rail fence the Americans stubbornly held their ground until the men from the redoubt had made good their retreat, then began to fall back themselves. As the others made their way over Bunker Hill, the men at the rail fence "gave ground, but with more regularity than could be expected of troops who had no longer been under discipline, and many of whom had never before seen an engagement."

It is probable that John Stark was at least partially responsible for this orderly retreat. Also there was General Seth Pomeroy, still clutching his musket, though the weapon had been shattered by a British bullet. Lord Rawdon wrote that the rebels "continued a running fight from one fence, or wall, to another, till we entirely drove them off the peninsula of Charlestown."

One man who did not take part in the rearguard action was Lieutenant

Samuel Webb. "We Ran very fast up the Hill," Webb wrote, "leaving some of our Dead and Wounded in the field—we retreated over Charlestown Neck, thro the thickest of the Ships fire,—here some principle Officers fell by Cannon & Bombs."

This was the point at which the American troops suffered their worst casualties. Bancroft observed, "Our loss was principally on the retreat." While many who had been at the rail fence retired fighting, most were simply fleeing across open ground, vulnerable to the muskets and artillery of the British troops in their wake and the still constant fire of the ships and floating batteries below. The Americans ran down the west slope of Bunker Hill and over the neck of land connecting Charlestown to the mainland, Putnam, Prescott, Stark, and the other officers with them. The men would not be rallied in the face of the British pursuit.

Many of the Americans retreated no farther than Winter Hill, about a mile beyond Charlestown Neck, where, under Putnam's tireless direction, they began entrenching. They did not know if the British would continue the pursuit or launch another attack over the neck and continue their offensive, but once clear of the immediate danger they were ready to once more make a stand.

Henry Clinton, to be sure, wanted very much to continue the attack, but most of the men who had been fully engaged during that bloody and trying day had had enough of battles for the time being. Howe explained in a letter to his brother that "the soldiers were so much harassed, and there were so many officers lost, that the pursuit was not followed with all the vigor that might be expected."

It was around 6:00 P.M. The Battle of Bunker Hill was over. The fighting had lasted about an hour. The echoes would be heard for years to come.

Epilogue

"WE ARE ALL WRONG AT THE HEAD"

The British were the victors at the Battle of Bunker Hill, but it did not feel like a victory. "We were exulting to see the flight of our enemies," wrote Boston Loyalist Ann Hulton, "but in an hour or two we had occasion to mourn and lament. Dear was the purchase of our safety! In the evening the streets were filled with the wounded and the dying."

The journal of the ship *Falcon* recorded, "Our Boats Emp[loye]d Carry Wounded men over to Boston," and the journal of every other ship in the harbor included a similar notation. Once again, for the second time in two months, a flotilla of boats was needed to carry the wounded, the dying, and the dead from Charlestown to Boston.

Once the fighting was over, Lieutenant Clarke wrote, "those persons who style themselves friends to government instantly sent out every sort of carriage they had, as coaches, chariots, single-horse chaises, and even hand-barrows, the water-side, to assist in bringing to Boston the wounded and killed officers and soldiers." Doctors, surgeons, and apothecaries turned out to help with the overwhelming number of wounded.

Lieutenant Clarke continued, "Then followed a melancholy scene of several carriages, with the dead and dying officers; in the first of which was Major Williams bleeding and dying, and three dead Captains of the Fifty second Regiment, but he lived till the next morning. The second contained four dead Officers, then another with wounded Officers; and this scene continued until Sunday morning, before all the wounded private men could be brought to Boston."

Peter Oliver, also in Boston, wrote, "It was truly a Shocking Sight and Sound, to see the carts loaded with those unfortunate Men and to hear the piercing Groans of the dying and those whose painful Wounds extorted the Sigh from the firmest Mind."

The British lost 226 men killed and 828 men wounded out of approximately 2,300 men engaged, not counting the late-arriving reinforcements, who did not really participate in the fighting. That's a casualty rate approaching 50 percent. Nor were the casualties spread evenly among the various regiments. The grenadiers and light infantry at the rail fence fared the worst. Out of an estimated 700 troops they suffered 465 casualties, nearly 70 percent. The troops who fell in the field were buried where they died. The officers "were decently buried in Boston," according to Clarke, "in a private manner."

The officers made up an inordinately high percentage of the casualties. Burgoyne wrote, "The day ended with glory, and the success was most important, considering the ascendency it gives the regular troops; but the loss was uncommon among the officers, considering the numbers engaged." He was not the only one to point out that discrepancy.

The reason is obvious. The Americans were targeting the officers, and unlike the British troops, they were taking aim before shooting. Protected as they were, with walls or fences to rest heavy muskets on, and with long experience in using their weapons in situations like hunting where accuracy mattered, the Americans were in a position to take care with their firing. They did, and the British officer corps suffered the brunt of it.

There was considerable outrage in some quarters at the way the battle was conducted. One officer, whose letter made it into the official parliamentary inquiry, was beside himself with anger. He thought it was absurd that the army had not taken Charlestown Neck and thus cut off the

Americans, or pursued them to Cambridge after the battle and scattered them. "We are all wrong at the head," he wrote. "My mind cannot help dwelling on our cursed mistakes . . . I have lost some of those I most valued. This madness or ignorance nothing can excuse. The brave men's lives were wantonly thrown away."

Eight days after the battle, General Gage wrote his official report to the Earl of Dartmouth. He gives a brief and generally accurate account of what took place, drawing largely on Howe's report written a few days after the battle. "This action shows the superiority of the King's troops," he wrote, "who under every disadvantage attacked and defeated above three times their own number, strongly posted and covered by breast-works . . . [T]he valour of the British officers and soldiers was at no time more conspicuous than in this action."

That was the report Gage understood would be published. On the same day he wrote another marked as private, a letter that carried a very different tone. It had something of an I-told-you-so quality, as written by a man too weary to care anymore that he was right. "The trials we have had, show that the rebels are not the despicable rabble too many have supposed them to be," he wrote, meaning to imply, no doubt, that Dartmouth himself belonged in that category.

"Wherever they find cover they make a good stand and the country, naturally strong, affords it them and they are taught to assist in natural strength by art, for they entrench and raise batteries," he went on. Gage explained that there were professional soldiers aiding them, specifically naming Gridley, and that they were fortifying every pass in and out of Boston. Though troops such as the Americans might be expected to "return home after such a check as they have got," Gage explained that they were not doing so. "In all their wars against the French," Gage wrote, and here was the bitterness of a veteran of the hard fighting in that last war, "they never showed so much conduct, attention and perseverance as they do now."

Perhaps sensing that Bunker Hill would mark the end of his tenure in America, Gage made no suggestions for future operations or strategy. He wrote simply, "I think it my duty to let your lordship know the true situation of affairs that administration may take some measures accordingly."

The next day Gage wrote to Lord Barrington, who was the secretary at war, and was more forthcoming with his ideas. Gage, of course, had been saying all along that the British army in America was too small. "A small body acting in one spot will not avail," he wrote. "You must have large armies, making diversions on different sides, to divide their force. The loss we have sustained is greater than we can bear." Gage would also mention a point that would become central to British thinking over the next year—that New York was the proper place from which to conduct the war.

It had apparently become popular in Boston to describe the army's approach to the Americans as "taking the bull by the horns." A number of letters and journals mention the use of that cliché. Gage relates this to Barrington, and the words seem to mock him after the frustration and struggle of his year as governor, a year that ended with the bloodshed he so dreaded and tried so hard to avoid. "We are here," he wrote, "to use a common expression, taking the bull by the horns, attacking the enemy in their strong parts. I wish this cursed place was burned."

Frustration with Gage had been building in London, as is clear from Dartmouth's letters urging more aggressive action. The Pyrrhic victory at Bunker Hill, coming on the heels of the humiliation of Lexington and Concord, was the end. Three days after Gage's report on Bunker Hill reached London, the decision was made to replace him.

The reaction in England was more shock than outrage. Unlike Lexington and Concord, Bunker Hill was a victory for British arms, which meant that the outrage was considerably less. It was rather the slaughter of British troops that took the people of England aback. No battle from the Seven Years' War came close to the casualty rate of Bunker Hill, not even Wolfe's capture of Quebec or the Battle of Minden, long considered to be examples of the worst kind of carnage.

Any number of reasons were put forth. It was supposed, incorrectly, that the Americans had rifles, and not just smooth-bore muskets, and with those they were able to accurately pick off the officers. The strength of the redoubt was greatly exaggerated, as was the number of Americans engaged, until the odds appeared to be two or three to one against the British.

Most of the blame for the great loss was heaped on Gage. He was criticized for not getting gunboats into the Mystic River, for not reconnoitering the defenses, for not concentrating an attack against the rail fence, and for not following up on the victory. They were legitimate criticisms all, but they were criticisms that should have been directed at Howe, not Gage.

From the evidence available, it seems clear that once Gage gave command of the attack on the rebel redoubt to Howe, he did not interfere with his subordinate's decisions. Had Bunker Hill been an unalloyed victory, Gage surely would have been praised for not trying to direct the action from headquarters. As it was, Gage as commander in chief took the blame, and the fall. His military reputation was ruined.

Howe in turn came in for considerable praise. Certainly his courage on the battlefield was extraordinary. Every one of his aides was wounded around him, many killed, but still Howe led from the front. For all his heroism, though, it was also his decision, and his alone, to twice fling the flank companies at the rail fence and to send Pigot's wing straight at the redoubt, in full packs and perfectly dressed lines, marching slowly up hill into the waiting muskets. Gage had nothing to do with that.

Dartmouth's letter of dismissal, sent to Gage in early August, was curt, its tone of disapproval unmistakable. "From the tenour of your letters of June twenty-fifth," he wrote, "and from the state of affairs after the action of the seventeenth, the King is led to conclude that you have little expectation of effecting any thing further this campaign, and has therefore commanded me to signify to you His Majesty's pleasure, that you . . . return to England." Gage was ostensibly recalled to report on conditions in America in preparation for the next year's campaign. In truth, they just wanted him removed from command.

On the same day, a letter was sent to Howe appointing him commander in chief of all British forces in the colonies on the Atlantic seaboard. General Guy Carleton, governor of Quebec, was to have command of the forces in Canada.

It was three months after Bunker Hill before Gage learned his fate, and he could not have been surprised. In that three months the British army in Boston had done little besides watch the Americans dig in even deeper around the city.

Once Charlestown was in British hands it stayed there. The troops not wounded or killed at Bunker Hill remained on the ground, and replacements were sent out to fill in the losses of the various regiments. The American redoubt on Breed's Hill was strengthened, and a proper fortification was built on Bunker Hill, with ditches and palisades and ramparts with artillery leering down Charlestown Neck. A genuine barracks was raised on the hill, and camps laid out in lines of straight white tents on the fields over which so many redcoats had marched to their death. William Howe remained in command of the division.

On October 10 Gage boarded a ship in Boston and sailed for England. Most of his professional life had been spent in America. It was there that he met and married his wife, and there that his children were born. He was never to return.

Various groups of citizens presented Gage with farewell addresses. One, from the "principal Inhabitants of the Town of Boston," came very close to the truth of Gage's situation. It assured the departing governor that if "a restoration of quiet and good order could have been effected in the Province, by the influence of personal character," then Gage was the man who could have done it. Unfortunately, "the general sentiments were too strong, and too far heightened," for Gage or anyone else to prevent the inevitable effusion of blood. While Gage's efforts were not widely applauded in London, the Loyalists in Boston, who really understood what he was up against, seem to have sincerely appreciated his efforts.

It would now be William Howe's turn to wade into the quagmire. What Dartmouth did not know, as he wrote the orders making William Howe commander in chief, was that Howe had just endured a wrenching and life-altering experience. The William Howe who commanded the orderly troops entrenched on Bunker Hill in August was not the same man who had led the flank companies against the rail fence in June. Howe had seen what entrenched Americans could do. He had been responsible for ungodly losses among his own men. It was a lesson he would not forget.

THE PATRIOT REACTION

Americans today do not look on the Battle of Bunker Hill as an American loss. Indeed, most Americans would probably be surprised to learn that the embattled farmers were not the winners. In the days and weeks following the fight, however, the Americans understood that they did indeed lose, and recriminations began to fly.

Hubris played a big part in the Battle of Bunker Hill, a big part on both sides. Certainly it was hubris that led to Howe's not bothering to reconnoiter and to his willingness to march his troops right into the guns of the entrenched Americans. Equally certain, it was American hubris that led to the battle in the first place.

Up until the fighting of June 17, American arms had fared well against the vaunted redcoats. At several alarms the minutemen had turned out and stood their ground, undaunted by the British columns. The Battle of Lexington and Concord had been an unmitigated American victory, a genuine routing of the enemy. At Grape Island, Noddle's Island, and Hog Island Americans had held their own and come off as victors. They had burned the *Diana* and locked the British up in Boston, where they held them besieged.

By the time Ward ordered Prescott to march for Charlestown, the various colonial armies were feeling confident about their ability to fight the British. The army's self-importance was growing out of proportion with its strength and professional competence. That was the circumstance that led Joseph Warren and the others to warn the members of Congress that they had better assume control before the military's sense of itself ended with its taking over the government of Massachusetts. It was in that context that Artemas Ward issued orders for the ill-conceived entrenchment on Bunker Hill.

Given their recent history, the various American armies did not look on a three-hour battle that ended in a Yankee rout as a particular victory. Courts-martial were convened for Gerrish, Callender, Gridley, and others. Artemas Ward was roundly criticized. Some believed that the American loss was due to actual treachery on the part of some officers, and not simple incompetence.

The American killed numbered 115, the wounded around 270, with 30 captured out of the 2,500 to 3,500 men who had fought in the battle. It was bad, but it was nothing compared with the British casualties. As more authentic reports of these reached their ears, the Americans began to see the results of the fighting in a new light.

James Warren wrote to John Adams a few days after the battle. His letter expressed the ambiguous feelings he and others had toward the outcome, and the high expectations left in the wake of Lexington and Concord. He wrote that the fighting "terminated with less success on our side than any one that has taken place before. However, they have nothing to boast of but the possession of the Ground. You will say that is enough. It is enough to mark with Infamy those who suffered [allowed] it; but they have paid very dearly for it, in the loss of many men."

Warren was ready to "mark with Infamy" the men who had yielded the ground to the British, harsh words for men who had fought so hard with so little support. Warren, like others, blamed the defeat on Artemas Ward's lack of leadership. Had the troops had "a Lee or Washington instead of a General destitute of all military Ability and Spirit to command them, it is my opinion that the day would have terminated with as much Glory to America as the 19th of April." Warren urged Congress to do something, as Massachusetts would not replace Ward.

As it happened, Congress already had. On June 15, two days before the Battle of Bunker Hill, "the President [of Congress, John Hancock] informed Colo. Washington that the Congress had yesterday, Unanimously made choice of him to be the General & Commander in Chief of the American Forces." Charles Lee was selected as a major general.

Washington, with some reservations, accepted the post. On June 23 he set out from Philadelphia for Boston, having not yet heard anything but vague rumors of the Battle of Bunker Hill. He was in New York on the

25th when an express rider from Boston arrived on his way to Philadelphia. The rider was carrying a letter to John Hancock containing the Provincial Congress of Massachusetts's full report on the Battle of Bunker Hill. Washington took the liberty of opening the letter, induced "by several Gentlemen of New York who were anxious to know the particulars of the Affair of the 17th Inst." Washington, apparently, was not personally motivated by anything so base as curiosity.

With that letter, Washington learned that the first real battle of the war had taken place after his appointment but before his arrival. The letter ended with a further plea from the Provincial Congress, which did not yet know of Washington's appointment, for a commander in chief in Boston. That plea no doubt spurred Washington on in his desire to get to Cambridge quickly.

The greatest single loss at the Battle of Bunker Hill, acknowledged by British and Americans alike, was that of Dr. Joseph Warren. The British soldiers and Loyalists paid Warren a backhanded compliment with the pleasure they took in his being killed. Boston Loyalist Ann Hulton, her pen dripping venom, wrote:

> Since Adams went to Philadelphia, one Warren, a rascally patriot and apothecary in this town, has had the lead in the Provincial Congress. He signed commissions and acted as President. This fellow happily was killed . . . You may judge what the herd must be when such a one is their leader.

Not all Loyalists, or British officers, dismissed Warren's contributions so easily, and many recognized his death as a great benefit to the Tory cause. One correspondent from Cambridge relates a conversation with a British officer who told him "the officers and soldiers triumph very much at the death of Doctor Warren, saying it is better to them than five hundred men." Lieutenant Francis, Lord Rawdon, writing to his uncle, related with triumph the death of Warren. There is arguably no better compliment paid to Warren's effectiveness as a revolutionary leader than the pleasure with which his enemies greeted his death.

A number of stories circulated concerning the treatment of Warren's body. Some suggested that the fine clothes were stripped off and sold. Others said that after burial Warren was disinterred several times so that curious British officers could take a look at him. Captain Walter Sloane Laurie, the British officer given the task of burying the dead, wrote, "Doctr. Warren . . . I found among the slain, and stuffed the scoundrell with another Rebel in one hole and there he and his seditious principles may remain."

Warren and his principles did not remain buried on Bunker Hill forever. Nine months after the battle, the British abandoned Boston for good, and Breed's Hill was once again in American hands. On April 4, 1776, after a week or so of searching, Warren's body was found under about three feet of ground by two of his brothers. Though badly decomposed, the body was identified by Warren's friend Paul Revere, who had made two false teeth for the doctor (this was perhaps one of the first examples of a body being identified through dental records).

The Massachusetts House of Representatives had already voted to erect a monument in Warren's honor, but before they could, the Lodge of Freemasons requested that they be allowed to bury Warren with their customary rights. On April 8 a funeral procession left from the statehouse. Freemasons, Continental troops, and Warren's many friends joined in the procession. Among the pallbearers were Artemas Ward and Colonel Richard Gridley.

Warren's body, enclosed in an elegant coffin, was placed in the tomb of George Richards Minot, a friend of the Warren family. As the years passed and Warren's fame was eclipsed by those who carried on the fight he had helped start, the location of his coffin was lost. In 1825 it was rediscovered and the bones identified by Warren's nephew based on the teeth and the bullet wound to the head. The remains were moved to the Warren tomb at St. Paul's Church in Boston, and later to Forest Hills Cemetery southwest of Boston.

In 1794 the King Solomon Lodge of Freemasons erected a monument to Warren on the spot where he was believed to have died. The monument stood for more than thirty years until it was superseded by the

Bunker Hill Monument. Today a fine marble statue of Warren stands in the visitors' center beside the monument, on ground that Warren walked as he took his place in the redoubt.

The Patriots' grief over Warren's death was immediate and widespread. "Here fell our worthy and much lamented Friend Doctor Warren," wrote James Warren, "with as much Glory as Wolfe on the Plains of Abraham, after performing many feats of Bravery . . . At once admired and lamented in such a manner as to make it difficult to determine whether regret or envy predominated."

Abigail Adams wrote to her husband, "I wish I could contradict the report of the Doctors Death, but it is a lamentable Truth,—and the tears of multitudes pay tribute to his memory." Even the official report of the Committee of Safety, of which Warren had been so integral a part, read, "Among the dead was Major General Joseph Warren, a man whose memory will be endeared to his countrymen, and to the worthy in every part and age of the world, so long as virtue and valour shall be esteemed among mankind."

Joseph Warren was the first great hero and martyr for the cause of liberty and American independence. He fit the role perfectly: young, handsome, a man who eschewed a profitable career and all but ruined himself financially for the cause, a man who was at once orator, scribe, and soldier for the rights of the colonists. There was no lack of eulogies, orations, and essays dedicated to Warren, at his death and for years to come. Now largely forgotten, Joseph Warren at the moment of his death was one of the most famous men in America, the shining light of the Glorious Cause, the very symbol of American virtue and patriotism.

THE ECHOES OF BUNKER HILL

The consequences of the Battle of Bunker Hill were many and long felt. The Americans, fearing a British assault and seeing firsthand what they could do when entrenched, began immediately to dig in all around

Boston. Washington's arrival only increased this activity, until the lines of the Continental Army were ringing the city with earthworks.

The British had also seen what the Americans could do when entrenched, and they did not care to see it again. Howe, taking over for Gage, had no interest in assaulting the American lines, in part because he could see no reason to do so. Even if he could roll them up, which would cost him dearly, he could not take or hold Massachusetts.

The lesson of Bunker Hill and the subsequent entrenchment bought the American army nine months of peace in the Massachusetts theater. In that time Washington's army was dissolved by the expiration of enlistments and built anew, right at the door of the British troops, but nothing was done to interfere. General James Wilkinson would later write that the Americans were indebted to the bold stance taken on Breed's Hill "for the unmolested occupancy of our position before Boston."

One would not expect William Howe to admit to having been unnerved by his experience at the rail fence, and of course he never did. Still, historians have long suspected that he was so shaken by the fighting on Breed's Hill that it prevented him from taking advantage of several extraordinary opportunities, the foremost being the rout of the Americans on Long Island. The idea that Howe grew overly cautious as a result of Bunker Hill crops up soon after the end of the war. American general Henry Lee, the great cavalry officer, writing after the war, suggested, "The sad and impressive experience of this murderous day sunk deep into the mind of Sir William Howe; and it seems to have had its influence on all its subsequent operations, with decisive control."

How could an experience such as the one William Howe endured at the rail fence, when he felt "a moment that I never felt before," not have an influence on his thinking? It was not any heightened concern for his own physical safety but an unwillingness to see his men butchered in such a manner again. "I freely confess to you," he wrote to a friend after the battle, "when I look to the consequences of it, in the loss of so many brave officers, I do it with horror."

William Howe served as commander in chief through the first years of the war and was presented with opportunities the like of which Henry

Clinton would never see once he in turn assumed the role of commander in chief. Howe's tenure took place when the Revolution was no more than a local fight in which the British army and hired German troops were trying to crush a ragtag insurrection. France and Spain were not part of the war; Howe did not have to worry about threats to the West Indies or a French invasion of England. There were no enemy fleets off the American coast. Yet he could never defeat the rebels, and on more than one occasion, at the Battle of Brooklyn and others, he was taken to task for what seemed an inexplicable timidity.

By the time Howe turned command of the army over to Clinton, the American Revolution was a world war. Clinton, who had desperately wanted to send his men after the fleeing Americans on Brooklyn Heights, now had to contend with French soldiers on American soil and a French fleet off the coast.

We do not know what motivated William Howe, but it is quite possible, indeed likely, that his ability to fling his troops at entrenched Americans, to prosecute the war to the full extent needed, might have died with all those men around him on the slopes of Breed's Hill. By an odd twist, the American Revolution may have been won even as it began, at the Battle of Bunker Hill.

Acknowledgments

As with every book, there are many, many people beyond the confines of my office to whom I owe a great debt of gratitude. I can name only a fraction of them here. There are first the librarians and archivists, the guides through the sources, both printed and original, on which such a book is built. In particular I am indebted to Peter Drummey, the Stephen T. Riley Librarian at the Massachusetts Historical Society. He and his fine, professional staff provided me with the primary resources in researching this book. Little work could be done on early Revolutionary War history without the Massachusetts Historical Society.

Closer to home, the staff and the collections of the Hawthorne-Longfellow Library at Bowdoin College provided invaluable support. What they could not provide was located by the reference staff at the Curtis Memorial Library in Brunswick, Maine. They are Janet Fullerton, Linda Oliver, Carol Lestock, Paul Dostie, and Marian Dalton, and they have supported me through many books over the years. As the Internet and other electronic resources become more useful, it is always a good idea to have on board an expert in navigating those waters. My quartermaster there is Charley Seavey, who has been a terrific and consistent help, and I owe him a great deal. Next round is on me.

The one constant in my writing career, which now spans sixteen books, has been my agent, Nat Sobel. Without his support I quite literally would not be able to continue on, and I am now and forever will be grateful to him for that and for all his kindness. That appreciation extends to Adia Wright and all the fine people at Sobel Weber Associates.

Peter Joseph at Thomas Dunne Books has supported this project from its inception. To him I owe the greatest debt of gratitude for his patience, understanding, and thoughtful insight. He has always displayed a level of courtesy more typical of the eighteenth century than the twenty-first, and for that I will always be grateful. My thanks as well to the many fine people at Thomas Dunne, including Margaret Smith and India Cooper.

Last here, but never least in my heart, is my wife, Lisa, whose support makes this strange occupation a possibility and a reality. Thank you.

Notes

ABBREVIATIONS

AA   *American Archives*

DAR   *Documents of the American Revolution*

JCC   *Journals of the Continental Congress*

MHSP   *Massachusetts Historical Society Proceedings*

NDAR   *Naval Documents of the American Revolution*

PGW, RWS   *Papers of George Washington, Revolutionary War Series*

PROLOGUE: THE BATTLE OF BROOKLYN

2. "your best men should": Washington to Putnam, *PGW, RWS* 6:128.

3. "The Enemy": Washington to Lund Washington, *PGW, RWS* 6:136.

3. "General Sullivan is to take command": General Orders, in Johnston, *Campaign of 1776* 3:26.

4. "His wants are common": Schecter, *Battle,* 122.

THE BRITISH COMMAND

5. "a shy bitch": Clinton, *Narrative,* xvii.

6. "though a subordinate officer": Ibid., 39.

7. with 5,000 British troops: Long Island Historical Society, *Battle of Long Island,* 173.

7. Howe family: Fischer, *Washington's Crossing*; Gruber, *Howe Brothers*; Mackesy, *War for America*; Middlekauff, *Glorious Cause*.

9. 19,000 British and German troops: Serle, *American Journal*, 77.

JAMAICA PASS

10. "the First Brigade and the Seventy-First": Howe to Germain, in Long Island Historical Society, *Battle of Long Island*, 379.

10. "Between eleven and twelve": Clinton, *Narrative*, 42.

12. "descried two men coming": "Letter from an Officer in Col. Atlee's Battalion," Long Island Historical Society, *Battle of Long Island*, 364.

12. "the enemy were advancing": Parsons to Adams, in Johnston, *Campaign of 1776*, 35.

12. "About 3 oClock": Stirling to Washington, *PGW, RWS* 6:159.

13. "cool clear & pleasant": Serle, *American Journal*, 78.

13. "Col: Atlee . . . Informed me": Stirling to Washington, *PGW, RWS* 6:159.

13. "to the great fire": "Atlee's Journal," Long Island Historical Society, *Battle of Long Island*, 353.

13. "repulsed them in every attack": Parsons to Adams, in Johnston, *Campaign of 1776*, 34.

14. "did not expect any good": Clinton, *Narrative*, 42n.

15. "convinced when the army": "Journal of Samuel Miles," Johnston, *Campaign of 1776*, 61.

OPPORTUNITY MADE AND LOST

16. "halted for the soldiers": Howe to Germain, in Long Island Historical Society, *Battle of Long Island*, 380.

16. "In this possition": Stirling to Washington, *PGW, RWS* 6:160.

17. "We took care to tell": "Account of the Massacre," Long Island Historical Society, *Battle of Long Island*, 402.

18. "Our men were most eager": "Journal of Captain Harris," ibid., 407.

18. "I had at that moment": Clinton, *Narrative*, 43.

19. "in evident confusion": "Account . . . by C. Stedmen," Long Island Historical Society, *Battle of Long Island*, 456.

19. "*frightened, defeated,* and *dismayed*": "Collier Journal," ibid., 412.

19. "Had they [the British troops]": Howe to Germain, ibid., 380.

CHAPTER 1: THE LEXINGTON ALARM

24. "I was forced to give": Percy to Duke of Northumberland, in Percy, *Letters,* 34.

24. "The people in this part": Ibid., 29.

24. "Our affairs here": Percy to Rev. Percy, ibid., 40.

25. "appeared to me": Dartmouth to Gage, *DAR* 9:39.

26. "the Grenadiers and Light Infantry": Barker, *British in Boston*, 29.

26. Gage's preparations: Fischer, *Revere's Ride;* Frothingham, *Siege;* Urban, *Fusiliers.*

27. "In consequence of this": Crozier to Rogers, in Commager and Morris, *Spirit of '76,* 77.

28. "with as much order": Lister, *Concord Fight,* 27.

29. "men had dropped": Frothingham, *Siege,* 72.

29. "The Country was an amazing": Barker, *British in Boston,* 37.

29. "At last": Fischer, *Revere's Ride,* 232.

30. "Very few Men had any": Barker, *British in Boston,* 37.

30. "In this critical situation": Ibid., 35.

"A CLEVER LITTLE ARMY"

30. "The town was a good deal": Mackenzie, *Diary,* 18.

32. "little suspecting": Evelyn, *Memoir,* 54.

32. "most delightfully varied": Percy, *Letters,* 32.

32. "This country is": Evelyn, *Memoir,* 54.

32. "In all the places we marched through": Mackenzie, *Diary,* 18.

32. "was informed that the Rebels": Percy, *Letters,* 50.

32. "as fast as good order": Ibid., 52.

33. "We heard some straggling shots": Mackenzie, *Diary,* 19.

33. "I immediately ordered": Percy, *Letters,* 50.

33. "As soon as the Rebels": Barker, *British in Boston,* 36.

33. "by reason of the Stone walls": Mackenzie, *Diary,* 19.

34. "anxious to know the reason": Lister, *Concord Fight,* 22.

35. "The rebels were in great no^s.": Percy, *Letters,* 52.

35. "We was then met": Lister, *Concord Fight*, 30.

35. "did not imagine there would be": Evelyn, *Memoir*, 98.

35. "rested ourselves a little while": Barker, *British in Boston*, 36.

35. "to examine my Arme": Lister, *Concord Fight*, 31.

35. "The Rebels endeavored": Mackenzie, *Diary*, 20.

36. "numbers of armed men": Ibid.

CHAPTER TWO: DR. JOSEPH WARREN

37. "Oppressions planted 'em": Middlekauff, *Glorious Cause*, 75.

37. "the famous Doctor": "Rawdon's Letter," Commager and Morris, *Spirit of '76*, 131.

38. Life of Warren: Cary, *Warren;* Frothingham, *Life and Times*.

39. "colonies had born": Fox, *Adventures*, 7.

THE POLITICS OF LIBERTY

42. Stamp Act and politics: Cary, *Warren;* Fischer, *Revere's Ride;* Frothingham, *Life and Times;* Middlekauff, *Glorious Cause*.

42. "scattered or destroyed": Hutchinson to Jackson, in Draper, *Struggle for Power*, 245.

42. "I was solicited": Adams autobiography, sheet 11 of 53, electronic ed.

43. "The whole continent": Warren to Dana, in Frothingham, *Life and Times*, 20.

43. "When a diabolical thirst": Ibid., 40.

44. list of seven groups: Fischer, *Revere's Ride*, 301.

"A NEW AND MORE TERRIFIC SCENE"

46. "long fateagueing March" and "retired from the right": Lister, *Concord Fight*, 31.

46. "I ordered the Gren[adiers]s": Percy, *Letters*, 52.

47. "Seeing Lt Col^l Smith": Lister, *Concord Fight*, 31.

47. "middling stature": Heath, *Memoirs*, 15.

48. "Keep up a brave heart": Frothingham, *Life and Times*, 457.

48. "About ten in the morning": Petition of Jacob Rogers, in Frothingham, *Siege*, 371.

49. "the old man": Frothingham, *Life and Times,* 457.

49. "had been broken": Heath, *Memoirs,* 22.

THE LONG RETREAT

50. "found the Balls": Lister, *Concord Fight,*

50. "our men had very few opportunities": Mackenzie, *Diary,* 21.

50. "came on pretty close": Ibid.

51. "What makes an insurrection": Percy, *Letters,* 38.

51. Almost 60 percent: Fischer, *Revere's Ride,* 319.

51. "Nor are several of their men": Percy, *Letters,* 53.

52. "They have men amongst them": Ibid.

53. "We did not fight as you did": Extracts from Intercepted Letters, *AA 4,* 2:440.

53. "If we had had time": Mackenzie, *Diary,* 22.

53. "imprudently posted themselves": Heath, *Memoirs,* 64.

53. "suffer'd for their temerity": Barker, *British in Boston,* 36.

53. "anything of value": Gordon's Account, *AA 4,* 2:630.

54. "On descending from the high grounds": Heath, *Memoirs,* 22.

54. "might either be broken down": Mackenzie, *Diary,* 21.

54. "being exceedingly fatigued": Ibid.

55. "It was the *Somerset* alone": Graves, "Conduct," *NDAR* 1:193.

55. "We then March'd": Lister, *Concord Fight,* 31.

55. "When the troops had drawn up": Mackenzie, *Diary,* 22.

55. "ordered a guard": Heath, *Memoirs,* 23.

56. British and American casualties: Fischer, *Revere's Ride,* 321.

56. "Damn them": Account of an Attack, *AA 4,* 2:488.

56. "I am still convinced": Percy, *Letters,* 35

56. "Whoever looks upon them": Ibid., 53.

CHAPTER THREE: "THE BUTCHERING HANDS OF AN INHUMAN SOLDIERY"

57. Oh! what a glorious": Gordon, *History,* 311.

58. "The barbarous murders": Frothingham, *Life and Times,* 466.

58. "If they proceed": Gage to Dartmouth, in Gage, *Correspondence,* 400.

59. Gage's background: Alden, *Gage in America;* Fischer, *Revere's Ride,* 319.

COMMANDER IN CHIEF

62. fifteen regiments stretched: "Queries of Chalmers," 367.

63. "*Resolved,* that his Majesty's": Middlekauff, *Glorious Cause,* 80.

63. "the Populace of Boston": Gage to Conway, in Gage, *Correspondence,* 67.

63. "Every thing is quiet": Ibid.

64. "They are of various Characters": Ibid., 69.

64. "enormous Engine": Adams, *Diary and Autobiography,* 1:263.

65. "If we enforce": Draper, *Struggle for Power,* 280.

65. "claimed to themselves": Declaratory Act, online at Avalon Project.

65. "Rejoicings on this Occasion": Gage to Conway, in Gage, *Correspondence,* 92.

GAGE IN BOSTON

68. "Quash this spirit": Gage to Barrington, in Alden, *Gage in America,* 159.

69. "The red-coats make": Frothingham, *Life and Times,* 100.

69. "Broils soon commenced": "Queries of Chalmers," 370.

70. "become more retired": Cary, *Warren,* 103.

71. "your Lordship's friendly": Gage to Hillsborough, in Gage, *Correspondence,* 334.

CHAPTER FOUR: WEED OF SLAVERY

72. Politics of tea: Cary, *Warren;* Frothingham, *Life and Times;* Labaree, *Boston Tea Party;* Mackesy, *War for America;* Middlekauff, *Glorious Cause.*

73. 265,000 pounds: Fleming, *Liberty,* 75.

73. "It must afford": *Boston Gazette,* January 11, 1773, in Frothingham, *Life and Times,* 221.

73. "The UNION of the colonies": *Boston Gazette,* June 14, 1773, in ibid., 220.

75. "What difficulties may arise": Drake, *Tea Leaves,* xv.

76. "From whom are you": Drake, *Tea Leaves,* xxvii.

77. one hundred and fourteen chests . . . : Quincy, *Memoir,* 122.

77. "weed of slavery": Adams to Warren, *Warren-Adams Letters,* 19.

THE BOSTON TEA PARTY

78. "Friends! Brethren!": Hutchinson, *History,* 429.

79. "My Heart beats": Adams to Warren, *Warren-Adams Letters,* 19.

80. "Who knows how tea": Drake, *Tea Leaves,* lxiii.

80. "a number of brave": *Massachusetts Gazette,* ibid., lxviii.

80. "Boston Harbor a tea-pot" and "Hurrah for Griffin's wharf": Ibid., lxxii.

83. "You cannot imagine": Frothingham, *Life and Times,* 281.

83. "the boldest stroke": Drake, *Tea Leaves,* lxxxvi.

83. "This destruction of the tea": Adams, *Diary,* 2:85.

INTOLERABLE ACTS

84. £9,659: Fleming, *Liberty,* 79.

84. "To engage the people": Hutchinson, *History,* in Commager and Morris, *Spirit of '76,* 10.

85. "The affair of Destroying": Cunningham, *Letters and Diary of John Rowe,* 258.

86. "The Doctor was so abused": Alden, *Gage in America,* 200n.

86. "do amount to the crime": Attorney and Solicitor General to Dartmouth, *DAR* 8:47.

86. "be completely effected": Dartmouth to Hutchinson, ibid., 61.

87. "His Majesty, upon information": King's Message, *AA 4,* 1:32.

87. "the *Americans* were": Order for Committee, *AA 4,* 1:42.

87. "the town of Boston": Ibid.

87. "instead of quieting": Question on the Passage of the Bill, *AA 4,* 1:38.

CHAPTER FIVE: GAGE'S RETURN

89. "I have not one magistrate": Hutchinson to Dartmouth, *DAR* 8:70.

90. "The King having thought": Dartmouth to Gage, ibid., 86.

92. "unconstitutional and unwarrantable": Hutchinson to Dartmouth, ibid., 72.

92. "The owners of the tea": Hutchinson to Dartmouth, ibid., 62.

93. "For flagrant injustice": Adams to Lee, *AA 4,* 1:332.

93. "We are of opinion": Providence Town Meeting, ibid., 333.

93. "thus to baffle": Resolves of Chestertown, ibid., 334.

93. "An union of the colonies": "To the Freemen of America," ibid., 335.

"I CANNOT GET A WORSE COUNCIL"

94. "not daring to reside": Gage to Dartmouth, *DAR* 8:116.

94. "to determine upon proper measures": Town Meeting in Boston, *AA 4,* 1:331.

94. "many of the principal gentlemen": Ibid.

95. "There were but very few": Cunningham, *Letters and Diary of John Rowe,* 271.

95. "The Lively, Man of Warr": Ibid., 269.

95. "We expect studied": Adams to Lee, *AA 4,* 1:333.

96. "I am afraid of the Consequences": Cunningham, *Letters and Diary of John Rowe,* 274.

97. "were upon moderate": Gage to Dartmouth, *DAR* 8:136.

97. "If the dissolution": Ibid.

MEN AND ARMS

98. "notwithstanding the violent threat": Evelyn, *Memoir,* 27.

98. "with a small park of artillery": Ibid.

99. "The Preston Man of Warr": Cunningham, *Letters and Diary of John Rowe,* 277.

99. "the honour of commanding": Percy, *Letters,* 30.

99. "Yesterday arrived at *Marblehead*": *AA 4,* 1:593.

99. Life of Putnam: Homans and Dearborn, *Cyclopedia of American Biography.*

100. "The old hero, Putnam": Frothingham, *Life and Times,* 341.

101. "Haste now prevents it": Warren to Adams, ibid., 352.

101. "for regulating the government": Gage to Dartmouth, *DAR* 8:163.

101. "Such a set of timid creatures": Percy, *Letters,* 30.

101. "by such means": Gage to Dartmouth, DAR VIII, 163.

102. "That as true and loyal": Middlesex Resolutions, *AA 4,* 1:750.

CHAPTER SIX: THE LOYAL AND ORDERLY PEOPLE

104. "the Governor is dispos'd": Andrews, "Letters," 339.

105. "near, or quite": Andrews, "Letters," 361.

105. "they would be watched": Gage to Dartmouth, *DAR* 8:181.

106. "obliging every Man": Kemble, *Journals,* 39.

106. "only step now": Gage to Dartmouth, *DAR* 8:181.

107. "cut a canal across": Andrews, "Letters," 355.

107. "to protect his Majesty's": Report of Selectmen, *AA 4*, 1:775.

108. "at the formidable appearance": Address to Gage, ibid., 779.

109. formidable battery: Frothingham, *Siege*, 16.

109. "such numbers going": Gage's Answer, *AA 4*, 1:780.

109. "refuse to be an actor": Committee to Gage, ibid., 781.

THE SUFFOLK RESOLVES

110. "The new Council": Gage to Dartmouth, *DAR* 8:201.

110. "persecuted, scourged": Suffolk Resolves, *AA 4*, 1:776.

113. "read with great applause": *JCC* 1:39n.

113. "one of the happiest": Ibid.

113. "By this treasonable vote": Galloway's Statement, *Letters of the Continental Congress*, 56.

113. "When you ask": Adams to Palmer, ibid., 48.

114. "tried patience": Adams to Warren, ibid., 47.

114. "I saw Ld Dartmouth": Hutchinson, *Diary*, 284.

CHAPTER SEVEN: A WELL-DIGESTED PLAN

115. "talk of fixing a plan": Gage to Dartmouth, *DAR* 8:198.

115. "at Concord": *Suffolk Resolves, AA 4*, 1:776.

115. "the present disordered": Gage's Proclamation, *AA 4*, 1:810.

115. "to resolve themselves": Provincial Congress, ibid., 829.

116. "The New England governments": George III to North, in Commager and Morris, *Spirit of '76*, 61.

116. "the least intention": Address to Gage, ibid., 836.

116. "some difficulty in contriving": Gage to Dartmouth, *DAR* 8:212.

116. "It is surely": Gage's Reply, *AA 4*, 1:837.

117. "moderation and forbearance": Gage to Dartmouth, *DAR* 8:212.

117. "the good people": Evelyn, *Memoir*, 34.

117. "Is this not encouraging": Barker, *British in Boston*, 3.

118. "a well digested Plan": *Provincial Congress, AA 4*, 1:844.

118. "Nothing of any consequence": Evelyn, *Memoir,* 38.

118. "persons unlawfully assembled": Gage's Proclamation, *AA 4,* 1:973.

A WINTER OF DISCONTENT

119. "Nothing has happened": Barker, *British in Boston,* 25.

120. "experienc'd the chief part": Lister, *Concord Fight,* 21.

120. "disposing of Arms": Mackenzie, *Diary,* 6.

121. "The officers and soldiers": Andrews, "Letters," 401.

121. "the most violent fellows": Mackenzie, *Diary,* 9.

121. "take notice of": Ibid.

122. "threw themselves": Warren's Oration, *AA 4,* 2:38.

122. "contained nothing so violent": Mackenzie, *Diary,* 9.

122. "a most seditious": Barker, *British in Boston,* 25.

122. "As there were numbers": Mackenzie Diary, 9.

123. "a grand exhibition": Lister, *Concord Fight,* 21.

123. "Country Fellow": Cunningham, *Letters and Diary of John Rowe,* 290.

123. "for breach of the Act": *Letter from Boston, AA 4,* 2:120.

124. "The streets and Neck lin'd": Andrews, "Letters," 402.

124. "The officers": Ibid., 401.

124. "It contained the most mischievous": Ibid.

124. "many Characters": Cunningham, *Letters and Diary of John Rowe,* 290.

RESISTANCE TO REBELLION

125. "would march but thirty rods": Diary of Ezra Stiles, *NDAR* 1:109.

126. "great numbers, completely armed": Warren to Lee, *AA 4,* 2:256.

126. "Expresses were sent": Barker, *British in Boston,* 27.

126. "Things now every day": Percy, *Letters,* 48.

127. "The most natural and most eligible": Gage to Dartmouth, DAR 9:37.

128. "rather encourages resistance": Gage to Dartmouth, *DAR* 8: 221.

128. "the acts of a tumultuous": Dartmouth to Gage, *DAR* 9:37.

129. "the talk of Government's": Andrews, "Letters," 332.

130. "a large quantity of military stores": Gage to Dartmouth, *DAR* 9:102.

130. "All things wear": Warren to Mercy Warren, *Warren-Adams Letters,* 44.

CHAPTER EIGHT: FROM THE PENN TO THE SWORD

135. "All the Boats": *Preston's* Journal, *NDAR* 1:195.

136. "were ordered to take": Mackenzie, *Diary,* 22.

136. "threw up a work": Barker, *British in Boston,* 37.

136. "The number of Guard Boats": Graves, "Narrative," *NDAR* 1:202.

137. "to act hostiley": Ibid., 193.

138. "be vigilant in moving": Heath, *Memoirs,* 23.

138. spread of the Lexington Alarm: Fischer, *Revere's Ride,* 324.

138. "five hundred armed": Diary of Ezra Stiles, *NDAR* 1:203.

139. "animated with resentment": Letter from New York, *AA 4,* 2:364.

139. "20th All confusion": Tudor, *Diary.*

139. "The Battle of Lexington": Adams, *Diary and Autobiography,* 314.

A MILITIA BECOMES AN ARMY

140. "large quantities of military stores," and list of items: Emerson, *Diaries,* 60.

140. "we are in want": Warren to Reed, in Reed, *Correspondence,* 104.

141. "heard that the Regulars": Ingalls, *War Journal,* 81.

141. "pass over the ground": Heath, *Memoirs,* 24.

141. "Colonel Gardiner repair immediately": "Orderly-Book," 88.

141. "All the eatables in the town": Heath, *Memoirs,* 24.

143. "every officer and soldier": "Orderly-Book," 88.

144. "In the morning [of April 20]": French, *First Year,* 26.

THE BRITISH IN BOSTON

145. "The town is now": Mackenzie, *Diary,* 29.

146. "I believe he was in": Lister, *Concord Fight,* 33.

147. "I stood upon the hills": Andrews, "Letters," 405.

147. "I had and supposed": Lister, *Concord Fight,* 34–35.

148. "frightened out of their wits": Percy, *Letters,* 29.

148. "The whole Country was assembled": Gage to Dartmouth, in Gage, *Correspondence,* 397.

148. "where a Battery is immediately": Mackenzie, *Diary,* 29.

148. "for the Officers to lay": Ibid.

148. "all scows, sloops, schooners": Graves, "Narrative," *NDAR* 1:202.

149. "kept constantly in readiness": Barker, *British in Boston,* 38.

150. "an Officer & a Party": Graves to LeCras, *NDAR* 1:211.

150. "until it is finished": Graves's Secretary to Captain LeCras, *NDAR* 1: 201.

CHAPTER NINE: OFFICERS AND MEN

151. "hasten and encourage": Committee of Safety Circular in Frothingham, *Life and Times,* 466.

151. "We pray your Honours": Committee of Safety Circular, *AA 4,* 2:370.

151. "We are all in motion": *Letter from Wethersfield, AA 4,* 2:362.

152. "I saw General Ward": Adams, *Diary and Autobiography,* 314.

153. 20,000 men turned out: French, *First Year,* 52.

153. "As to the Army": Warren to Adams, *Warren-Adams Letters,* 47.

153. "they have a sufficient": Greenleaf to Hampton Committee, *AA 4,* 2:174.

154. "But for counterintelligence": Livingston, *Putnam,* 185.

155. "as speedily as possible": Putnam to Williams, ibid., 194.

155. "This day, General Putnam": "Orderly-Book," 89.

155. John Stark history: Caleb Stark, *Memoir and Official Correspondence.*

156. "to defend the inhabitants": "Orderly-Book," 89.

156. "This night was Alarmed": Farnsworth, "Diary," 78.

A MOST DISTRESSED CONDITION

157. "I cannot precisely tell": Warren to Lee, *AA 4,* 2:619.

158. "Your Excellency knows": Warren to Gage, ibid., 370.

158. "the Freeholders": Ibid., 375.

158. "After much debate": Cunningham, *Letters and Diary of John Rowe,* 293.

159. "he had no intention": Agreement Between Gage and Town of Boston, *AA 4,* 2:375.

159. "All Business at an end": Cunningham, *Letters and Diary of John Rowe*, 293.

159. "he would desire the Admiral": Report of the Selectmen, *AA 4*, 2:376.

160. "none but the ill inclined": Gage to Dartmouth, in Gage, *Correspondence*, 397.

160. "I can escape": Andrews, "Letters," 405.

161. "The general is perpetually": Warren to Trumbull, in Frothingham, *Life and Times*, 475.

161. "A delay of justice": Provincial Congress to Gage, *AA 4*, 2:798.

161. "As no living Person": Warren to Gage, in French, *First Year*, 125.

162. "General Gage, I fear": Warren to Adams, in Frothingham, *Life and Times*, 483.

CAPTAIN DERBY'S MISSION

162. "to be sent to *England*": Provincial Congress, *AA 4*, 2:483.

162. "Friends and Fellow-Subjects": Letter to Great Britain, ibid., 487.

163. "It is Strange to see": Germain to Irwin, *NDAR* 1:476.

163. "The Opposition here": Hutchinson, *Diary*, 455.

164. "It is very much to be": Dartmouth to Gage, ibid., 481.

164. "I assured many gentlemen": Hutchinson, *Diary*, 466.

164. 'How often have I heard,' ": Hutchinson, *Diary*, 461.

164. "The sword of civil war": "To the Publick," *AA 4*, 2:948.

165. "a test of the people's": Dartmouth to Gage, *DAR* 9:37.

166. "The prospect is dark": Hutchinson, *Diary*, 466.

CHAPTER TEN: THE MASSACHUSETTS ARMY

168. "attended with many difficulties": Warren to Adams, *Warren-Adams Letters*, 47.

168. "The Committee of Safety": Huntington to Trumbull, *AA 4*, 2:423.

168. "The principal Objects": Warren to Adams, *Warren-Adams Letters*, 47.

168. "orders be given to Captain Dexter": Committee of Safety, *AA 4*, 2:745.

169. "My situation is such": Ward to Congress, *AA 4*, 2:384.

169. "As many of the persons": Committee of Safety to Several Towns, *AA 4*, 2:446.

170. "On Monday my Brother": Farnsworth, "Diary," 82.

170. "I came into this place": Huntington to Trumbull, *AA 4*, 2:423.

171. "an army of Thirty Thousand": Provincial Congress, *AA 4*, 2:765.

171. "Mr. S Adams and myself": Hancock to Committee, ibid., 384.

172. "a Coat for a uniform": Provincial Congress, ibid., 766.

THE CONTINENTAL ARMY

172. "better to dig a ditch": Livingston, *Putnam,* 199.

172. "Four captains, eight subalterns": "Orderly-Book," 96.

173. "Shoe themselves": Farnsworth, "Diary," 79.

173. "This movement produced": Warren to Mercy Warren, *Warren-Adams Letters,* 50.

173. "Between 2 and 3000": Barker, *British in Boston,* 46.

174. "truly and faithfully serve": Provincial Congress, *AA 4,* 2:791.

174. returns of the Army: Frothingham, *Siege,* 101.

174. "We are all embarked": Warren to Reed, in Reed, *Correspondence,* 104.

174. "an application to the Continental Congress": Provincial Congress, *AA 4,* 2:801.

175. "But remember to revere": Warren to Mercy Warren, *Warren-Adams Letters,* 50.

175. "There is a degree of timidity": Warren to Adams, ibid., 47.

175. "the Committee appointed": Provincial Congress, *AA 4,* 2:801.

176. "We have the greatest confidence": Letter from the Provincial Congress *AA 4,* 2:487.

176. "seem to me to want": Warren to Adams, *Warren-Adams Letters,* 47.

177. "equally affected our sister Colonies": Provincial Congress to Continental Congress, *AA 4,* 2:621.

178. "I would just observe": Warren to Adams, in Frothingham, *Life and Times,* 485.

"THE MOST RIDICULOUS EXPEDITION THAT EVER WAS PLAN'D . . ."

179. "a strong Redoubt raised": Committee Report, *AA 4,* 2:756.

180. Lieutenant Thomas Innis: Barker, *British in Boston,* 49n.

181. "People, women and children": Abigail Adams to John Adams, in French, *First Year,* 189.

181. "The distance from Weymouth": *Essex Gazette,* Frothingham, *Life and Times,* 492.

181. "There was many guns": Farnsworth, "Diary," 80.

181. "gained honor for their good": Abigail Adams to John Adams, in French, *First Year,* 189.

182. "Thay was mad": Farnsworth, "Diary," 80.

182. "the most ridiculous expedition": Barker, *British in Boston,* 49.

CHAPTER ELEVEN: THREE GENERALS

184. "Captain De Lancy went": Gage to Dartmouth, *DAR* 9:130.

184. "I have the farther satisfaction": Dartmouth to Gage, ibid., 54.

184. "I must then lament": Germain to Suffolk, in Commager and Morris, *Spirit of '76,* 119.

185. "You seem in England": Oliver to Hutchinson, in Hutchinson, *Diary,* 459.

185. "Once these rebels have felt": George III to Sandwich, in Commager and Morris, *Spirit of '76,* 97.

186. "About eight o'clock": Price, "Diary," 185.

187. "I look upon America": Burgoyne to the Commons, in Fonblanque, *Episodes,* 117.

"THE BAULS SUNG LIKE BEES"

188. "all the live-stock": Committee of Safety, *AA 4,* 2:757.

188. "I have this moment": Gage to Graves, *NDAR* 1:523.

189. "strictest look out": Graves to Gage, ibid., 254.

189. "two large Cargoes": Graves to Stephens, ibid., 622.

189. "tar, pitch, junk": Graves to Stephens, *DAR* 9:173.

189. "Went on hog island": Farnsworth, "Diary," 80.

190. "at 2 P.M. Saw a Number": *Preston*'s Journal, *NDAR* 1:546.

190. "disembarked our party": *Cerberus*'s Journal, ibid.

190. "The Adml made the Signal": *Glasgow*'s Journal, ibid., 547.

191. "Kil^d Some hoses": Farnsworth, "Diary," 81.

192. "the Rebels kept a Continual": *Preston*'s Journal, *NDAR* 1:546.

192. "Two of our 3pdrs": *Cerberus*'s Journal, ibid.

192. "About sundown, the firing": Price, "Diary," 185.

193. "About ten At night March^d": Farnsworth, "Diary," 81.

193. "unfortunately got aground": Graves to Stephens, *NDAR* 1:622.

194. "we sot fiar to hur": Farnsworth, "Diary," 81.

194. "it is said that this success": Price, "Diary," 186.

ORDERS FROM LONDON

194. "the people's minds are greatly cooled": Gage to Dartmouth, *DAR* 9:29.

195. "On our arrival we found": Clinton, *Narrative,* 18.

195. "It would be unnecessary": Burgoyne to Rochford, in Fonblanque, *Episodes,* 142.

195. "the want of preparation": Ibid., 144.

196. "this war may be spun out": Howe to Harvey, in French, *First Year,* 207.

196. "tolerably quiet": Evelyn, *Memoirs,* 59.

196. "The two first of these objects": Dartmouth to Gage, *DAR* 9:98.

197. "Whereas, the infatuated multitude": Gage's Proclamation, *AA 4,* 2:967.

198. "Gages Proclamation read": Jenks, *Diary,* 48.

199. "Satan, when driven": Abigail to John Adams, Warren-Adams Letters, 53.

CHAPTER TWELVE: THE SIEGE OF BOSTON

200. "You who riot in pleasure": Oliver to Hutchinson, in Hutchinson, *Diary,* 469.

200. "We have now": Andrews, "Letters," 406.

201. "We are every hour": Oliver Jr. to Hutchinson, in Hutchinson, *Diary,* 458.

201. "issued a proclamation": Gage to Dartmouth, *DAR* 9:171.

202. "surprise and concern": Burgoyne Memorandum, in Fonblanque, *Episodes,* 125.

203. "effects on the spirit": Burgoyne to Rochford, ibid., 145.

203. "command the Town": Burgoyne to Stanley, *AA 4,* 2:1094.

203. "First to possess": Howe to Richard Howe, in French, *First Year,* 208.

204. "*Howe* was to land": Burgoyne to Stanley, *AA 4,* 2:1094.

204. "would then go over": Howe to Richard Howe, in French, *First Year,* 208.

204. "the operations must have been": Burgoyne to Stanley, *AA 4,* 2:1094.

AN APPEAL TO CONGRESS

204. "unless some authority": Warren to Adams, in Frothingham, *Life and Times,* 495.

206. "They now feel rather": Gerry to Congress, *AA 4,* 2:905.

206. "The Army at Cambridge": Oliver to Hutchinson, in Hutchinson, *Diary,* 469.

207. "the inconveniences": *JCC* 2:83.

208. "the Congress have been": Burnett, *Letters of Members,* 116.

208. "borrow the sum of": *JCC* 2:79.

208. "for the use of the continent": Ibid., 85.

209. "a soldier": Ibid., 90.

COUNTERSTROKE

209. "By a gentleman of undoubted": New Hampshire Committee of Safety to Provincial Congress, *AA 4,* 2:979.

210. "it is daily expected": *Committee of Safety,* ibid., 1352.

210. "good intelligence that": *Provincial Congress to Continental Congress, AA 4,* 2:1040.

210. "heard General Burgoyne": Hutchinson, in French, *First Year,* 209.

210. "Whereas it appears": *Committee of Safety, AA 4,* 2:1354.

211. "Yes, yes, they must": Livingston, *Putnam,* 275.

212. "wait on the Hon.": Frothingham, *Life and Times,* 503.

CHAPTER THIRTEEN: CHARLESTOWN HEIGHTS

217. Description of Charlestown peninsula: Frothingham, *Battle-Field,* 4; Frothingham, *Siege.*

219. "almost every housekeeper": "Description of Charlestown Neck," *Detail and Conduct,* 13.

MARCHING ORDERS

220. "Possibly the whole": Chester to Fish, in Frothingham, *Siege,* 390.

220. "the New England army": Committee of Safety Report, *AA 4,* 2:1373.

221. "Frye's, Bridge's, and Wm. Prescott's": "Orderly-Book," 109.

221. "Expecting an engagement": Storrs, *Diary,* 85.

222. "Friday the 16 of June": Brown, "Letter."

223. "we had orders to be redy": Farnsworth, "Diary," 83.

223. "fervent and impressive": "Judge Prescott's Account," 68.

223. "And about Dusk Marched": Farnsworth, "Diary," 83.

224. "the Americans are not": Livingston, *Putnam,* 212.

224. "Colonel Prescott was constantly": Grovesnor in *Particular Account,* 10.

"A SMALL REDOUBT, ABOUT EIGHT RODS SQUARE"

225. "Jest before we turned": Farnsworth, "Diary," 83.

227. "The Rebels . . . flung up": Percy, *Letters,* 56.

227. "a very confused": Gray to Dyer, in Frothingham, *Siege,* 393.

228. "called Colonel Gridley": "Judge Prescott's Account," 69.

228. "proceeded to Breed's Hill": *Report of the Committee of Safety, AA 4,* 2:1373.

229. "the clocks of Boston": "Thatcher's Narrative," Commager and Morris, *Spirit of '76,* 127.

229. "a small redoubt": Ibid., 1374.

229. "ten Rod long": Brown, "Letter."

230. "begun thair intrenchment": Farnsworth, "Diary," 83.

230. "were almost Suffocating": Gearfield Letter.

CHAPTER FOURTEEN: FIRST LIGHT

232. "Modt and fair weather": *Lively's* Journal, *NDAR* 1:700.

233. "Insensibly": Graves, in French, *First Year,* 220.

233. "Carried out the Stream Anchor": *Glasgow's* Journal, *NDAR* 1:701

233. "As a specimen": "Howe's Letter," Commager and Morris, *Spirit of '76,* 131.

233. "Friday night just returned": Clinton Note, in French, *First Year,* 210.

234. "pushed entrenchments": Burgoyne to Stanley, in Drake, *Bunker Hill,* 41.

235. "This work was no sooner": Howe to Richard Howe, in French, *First Year,* 222.

235. "S.D. 2": Clinton MS, ibid., 221.

"THE ENENMY APPEARED TO BE MUCH ALARMED"

237. *"Saturday June ye 17"*: Farnsworth, "Diary," 83.

238. "neither picketted pallasaded": Clinton MS, French, *First Year,* 221.

238. "We not having more": Brown, "Letter."

239. "Having thrown up": Prescott to Adams, in Frothingham, *Siege,* 395.

239. "the fort was in considerable forwardness": Parker, in Coffin, *History of the Battle,* 34.

240. "were prevented completing it": *Report of the Committee of Safety, AA 4,* 2:1374.

240. "half of stone and two rayles": Chester to Fish, in Frothingham, *Siege,* 390.

241. "Without prayers?": Swett, *History of Bunker Hill,* 22.

241. "We began to be almost beat out": Brown, "Letter."

242. "It had the effect intended": "Judge Prescott's Account," 70.

243. "The men who had raised the works": Swett, *History of Bunker Hill,* 23.

BRACING FOR THE BLOW

244. "General Putnam rode": Livingston, *Putnam,* 220.

244. "was only entertained": Percy, *Letters,* 57.

245. "our men had left work": Bancroft, "Narrative," Hill, *Reminiscences,* 58.

246. "began to fire as brisk": Brown, "Letter."

246. "My lads": Bancroft, "Narrative," Hill, *Reminiscences,* 58.

247. "Our Officers sent time after time": Brown, "Letter."

247. "We with little loss": Farnsworth, *Diary,* 88.

CHAPTER FIFTEEN: REDCOATS AND BLUEJACKETS

248. "By Springs on our Cable": *Falcon*'s Journal, *NDAR* 1:703.

249. "but there was not": Graves, "Narrative," ibid., 704.

250. "The 10 Eldest Companies": General Orders, in French, *First Year,* 740.

251. "Howe's troop strength: Murdoch, *Bunker Hill.*

251. "As the shore where it was judged": Howe to Richard Howe, ibid., 147.

252. "alter our plan": Burgoyne to Stanley, in Drake, *Bunker Hill,* 41.

252. "This plan . . . did not": Clinton, *Narrative,* 20.

253. "At Noon the Signal was Made": *Cerberus*'s Journal, *NDAR* 1:703.

253. "P M at 1 The Boats": *Preston*'s Journal, ibid., 701.

"MORE CONFUSION AND LESS COMMAND"

253. "To be plain it appears": Pitts to Adams, in French, *First Year,* 229.

254. "Lieut.-col Robinson and Major Woods": Prescott to Adams, in Frothingham, *Siege,* 395.

255. "whole regiment to proceed": Stark, "Colonel Stark to . . . Thornton," 112.

255. "orders were immediately": "Dearborn's Account," Coffin, *History of the Battle,* 18.

THE FIRST WAVE

258. "It was the heaviest": Joseph Pearce, in Frothingham, *Siege,* 131n.

258. "and continued firing": Graves, "Narrative," *NDAR* 1:704.

258. "solemn procession": Jones, "Letter," 91.

260. "Lord Rawdon behaved": Burgoyne to Stanley, Fonblanque, *Episodes,* 157.

260. "The work we had seen": Rawdon to Huntington, in Commager and Steele, *Spirit of '76,* 130.

260. "Gondolas": Barker, *British in Boston,* 62.

261. "He quitted the first": Clinton MS, in French, *First Year,* 230.

261. "We went to battle": "Letter of a British Officer," Commager and Morris, *Spirit of '76,* 135.

261. "went on shore with Brig. General Pigot": "Howe's Letter," ibid., 131.

REINFORCEMENTS AND RESERVES

263. "who has the command": Storrs, "Diary," 85.

264. "About one O'clock P. M.": Webb to Webb, in Commager and Morris, *Spirit of '76,* 36.

264. "I was walking out": Chester to Fish, in Frothingham, *Siege,* 389.

265. "alleging that his Life": "Belknap's Note-books," 92.

265. "from appearances we shall have": Swett, *History of Bunker Hill,* 31.

CHAPTER SIXTEEN: THE BATTLE OF BUNKER HILL

267. "to be near General Howe": Graves, "Narrative," *NDAR* 1:704.

268. "Clinton and myself": Burgoyne to Lord Stanley, in Drake, *Bunker Hill,* 40.

268. "The rest of the army": Jones, "Letter," 91.

268. "Howe's disposition": Burgoyne to Lord Stanley, in Drake, *Bunker Hill,* 40.

269. "set fire to one of the old houses": Cockran's Deposition, *AA 4,* 2:1376.

270. "almost all laid in ashes": Farnsworth, "Diary," 84.

THE AMERICAN POSTS

271. "a party of the enemy": Prescott to Adams, in Frothingham, *Siege,* 395.

272. "I was now left": Ibid., 396.

272. "about 700 of us left": Brown, "Letter."

273. "more the result of accident": "Dearborn's Account," Coffin, *History of the Battle*, 22.

273. "our officers in command": Chester to Fish, in Frothingham, *Siege*, 390.

273. "There was a party of Hampshire": Prescott to Adams, ibid., 395.

274. "take good aim": "Judge Prescott's Account," 70.

275. "Gen. Putnam . . . was riding": Notes's Deposition, Swett, *History of Bunker Hill*, 13.

275. "Men, you know": Johnson's Deposition, ibid., 17.

275. A careful analysis: Murdoch, *Bunker Hill*, 78.

THE RAIL FENCE

276. "Gentlemen": *Clark's Narrative*, in Drake, *Bunker Hill*, 40.

276. "Our men at last grew": Rawdon to Huntingdon, in Commager and Morris, *Spirit of '76*, 130.

276. "We began the attack": Howe to Richard Howe, in Murdoch, *Bunker Hill*, 148.

277. "entrenched up to their chins": Jones, "Letter," 91.

278. "The intermediate space": Ibid., 149.

278. "set forward to the attack": Howe to Adjutant General, in Commager and Morris, *Spirit of '76*, 132.

278. "did not carry into the field": "Dearborn's Account," Coffin, *History of the Battle*, 22.

279. "poured in so heavy": Rawdon to Huntingdon, in Commager and Morris, *Spirit of '76*, 130.

279. "under a heavy fire": Howe to Adjutant General, in Commager and Morris, *Spirit of '76*, 133.

280. "The dead lay as thick": Wilkinson, in Coffin, *History of the Battle*, 13.

280. "the prudence of the officers": Chester to Fish, Frothingham, *Siege*, 390.

THE BRITISH LEFT

280. "And now ensued": Burgoyne to Stanley, in Drake, *Bunker Hill*, 40.

281. "Upon the left": Howe to Adjutant General, in Commager and Morris, *Spirit of '76*, 132.

281. "sufficient employment": Howe to Richard Howe, in Murdoch, *Bunker Hill*, 149.

282. "The enemy landed": Brown, "Letter."

282. "It was an awful moment and following": Bancroft, "Narrative," Hill, *Reminiscences,* 60.

282. "had got hardened": Chester to Fish, in Frothingham, *Siege,* 390.

CHAPTER SEVENTEEN: ATTACK AND REPULSE

284. "met with a thousand": Burgoyne to Stanley, in Drake, *Bunker Hill,* 40.

285. "A firing of eight or ten guns": Bancroft, "Narrative," Hill, *Reminiscences,* 60.

285. "a simultaneous discharge": "Judge Prescott's Account," 70.

285. "On the left Pigot": "Letter from Boston," *Detail and Conduct,* 14.

285. "There was no need": *Rivington's Gazette,* Frothingham, *Siege,* 397.

287. "As soon as landed": Barker, *British in Boston,* 60.

287. "Stopt by the Marsh": De Berniere's Map, in French, *First Year,* 227.

287. "was told they got": "Letter from Boston," *Detail and Conduct,* 14.

287. "The wretched blunder": Ibid., 15.

287. "At Bunkers Hill I sent": Cleaveland's Statement, in French, *First Year,* 749.

288. "When our officers saw": Brown, "Letter," Masshist.org.

289. "The General dismounted": Committee Report, *AA 4,* 2:1438.

289. "being deficient in his duty": Frothingham, *Siege,* 185.

THE SECOND ADVANCE

290. "Here the officers were observed": Committee of Safety Report, in Frothingham, *Siege,* 383.

291. "As we approached": "Letter from Boston," *Detail and Conduct,* 14.

291. "Several attempts were made": "Dearborn's Account," Coffin, *History of the Battle,* 20.

291. "attended the whole time": Frothingham, *Siege,* 199.

291. "'Tis astonishing what a number": Waller in Drake, *Bunker Hill,* 29.

292. "Place, from whence the Grenadiers": De Berniere's Map, in French, *First Year,* 227.

292. "were compelled a second time": "Dearborn's Account," Coffin, *History of the Battle,* 20.

292. "more destructive": Ibid., 20.

292. "but never without a sure aim": Ibid., 26.

293. "a scattering fire": Bancroft, "Narrative," Hill, *Reminiscences,* 61.

293. "After a considerable time": Prescott to Adams, in Frothingham, *Siege,* 396.

293. "As fast as the front man": *Rivington Gazette,* ibid., 398.

293. "We within the intrenchment": Farnsworth, "Diary," 84.

293. "till the enemy advanced": Prescott to Adams, in Frothingham, *Siege,* 396.

294. "A moment of the day": Burgoyne to Lord Stanley, in Drake, *Bunker Hill,* 40.

294. "Enimy appeared in great force": Clinton Note, in French, *First Year,* 241n.

295. "repulsed": Howe to Adjutant General, in Commager and Morris, *Spirit of '76,* 132.

295. "The ministerial army now made": Committee of Safety Report, Frothingham, *Siege,* 383.

295. "wisely gave orders": "Judge Prescott's Account," 71.

295. "the ground . . . covered": "Dearborn's Account," Coffin, *History of the Battle,* 20.

296. "exhorting them not to waste": "Judge Prescott's Account," 71.

"GOOD GOD HOW THE BALLS FLEW"

296. "On our March down": Webb to Joseph Webb, in Commager and Morris, *Spirit of '76,* 36.

297. "When we arrived": Chester to Fish, in Frothingham, *Siege,* 391.

298. "The Regulars fell": Webb to Joseph Webb, in Commager and Morris, *Spirit of '76,* 36.

298. "The artillery was directed": "Judge Prescott's Account," 71.

298. "When we came immediately": "Waller's Account," Drake, *Bunker Hill,* 29.

299. "Our ammunition being": Prescott to Adams, in Frothingham, *Siege,* 396.

299. "fir'd away all his Cartridges": Perkins Letter.

299. "I had twice mounted": "Account of Captain Harris," Drake, *Bunker Hill,* 37.

300. "Two companies of the first battalion": "Waller's Account," Drake, *Bunker Hill,* 28.

300. "The day was over": Bancroft, "Narrative," Hill, *Reminiscences,* 61.

300. "I Did not leave the Intrenchment": Farnsworth, "Diary," 83.

300. "Oh may I never forget": Brown, "Letter."

301. Death of Warren: Frothingham, *Life and Times,* 517.

302. "desired General Burgoyne": Clinton, *Narrative,* 19n.

303. "The whole of our line": "Dearborn's Account," Coffin, *History of the Battle,* 20.

303. "checked by a party": Committee of Safety Report, Frothingham, *Siege,* 383.

303. "continued a running fight": Rawdon to Huntingdon, in Commager and Morris, *Spirit of '76,* 130.

303. "We Ran very fast": Webb to Joseph Webb, *ibid,* 37.

303. "Our loss was principally": Bancroft, *Narrative,* in Hill, *Reminiscences,* 61.

304. "the soldiers were so much": Howe to Richard Howe, in Murdoch, *Bunker Hill,* 148.

EPILOGUE: "WE ARE ALL WRONG AT THE HEAD"

305. "We were exulting": "Hulton Letter," Commager and Morris, *Spirit of '76,* 136.

305. "Our Boats Emp[loye]d": *Falcon's* Journal, *NDAR* 1:703.

305. "Then followed a melancholy scene": *Clarke's Narrative* in Drake, *Bunker Hill,* 44.

306. "It was truly a Shocking Sight": Oliver, in French, *First Year,* 257.

306. The British lost 226 men killed: Murdock, *Bunker Hill,* 32.

306. "The day ended with glory": Burgoyne to Lord Stanley in Drake, *Bunker Hill,* 40.

307. "We are all wrong": "Letter from Boston," *Detail and Conduct,* 15.

307. "This action shows the superiority": Gage to Dartmouth, *DAR* 9:199.

307. "The trials we have had": Gage to Dartmouth, Private, ibid.

308. "A small body acting": Gage to Barrington, Commager and Morris, *Spirit of '76,* 134.

309. "From the tenour of your letters": Dartmouth to Gage, *AA 4,* 3:7.

310. "principal Inhabitants of the town": Ibid., 976.

THE PATRIOT REACTION

312. "terminated with less success": Warren to Adams, *Warren-Adams Letters,* 62.

312. "the President": Address to Congress, *PGW, RWS* 1:1.

313. "by several Gentlemen": Washington to Hancock, ibid., 34.

313. "Since Adams went to Philadelphia": "Hulton Letter," Commager and Morris, *Spirit of '76,* 137.

314. "Doctr. Warren . . . I found": Laurie Letter, in French, *First Year,* 263n.

315. "Here fell our worthy": Warren to Adams, *Warren-Adams Letters,* 63.

315. "I wish I could contradict": Abigail Adams to John Adams, June 18, 1775, Massachusetts Historical Society Web site, http://www.masshist.org/bh/adamsp1text .html (accessed August 19, 2010).

315. "Among the dead was": Committee of Safety Report, *AA 4,* 2:1375.

THE ECHOES OF BUNKER HILL

316. "for the unmolested occupancy": Wilkinson, in Frothingham, *Siege,* 157n.

316. "The sad and impressive experience": Lee, in ibid.

316. "a moment that I never felt": Howe to Adjutant General, *Spirit of '76,* 132.

Bibliography

PRIMARY SOURCES

BOOKS

Adams, John. *Diary and Autobiography of John Adams*. Vol. 3. Edited by L. H. Butterfield. Cambridge, Mass.: Belknap Press, 1961.

Adams, John. Autobiography, part 1, "John Adams," through 1776. *Adams Family Papers: An Electronic Archive.* Massachusetts Historical Society. http://www.masshist.org/digitaladams/ (accessed January 18, 2010).

Avalon Project. *Documents in Law, History and Diplomacy.* Lillian Goldman Law Library, Yale Law School. http://avalon.law.yale.edu (accessed January 23, 2010).

Barker, John. *The British in Boston: The Diary of Lt. John Barker.* New York: Arno Press, 1969, reprint of 1924 edition.

Burnett, Edmund C., ed. *Letters of Members of the Continental Congress.* Vol. 1. Washington, D.C.: Carnegie Institute of Washington, 1921.

Clark, William Bell, ed. *Naval Documents of the American Revolution.* Vol. 1. Washington, D.C.: Government Printing Office, 1964.

Clinton, Henry. *The American Rebellion: Sir Henry Clinton's Narrative of His Campaigns, 1775–1782, with an Appendix of Original Documents.* Edited by William Willcox. New Haven: Yale University Press, 1954.

Coffin, Charles, ed. *History of the Battle of Breed's Hill, by Major-Generals William Heath, Henry Lee, James Wilkinson and Henry Dearborn.* Portland, Me.: D. C. Colesworthy, printer, 1835.

Commager, Henry Steele, and Richard B. Morris, eds. *The Spirit of '76: The Story of the American Revolution as Told by Its Participants.* New York: Castle Books, 2002, reprint of 1967 edition.

Cunningham, Anne Rowe, ed. *Letters and Diary of John Rowe, Boston Merchant.* Boston: W. B. Clarke Company, 1903.

Davies, K. G., ed. *Documents of the American Revolution, 1781.* Dublin: Irish University Press, 1979.

Detail and Conduct of the American War Under Generals Gage, Howe, Burgoyne and Vice Admiral Richard Howe. London: Richardson and Urquhart, 1780.

Drake, Francis S. *Tea Leaves: Being a Collection of Letters and Documents Relating to the Shipment of Tea to the American Colonies in the Year 1773.* Boston: A. O. Crane, 1884.

Drake, Samuel Adams. *Bunker Hill: The Story Told in Letters from the Battle Field by British Officers Engaged.* Boston: Nichols and Hall, 1875.

Emerson, William. *Diaries and Letters of William Emerson, 1743–1776, Minister of the Church in Concord, Chaplain in the Revolutionary Army.* Edited by Amelia Forbes Emerson. Boston: N.p., 1972.

Evelyn, W. Glanville. *Memoir and Letters of Captain W. Glanville Evelyn of the 4th Regiment ("King's Own").* Edited by G. D. Scull. New York: Arno Press, 1971, reprint of 1879 edition.

Force, Peter, ed. *American Archives.* Fine Books Company, CD-ROM of 1890 edition.

Fox, Ebenezer. *The Adventures of Ebenezer Fox in the Revolutionary War.* Boston: Charles Fox, 1847.

Gage, Thomas. *The Correspondence of General Thomas Gage with the Secretaries of State, 1763–1775.* Vol. 1. Edited by Clarence Edwin Carter. New Haven: Yale University Press, 1931.

Haskell, Caleb. *Caleb Haskell's Diary.* Edited by Lothrop Withington. Newburyport, Mass.: William H. Huse & Company, 1881.

Heath, William. *Heath's Memoirs of the American War.* New York: A. Wessels Company, 1904.

Hill, John B. *Reminiscences of Old Dunstable. With sketches of events and persons of the early times of that town, and Colonel Bancroft's personal narrative of the battle of Bunker Hill.* Nashua, N.H.: Printed for E. H. Spalding, 1878.

How, David. *Diary of David How: A Private in Colonel Paul Dudley Sargent's Regiment of the Massachusetts Line, in the Army of the American Revolution.* Morrisania, N.Y.: Printed by H. O. Houghton and Company, 1865.

Hutchinson, Thomas. *The Diary and Letters of His Excellency Thomas Hutchinson, Esq.* Edited by Peter Orlando Hutchinson. Boston: Houghton Mifflin & Co., 1884.

———. *The History of the Province of Massachusetts Bay, from 1749 to 1774.* London: John Murray, 1828.

Jenks, John. *John Jenks's Diary.* Massachusetts Historical Society.

Journals of the Continental Congress, 1774–1789. Edited by Worthington Chauncey Ford. Washington, D.C.: Government Printing Office, 1905; http://memory.loc.gov.

Kemble, Stephen. *Journals of Lieut.-Col. Stephen Kemble, 1773–1789; and British Army Orders: Gen. Sir William Howe, 1775–1778; Gen. Sir Henry Clinton, 1778; and Gen.*

Daniel Jones, 1778. Edited by George Athan Billias. Boston: Gregg Press, 1972, reprint of 1883 edition.

Lister, Jeremy. *Concord Fight*. Cambridge, Mass.: Harvard University Press, 1931.

Long Island Historical Society. *Memoirs of the Long Island Historical Society,* vol. 2, *The Battle of Long Island*. Brooklyn, N.Y.: Published by the Society, 1869.

Mackenzie, Frederick. *The Diary of Frederick Mackenzie*. Cambridge, Mass.: Harvard University Press, 1930.

Massachusetts Historical Society. *Warren-Adams Letters*. Vol. 1. Boston: Massachusetts Historical Society, 1917.

The Nineteenth of April, 1775: A Collection of First Hand Accounts. Lincoln, Mass.: Sawtells of Somerset, 1968.

Percy, Hugh. *Letters of Hugh, Earl Percy, from Boston and New York, 1774–1776*. Edited by Charles *Knowles Bolton*. Boston: Charles E. Goodspeed, 1902.

Perkins Letter, Miscellaneous Bound Manuscripts, Massachusetts Historical Society.

Reed, William B. *Life and Correspondence of Joseph Reed*. Vol. 1. Philadelphia: Lindsay and Blakiston, 1847.

Rhodehamel, John, ed. *The American Revolution: Writings from the War of Independence*. New York: Library of America, 2001.

Serle, Ambrose. *The American Journal of Ambrose Serle, Secretary to Lord Howe, 1776–1778*. Edited by Edward H. Tatum Jr. Los Angeles: Arno Press, 1969, reprint of 1940 edition.

Stark, Caleb. *Memoir and Official Correspondence of John Stark, with Notices of Several Other Officers of the Revolution*. Concord, N.H.: G. Parker Lyon, 1860.

Tudor, John. *Deacon Tudor's Diary: A Record of More or Less Important Events in Boston, from 1732 to 1793, by an Eye Witness*. Edited by William Tudor. Boston: Press of Wallace Spooner, 1896.

Twohig, Dorothy, ed. *The Papers of George Washington, Revolutionary War Series*. Vol. 6. Charlottesville, Va., and London: University Press of Virginia, 1994.

PUBLISHED MANUSCRIPTS

Andrews, John. "Letters of John Andrews." *Massachusetts Historical Society Proceedings* 8, 1864–65.

Belknap, Jeremy. "Extracts from Dr. Belknap's Note-books." *Massachusetts Historical Society Proceedings* 14, 1875–76.

Boynton, Thomas. "Thomas Boynton's Journal." *Massachusetts Historical Society Proceedings* 15, 1876–77.

Brown, Peter. "Letter from Peter Brown to His Mother June 25, 1775." Massachusetts Historical Society, http://www.masshist.org/bh/brown.html (accessed April 3, 2010).

Farnsworth, Amos. "Amos Farnsworth's Diary." *Massachusetts Historical Society Proceedings*, Ser. 2, vol. 12, 1897–99.

French, Allen. *The First Year of the Revolution,* New York: Octagon Books, Inc. 1968.

Gearfield, Elisha. Letter, June 23, 1775. Massachusetts Historical Society, Miscellaneous Bound Manuscripts.

Ingalls, Phineas. "Revolutionary War Journal, Kept by Phineas Ingalls of Andover, Mass., April 19, 1775–December 8, 1776." *Essex Institute Historical Collections* 53 (1917): 81–92.

Jones, Val. "Letter of Brigadier-General Jones." *Massachusetts Historical Society Proceedings* 14, 1875–76.

"Orderly-book." *Massachusetts Historical Society Proceedings* 15, 1876–77.

Price, Ezekiel. "Diary of Ezekiel Price." *Massachusetts Historical Society Proceedings*, November 1863.

Prescott, William. "Judge Prescott's Account of the Battle of Bunker Hill." *Massachusetts Historical Society Proceedings* 14, 1875–76.

"Queries of George Chalmers, with the Answers of General Gage." *Collections of the Massachusetts Historical Society,* 4th ser. vol. 4. Boston: Little, Brown, and Company, 1858.

Stark, Caleb. *Memoir and Official Correspondence of Gen. John Stark.* Concord, Mass.: Parker Lyon, 1860.

Storrs, Experience. "Diary of Lieutenant-Colonel Storrs." *Massachusetts Historical Society Proceedings* 14, 1875–76.

Webb, Samuel. "Letter of Samuel B. Webb to Silas Deane." *Massachusetts Historical Society Proceedings* 14, 1875–76.

SECONDARY SOURCES

Alden, John Richard. *General Gage in America, Being Principally a History of His Role in the American Revolution.* Baton Rouge: Louisiana State University Press, 1948.

Cary, John. *Joseph Warren: Physician, Politician, Patriot.* Urbana: University of Illinois Press, 1961.

Draper, Theodore. *A Struggle for Power: The American Revolution.* New York: Times Books, 1996.

Fischer, David Hackett. *Paul Revere's Ride.* New York: Oxford University Press, 1994.

———. *Washington's Crossing.* New York: Oxford University Press, 2004.

Fleming, Thomas. *Liberty! The American Revolution.* New York: Viking, 1997.

Fonblanque, Edward Barrington de. *Political and Military Episodes in the Latter Half of the Eighteenth Century: Derived from the Life and Correspondence of the Right Hon. John Burgoyne.* Boston: Gregg Press, 1972, reprint of 1876 edition.

Frothingham, Richard. *The Battle-Field of Bunker Hill: With a Relation of the Action by William Prescott.* Boston: Printed for the Author, 1876.

———. *History of the Siege of Boston, and of the Battles of Lexington, Concord, and Bunker Hill.* Boston: Little, Brown, and Company, 1873.

————. *Life and Times of Joseph Warren.* Boston: Little, Brown, and Company, 1865.

Gordon, William. *The History of the Rise, Progress, and Establishment of the Independence of the United States of America.* New York: Printed for Samuel Campbell, 1801.

Gross, Robert A. *The Minutemen and Their World.* New York: Hill and Wang, 1976.

Gruber, Ira D. *The Howe Brothers and the American Revolution.* New York: Atheneum, 1972.

Homans, J. E., and L. E. Dearborn, eds. *The Cyclopedia of American Biography.* Supplementary ed. New York: The Press Association Compilers, 1918–31.

Johnson, William. *Sketches of the Life and Correspondence of Nathanael Greene.* Charleston, S. C.: Printed for the Author by A. E. Miller, 1822.

Johnston, Henry P. *The Campaign of 1776 Around New York and Brooklyn.* Brooklyn, N.Y.: Long Island Historical Society, 1878.

Labaree, Benjamin Woods. *The Boston Tea Party.* New York: Oxford University Press, 1964.

Livingston, William Farrand. *Israel Putnam: Pioneer, Ranger, and Major-General, 1718–1790.* New York: G. P. Putnam's Sons, 1901.

McCullough, David, *1776.* New York: Simon & Schuster, 2005.

Mackesy, Piers. *The War for America, 1775–1783.* Cambridge, Mass.: Harvard University Press, 1964.

Middlekauff, Robert. *The Glorious Cause: The American Revolution, 1763–1789.* New York: Oxford University Press, 1982.

Murdock, Harold. *Bunker Hill: Notes and Queries on a Famous Battle.* Boston: Houghton Mifflin Company, 1927.

Nelson, James L. *George Washington's Secret Navy: How the American Revolution Went to Sea.* New York: McGraw-Hill, 2008.

A Particular Account of the Battle of Bunker, or Breed's Hill, on the 17th of June, 1775, by a Citizen of Boston. Boston: Cummings, Hilliard & Company, 1825.

Quincy, Josiah. *Memoir of the Life of Josiah Quincy, Junior, of Massachusetts Bay, 1744–1775, by His Son.* Boston: Little, Brown, and Company, 1875.

Schecter, Barnet. *The Battle for New York: The City at the Heart of the American Revolution.* New York: Walker & Company, 2002.

Swett, Samuel. *History of Bunker Hill Battle, with a Plan.* Boston: Munroe and Francis, 1827.

Urban, Mark. *Fusiliers: The Saga of a British Redcoat Regiment in the American Revolution.* New York: Walker & Company, 2007.

Index